Standards for Online Communication:

Publishing Information for The Internet/World Wide Web/Help Systems/Corporate Intranets

Standards for Online Communication:

Publishing Information for The Internet/World Wide Web/Help Systems/Corporate Intranets

JoAnn T. Hackos
Dawn M. Stevens

Wiley Computer Publishing

WILEY

John Wiley & Sons, Inc.
New York • Chichester • Weinheim • Brisbane • Singapore • Toronto

Publisher: Katherine Schowalter
Editor: Theresa Hudson
Managing Editor: Micheline Frederick
Electronic Products, Associate Editor: Mike Green
Text Design & Composition: Rodney Sauer, RDD Consultants, Inc.

Designations used by companies to distinguish their products are often claimed as trademarks. In all instances where John Wiley & Sons, Inc., is aware of a claim, the product names appear in inital capital or ALL CAPITAL LETTERS. Readers, however, should contact the appropriate companies for more complete information regarding trademarks and registration.

This text is printed on acid-free paper.

This publication is designed to provide accurate and authoritative information in regard to the subject matter covered. It is sold with the understanding that the publisher is not engaged in redering legal, accounting, or other professional service. If legal advice or other expert assistance is required, the services of a competent professional person should be sought.

Library of Congress Cataloging-in-Publication Data:

Hackos, JoAnn T.
    Standards for online communication : publishing information for
  the Internet/World Wide Web/Help Systems/Corporate Intranets
  JoAnn Hackos, Dawn Stevens
       p.   cm.
  Includes index
  ISBN 0-471-15695-7 (pbk. alk. paper)
    1. Computer networks. 2. Electronic publishing. I. Stevens, Dawn. II. Title.
  ZA4375.H33   1997
808.066'005--dc21   96-39029
                                                         CIP

Printed in the United States of America
10 9 8 7

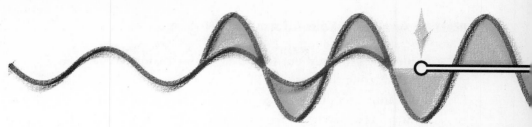

Table of Contents

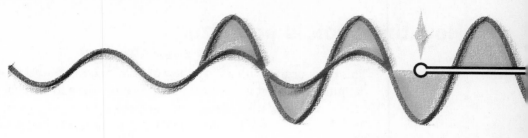

Preface

The field of information design and development is not the same today as it was yesterday or as it will be tomorrow. Technological advances demand that information designers constantly examine new ways to disseminate information other than traditional hardcopy books or even online help systems. As they struggle to learn the tools to create new information systems, however, those learning the new tools often overlook a very important part of the process—sound design. Far too often, given the demands of fast-paced corporate life, information is being thrown into an online tool for use on the Web, a company intranet, or in online help without regard for the basics of good information design—is the information accessible and usable?

This book reintroduces the design principles overlooked in the rush to be the first. We remind information designers of the importance of planning thoroughly and making design decisions based on audience needs. We list guidelines to consider when creating your plans and the systems themselves—guidelines that you may ultimately decide to follow or ignore, but that should nevertheless always be part of your conscious decision making.

In this book, we do not provide information about the mechanics of implementing the design features discussed. Nor do we explore every aspect of an issue. Rather we intend the guidelines to serve simply as a springboard into the world of online communication, to get you thinking about the issues that affect the usability of your information. We hope that we peak your interest and encourage further exploration into this rapidly changing arena.

How this book is organized

This book begins with an overview of online communication, including definitions of what is included under its umbrella and a global look at the process to follow when designing and implementing an online system. The book is then divided into three parts, representing the major milestones in an online project:

- Part 1, *Analyzing Your Information Needs,* guides you through the creation of an information plan. The chapters in this part explain how to conduct and interpret front-end analysis of audience and task, so that you thoroughly understand the goals of the system you are creating.

- Part 2, *Designing Your Online System,* guides you through the creation of an information content specification. In these chapters, you learn how to structure your online system, both at a high-level and at the detailed topic level.

- Part 3, *Implementing Your Design,* provides a series of chapters containing guidelines to follow while implementing your online system. The chapters take the form of checklists with brief explanations and examples. They are not intended to be a comprehensive discussion of any single recommendation. Rather, they are intended cumulatively to provide a detailed but high-level description of good implementation strategies for online documents of any type.

Each chapter includes recommendations for further reading on the topics discussed. The guidelines and recommended reading presented in each chapter are summarized in the appendices.

Using the CD

The information in this book is also presented on an accompanying CD. Appendix C describes how to install and use the CD. It also discusses the design decisions we made in creating the CD, so that the entire CD serves as a case study of the principles in this book.

Conventions

Although this book is designed to apply to all forms of online communication, occasionally we provide information specific to a certain form. This information is set apart by the following icons:

 Computer-based training. Information following this icon applies to tutorials and training presented online.

 CD-ROM. Information following this icon applies to libraries, catalogs, and so on that are delivered on a CD-ROM.

 Help. Information following this icon applies to online help systems.

 Web. Information following this icon applies to the Worldwide Web and corporate intranets.

About the Authors

Dr. JoAnn T. Hackos and Dawn Stevens lead the designers and developers at Comtech Services, Inc. of Denver, Colorado, and San Jose, California. Comtech designs, produces, and helps others produce technical information in support of products and processes. The company develops user interfaces, online information, paper documentation, and training systems and conducts usability testing of products and documentation. Dr. Hackos founded the company in 1978 to provide project-oriented information designservices to the business community. Comtech's clients include Hewlett-Packard, Federal Express, Dupont, Cadence, Octel Communications, IBM, Storage Technology, Ungermann-Bass, Oracle, Compaq, Northern Telecom, Wells Fargo, the Veterans Administration, and many others.

Dr. Hackos is president of Comtech Services, Inc. She consults with companies worldwide on benchmarking, strategic planning and customer needs analyses, performance support systems, and developing training and documentation using a minimalist philosophy. She also conducts research into the information customers need to learn and use products and into the processes used by organizations to produce products and documentation. Using the research studies as a base, she helps organizations develop strategic plans to design more usable products and better technical information to accompany those products, as well as better information to train and inform employees of company procedures and policies through the internet and corporate Intranets. JoAnn presents courses in project management and the design of usable products and information to public and inhouse groups all over the world.

JoAnn has published articles on management and technical information appearing in technical journals such as *Technical Communication, IEEE Transactions on Professional Communications*, the *Proceedings of the International Technical Communication Conference*, the *Proceedings of the STC Annual Conference, Franchise Update Magazine*, and many others. Her books and monographs include an article on total quality management in *The Franchise Handbook*, published by the American Management Association; a book on typography called *About Type: IBM'S Guide for Type Users*; and NBI's *Designing High-Impact Documents* (Legend 2.0). Her book, *Managing Your Documentation Projects*, was published by John Wiley & Sons in 1994.

JoAnn holds a PhD from Indiana University. She is a fellow of the international Society for Technical Communication (STC) and a Past President (1992–3). She is also the editor of the Usability Professional Association's national newsletter. She enjoys birdwatching and traveling the world with her husband, Bill.

Dawn Stevens is Comtech's vice-president. She has performed at all levels in online information projects—as writer, designer, programmer, editor/quality assurance, and manager—and she brings the experience of all these projects and perspectives to this book. Currently, she oversees the day-to-day management of all projects performed by Comtech and has had a key role in designing and delivering new information technologies to clients.

Dawn has served as a judge at both local and national levels in online competitions of the Society for Technical Communication, and has spoken at many conferences nationwide about the design of online systems. *Standards for Online Communication* is her first book for John Wiley & Sons.

Dawn has a BS in engineering physics from the Colorado School of Mines and an MS in technical communication from the University of Colorado, Denver.

She is patiently waiting for her husband to complete his master's degree before pursing a doctorate. Dawn is a senior member of the Society for Technical Communication. She admits that she is obsessed with Disney, Hallmark Christmas ornaments, and preserving her family's lives through photographs. Dawn is married to John and her children are Andrea and Brianna.

Acknowledgments

Many people and many diverse ideas have contributed to the design and development of this book. We cannot begin to list here the nearly 20 years of accumulated experience with the design of electronic information. However, we must thank many members of the Society for Technical Communication for their contributions to the development of online communication. Especially, we want to thank Bill Horton for his seminal work in online documentation—he has clearly influenced the entire field to think about good design. We also want to thank major contributors to the field of online help design like John Brockmann, Mary Deaton, Joe Welinske, Dave Farkas, Cheryl Zuback, and others. We acknowledge the contributions of the consortium of designers who are attempting to define minimalism as a school of information design, especially John Carroll, Hans van der Meij, Ginny Redish, Stephanie Rosenbaum, Barbara Mirel, as well as Patricia Wright of Cambridge University, whose research on information users has influenced our thinking about the field. We also greatly appreciate the participation in the development of the chapters on graphics and multimedia design of JoAnn's sister, Marilyn Whitesell, a consummate visual artist, graphic designer, and creative director of multimedia projects.

In addition to contributors to these standards and guidelines worldwide, we have many to thank who are closer to home. The staff at Comtech Services, Inc. were instrumental in seeking out many of the wonderful examples of online communication that you see in the more than 200 illustrations presented here. They often found the right examples and spent many hours taking the screen captures. We especially want to acknowledge the assistance of Robin Bellerson, Tim Keirnan, and Jeni Halingstad. A key contributor to the final assembly of all the pieces that make up a major text has been Lori Maberry, Comtech's intrepid production manager.

We must also acknowledge the design talent of Rodney Sauer of RDD Consultants, who designed the book and handled the final production of camera-ready copy. Rodney always manages to shake up our thinking about typography, a field that he loves and in which he offers an innovative eye for the details of design. We are also pleased with the interesting graphic elements that Rodney has contributed to the design. We hope you like them too.

The CD could not have been completed were it not for the expertise of Connie Kiernan, Comtech's newest staff member. Her experience with RoboHelp and quickness in learning HDK helped complete the system within our final deadlines.

Finally, we cannot forget the people who provided support throughout the long hours of planning, writing, rewriting, and more rewriting. Bill Hackos and John Stevens are happily skilled chefs who assumed the tasks of keeping the troops fed. We also want to thank Andrea and Brianna Stevens for tolerating their mother's long hours at the computer. These contributors help to keep us focused on what is really important in the world.

1 Defining the Process

Electronic information, information databases, corporate knowledge bases—
they're the wave of the future and becoming more commonplace every day.
The pressure is on to move our organizations into the 21st century while we're
still in the 1990s. Managers hope that delivering information electronically
will save costs. Employees want information that is up-to-date and
immediately and easily accessible. Customers want to know everything we
know about the products they have purchased. Business partners want access
to information. From every side, we are pressured to do something—install a
document management system, get up on the Web, develop an intranet, find
ways of disseminating information more quickly and comprehensively than
ever before. But the reality is that we don't know how to respond to all these
wants. Questions rather than solutions dominate:

- What exactly do users mean when they say they want information
  online? Does that mean dumping existing manuals onto a CD-ROM?
  Establishing information Web pages or disseminating information
  through corporate intranets? Creating an online help system?
  Designing a multimedia whizbang information database? Supporting
  user goals through wizards, coaches, and other performance-centered
  tools?

- What information should an electronic system include and how
  should it be organized? What information is appropriate for
  electronic distribution? What information is not? What information
  is most important? What should go online first?

- How should the information look? What graphic design features do
  users need? What about video and sound—where do they fit in?

- Will users want to read information on their computer screens or print it out?

- What capabilities should the electronic information system have? How will users access information? Can they find their way around? Will they need a library-like catalog? Will individual documents or document sets have single or multiple tables of contents? What about indexes? Keyword searches? Full-text searches?

- What is the best way to proceed?

- Where do we begin?!

In this book, we provide a comprehensive approach to answering such questions and getting started in the process of creating an effective electronic information design. But before we can do that, we need to establish exactly what *we* mean by "electronic information." This chapter provides our definition and outlines a development process that will be expanded on in the rest of this book.

What is electronic information?

Electronic information includes any form of communication that depends on a computer for its distribution and maintenance, including such diverse systems as these:

- A kiosk that provides immediate information or demonstrates the key features of a product

- An interactive demonstration that teaches general techniques for using the features and capabilities of a software product

- A context-sensitive online help system that answers specific questions about an application screen currently displayed

- A CD-ROM containing all regulations governing a particular industry

- A wizard that walks a user through a difficult and rarely used task within an application program

- A Web page providing shortcuts and expert-level hints for improving system performance

■ A virtual world in which users can explore the parts of a complex machine without taking their own machines apart

Although each type of electronic information differs in purpose and presentation, the design processes for each is frequently similar. The process may be likened to creating an ice-cream sundae: the end products are similar, but the ingredients (chocolate or vanilla ice cream? hot fudge or caramel?) and presentation (whipped cream? cherry? nuts?) may be quite different. Yet all the employees at the local Dairy Queen can create any sundae. They know the implications of their customers' requests and can translate customer needs into a set of specifications to use when creating the final product. We hope to give you the skills you need to translate the demands of your customers, staff members, and management into a set of specifications. We provide guidelines for the implementation of those specifications into a usable, effective presentation of information.

When is electronic information the right choice?

The key to your decision-making process about moving from paper to electronic distribution must be focused on the needs of the users. If you make the right decision, the outcome will be clear. When we look at a well-supported learning environment, we encounter the following:

■ Fewer user errors

■ More rapid correction of mistakes

■ More rapid and effective problem solving

■ Lower training requirements

■ More effective learning

■ A more global understanding of the work environment

In short, users who are well supported by information are more productive in their work environments. They are perceived as having greater expertise and therefore earn more respect. As a result, they are usually more satisfied with their jobs.

A user who has access to the right information at the right time has a tremendous opportunity to learn and perform effectively. The better the sources of information are for access and usability, the more likely it is that they will continue to be used effectively and promote the development of a learning organization.

How do I sell electronic information distribution in my organization?

The most obvious advantage of distributing information electronically is cost. Delivering information electronically is less expensive than delivering it on paper. You save the expense of printing and binding the paper copies and the expense of physical delivery. With the steep increase in the cost of paper over the past few years, electronic dissemination of information has become increasingly attractive to managers trying to contain costs.

However, the cost of goods and delivery is not the only reason why creating an electronic information system might be a good idea. When we study users of information in both high-tech and low-tech environments, we find that they rarely have immediately at hand the information they need to perform tasks, understand concepts, and solve problems. The reasons for this lack of information are myriad:

- Print manuals are often bulky and contain multiple volumes that are difficult to access quickly.

- The printed manuals users receive are generally out of date before they are delivered.

- Print manuals are rarely updated in a timely manner if at all.

- Even when information is updated, it is rarely integrated into the original paper information set and is often misplaced.

- Information gathered after a product is in use or a service begun is rarely integrated with the initial information developed to support a product release or service initiation.

- Print manuals are often lost in the users' environment—carried off by a single user and not returned, never included in the original packaging, misplaced on the loading dock or in the purchasing department, and so on.

■ Even when users have the information at hand, they often lack the skills needed to find answers to specific questions in the complex organization of user manuals. They may not know how to use indexes or even tables of contents. They may not know how to relate the information in the text to the questions they have.

It should be quite obvious that you have many reasons to find better ways of disseminating information to your users. You will reduce their confusion and frustration if they always know where to find information and can feel assured that the information they find is the most current information available.

Information delivered electronically and designed for online use provides many advantages for users:

■ CD-ROMs take up less space than paper manuals and are more conveniently stored.

■ Information that can be accessed from system servers takes no local space at all and is available to everyone attached to the network.

■ Information that can be downloaded from bulletin boards or through the Internet may not require any local storage.

■ Electronically delivered information can be updated at the source so that the most recent versions of the information are available to everyone with access.

■ Information distributed among well-conceived information objects can be updated as soon as the content of a topic changes.

■ Updated information is not present as addenda (point pages, errata, and so on) but is immediately incorporated into the appropriate context.

■ Users have current information available at any workstation without having to carry heavy manuals around.

■ Information loaded onto laptop computers is available in the field at the moment of need.

■ Well-organized online information that may have once been presented in myriad volumes of paper documentation can be integrated into a single, accessible whole.

These and many more arguments can be made in favor of delivering information electronically, in addition to the basic cost reductions that may result when manuals are no longer printed and distributed in paper. For example, SUNCORP Building Society, a Brisbane, Australia, insurance company, witnessed a substantial increase in the use of policies and procedures when it provided users with a well-designed, easy-to-access online system delivered through their Wide Area Network (WAN). Network system administrators whose information use we studied told us that they prefer information delivered through CD-ROM and the Internet because it takes less shelf space and is more easily accessible.

However, it is also true that not every situation lends itself to electronic distribution. Paper often works better in meeting the needs of users. Even then, you will encounter many circumstances where providing users with the opportunity to print their own copies when they are needed may be more practical than distributing paper.

For example, some years ago, one of the government labs decided to place its policies and procedures online, principally to reduce the cost of printing. Users preferred the online information, but instead of declining, printing costs increased. Upon investigation, the designers discovered that not only were users printing copies for themselves, they were printing the copies more than once. It was no longer practical to store paper copies but simply to use them and throw them away. People preferred to read from paper but get their delivery online.

Whom should I involve?

The design of an electronic information delivery system is rarely the responsibility of a single individual or even a single department. Most often you will find yourself working with managers and colleagues from many parts of your organization. If you are providing information for customers outside your organization, you may find yourself on a team involving

- Marketing
- Customer support
- Training
- Development
- Field engineering/field support

- Information technology (IT or IS departments)

and others interested in supporting customer needs.

If you are designing an information library for employees of your organization, you may find yourself on a team of people from various areas:

- Human resource development

- Training

- Hotline support

- Business leaders

- Information technology

All team members should participate in the analysis activities so that the decisions they make are directly influenced by data about user needs and a thorough understanding of the opportunities and challenges to be addressed during design and implementation.

What skills do I, as information designer, need?

The transition from paper-based to electronic information sends many people into a cold sweat. Fear of the unknown is real and difficult to overcome and, of course, is a likely reason you are reading this book. But the reality is that you don't need to be a computer whiz to design electronic information. Many of the same practices that were effective for designing print information remain effective for designing electronic information:

- Information must be well organized for ease of access.

- Information must be written so that instructions are easy to follow.

- Instructions must be easy for experts to skim, yet provide sufficient information for novices.

- Types of information, such as concepts, background, purpose, feedback, and actions, must be clearly differentiated.

- Text should be supported by graphics to clarify concepts and instructions and reduce words.

■ Explanations should be supported by examples to help users apply new information to their particular circumstances.

On the other hand, designing and developing information for online access and electronic distribution also requires a perspective not ordinarily encountered in designing paper documentation. CD-ROMs, intranets, and the Web allow us to create libraries of information that encompass multiple products, services, and activities rather than focusing on only one information set for one product. This expansion of information means that users may have to make a more complex set of decisions to reach the information they need. You must support that decision-making process.

The new electronic media also invite you to organize information differently than you have in the past. When technical communicators had to publish information in physical books, they had to accommodate trade-offs between books or libraries that were too large and cumbersome to use. They tended to repeat information in each context to which it applied. Users had conflicting demands—they said they preferred smaller documents, but at the same time, they wanted all the information needed to support a task in one place. Communicators often had to decide between repeating information and making books longer, and providing a complicated net of cross-references to support a single task.

With electronic media, you now have the ability to repeat everything that users might need or want to know in the context in which they are accessing the information. You can provide information for both expert and novice users through a network of hypertext links. You can support those who learn by example and those who prefer to begin with conceptual overviews. However, to do so, you must learn to design and write differently than you have for paper. You must create information objects that can be reused in a variety of circumstances. You must consider information designed as discrete topics to be linked together in a web rather than read (or written) as continuous expository prose. You must eschew transitions in favor of well-orchestrated networks of related topics.

Although you have many opportunities to redesign the information you have so that you take advantage of the capabilities of electronic information, the processes you use to analyze, design, and implement our ideas will be the same. You still have to understand your users and their requirements, the product or service environment that you have to discuss, and the tasks that you need to support. In the following section, we briefly outline a process that has proven successful for both paper and electronic information.

What process should I follow?

Just as in the design of paper-based information, it's important to follow a consistent, proven process in developing electronic information. We have found, in fact, that the same process that has been successful in creating paper-based information also works for electronic information; that is, a five-phase development life cycle, as shown in Figure 1.1:

- Information plan

- Content specification

- Implementation

- Testing and production

- Evaluation

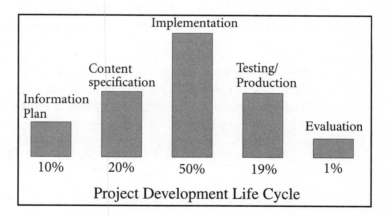

Figure 1.1: Plan to allot the shown percentages for each phase of the project life cycle.

In the sections that follow, we provide a high-level overview of each of these development phases. The rest of the book is then divided into three parts that parallel the life-cycle phases: analysis (information plan), design (content specification), and implementation, including testing and evaluation.

Information plan

The information plan is the document that results from your initial investigation into the requirements of an information project. Your investigation should answer the following questions:

- Who will use the information? What personal characteristics, including learning styles, will influence your information design? How much prior knowledge and skill do users bring to understanding the information you will provide?

- What are the information goals of your users? What do they want to learn? How do they articulate their goals and attempt to translate their goals into actions?

- What tasks do your users need to perform that must be supported by the information environment you hope to design? Will they be performing tasks that are simple, complex, or somewhere in between? Will the tasks be performed frequently or infrequently? Must they learn new skills to perform effectively, or simply look up information that supports their performance of tasks already well understood?

- In what environment will the information be used? What computer infrastructure is available to support information access? What challenges presented by the environment and the infrastructure will affect your design decisions?

- How will the usability (or lack thereof) of products you are supporting affect the users' information needs?

- What information must be provided to users because of regulations or legal requirements?

These and other questions should direct your analysis of the information needs of the community you hope to support through the electronic delivery of information. Armed with the fruits of this early investigation, you are ready to construct an information plan that outlines the information you believe will best meet the needs of your user community, as well as the internal requirements of your own organization. Your information plan should reflect your approach to the design of your information library, including the usability goals of the design, as well as the corporate goals and objectives.

In Part 1, *Analyzing Your Information Needs,* we present guidelines for this phase of your development process and suggest the types of information you should include in your plan to convince your managers, peers, and colleagues on the design team that you have

- Conducted your preliminary research thoroughly

- Thought through the alternatives carefully

- Presented sound recommendations for addressing the needs you have identified

- Presented a strong argument for the information design that you have recommended

Once the strategic design is complete in the information plan and has been thoroughly reviewed and revised by the design group, it should be presented to appropriate managers for review and decision making. Without the support of senior management, you may find many organizational roadblocks in your way toward implementing your design ideas. With support from senior managers, you may be better able to enlist the cooperation and participation of the diverse parts of your organization that will need to contribute to a successful implementation.

Content specification

Once the information plan has been reviewed and accepted, you are ready to move into a detailed design stage. The content specification documents your detailed analysis of what you plan to develop and how you intend to organize it for your information library. With thorough content analysis and a substantial understanding of user needs, you can

- Understand the information you will provide and how it will support users and their tasks

- Organize the details of the information library

- Confirm your earlier audience and task analyses and extend them with more information as the project develops

Documenting this information enables you to obtain early agreement about the information organization from all team members and avoid reorganizing the information library or its details late in the development cycle. Part 2, *Designing Your Online System,* concentrates on what you must consider when developing your detailed specifications.

Detailed specifications should include

- The list of topics

- The topic categories and their proposed design

- The links between topics

In addition to a document that explains the details of your design, you should provide prototypes of your design ideas. For example, prototypes might consist of storyboards of the topics and hypertext links that you will develop. Prototypes assist you in informing both your team members and management about your design. Early prototypes might also be created in tools such as presentation programs. These programs enable you to quickly and easily show users (and managers) what the information library access and display screens might look like. Physical prototypes are easier for people outside the collaborative team to understand than are analytical discussions and textual descriptions of your intended information library.

Prototypes also provide you with an opportunity to obtain early user feedback. You can use the storyboards to walk users through a variety of information-access scenarios to gauge their response to your system before you develop it.

Implementation

The implementation phase begins the actual design and development of the electronic information. During this phase, you make additional detailed design decisions and sometimes revise your content specifications as new analysis takes place. You produce many drafts of the information, conduct reviews, and make revisions.

During this phase of the project you may encounter questions about the style or approach to take with the presentation of text and graphics. Part 3, *Implementing Your Design,* provides guidelines that anticipate those questions. However, the chapters in Part 3 are not intended to be a comprehensive discussion of any single recommendation. Rather, they are intended cumulatively to provide a detailed, but high-level, description of good implementation strategies for online information of any type.

Testing and production

Analysis and design eventually must end if you are to construct and deliver an information product. That product must itself be tested to ensure that the dynamic structure of hypertext you have created actually behaves as designed. The production phase includes both functional and final evaluative testing to ensure that the design you have created is usable and useful.

In addition to testing, Phase 4 is the manufacturing part of the development cycle. The production process for electronic media may include

- Compiling and testing the electronic information

- Pressing CD-ROMs

- Compressing files onto diskettes

- Uploading information to a Web site or intranet server

Finally, Phase 4 is also the time to release the information for translation if necessary. Remember, however, that the groundwork for translation and localization must be laid during information planning and should include the development of translation aids, such as glossaries, during the implementation phase.

Evaluation

In the final phase of the development cycle, you evaluate the project that just ended and plan for the next project. Surveys, interviews, and observations of users at work all assist in determining the successes and challenges of your initial efforts, providing opportunities for improvement during the next development cycle.

During this phase, you may find it useful to compare the final product with the product you originally defined in your information plan. If you estimated a project scope and the hours required to complete your project, you might compare those estimates to the actual scope and hours at the end of the project. Such a comparison allows you to assess how the project might have changed (grown in scope, increased in difficulty) since its beginning. You will also have information that will help you estimate more effectively in the future.

For example, when the Association for the Advancement of Retired Persons (AARP) completed their project to move policies and procedures online, they discovered that they averaged 1 1/2 to 2 hours per page to convert their original information into SGML-coded information for delivery to multiple operating system environments. Using this information, they were able to more effectively plan the effort required for their next conversion.

Besides looking internally at the success of your project, you must look externally to your information users. Evaluations by users might include survey responses, the results of interviews, or an informal compilation of comments to customer support. The feedback you receive from your users will assist you in improving your information design for the next release. However, because much electronic information can be continuously updated, you may be able to make critical improvements long before a major redesign.

For example, one company received feedback that users found the initial graphic on its Web page too slow to load. Users couldn't access the information they needed in a timely manner. Once the feedback was analyzed, the graphic designers were able to quickly change the graphic and eliminate the problem even though the overall organization and structure of the information remained the same.

Further reading

Brockmann, R. John, *Writing Better Computer User Documentation: From Paper to Hypertext* (New York: John Wiley & Sons, 1990).

Hackos, JoAnn T., *Managing your Documentation Projects* (New York: John Wiley & Sons, 1994).

Horton, William, *Designing and Writing Online Documentation*, 2nd edition (New York: John Wiley & Sons, 1995).

Price, Jonathan and Henry Korman, *How to Communicate Technical Information: A Handbook of Software and Hardware Documentation* (Redwood City, CA: Benjamin/Cummings, 1993).

Senge, Peter, *The Fifth Discipline: The Art and Practice of the Learning Organization* (New York: Doubleday, 1990).

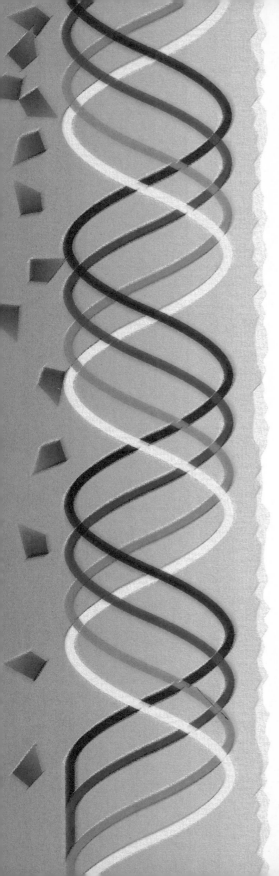

PART 1

Analyzing Your Information Needs

As you begin to plan the design of your online information and embark on Phase 1 of the information development life cycle, you must consider a variety of requirements that focus on assisting your users to find information they need to do their jobs effectively. These requirements will be determined by

- The users' personal characteristics

- The nature of the information

- The users' goals for the information

To determine this information, you must thoroughly research your user community and the information you are providing them. The chapters in this part provide guidelines for conducting that research, analyzing the results, and understanding the implications:

- Chapter 2, *Learning About Your Users' Information Needs,* focuses on how to gather information about your users and their tasks. It discusses various methods for conducting your research and then describes how to create user profiles and use scenarios that reflect the information you gather from that research.

- ■ Chapter 3, *Determining the Stages of Use,* further expands on the design issues surrounding your users and their characteristics. It presents the Stages of Use model for classifying your users and discusses the most effective approaches for the classification mix that you are addressing.

- ■ Chapter 4, *Categorizing Information Needs,* focuses on the kind of information you will be presenting. It introduces four classifications of information and provides guidelines for dividing the information you will present into those classifications.

- ■ Chapter 5, *Recognizing the Implications of Design Research,* summarizes the design implications introduced in the previous chapters. It then brings together these elements in case studies of effective design decisions—designs currently in production that have led to usable and accessible information.

We hope that this part will help you build a foundation of thinking about and gathering data about users and the information they need. It is crucial to understand these issues fully before you tackle the design issues discussed in the later parts of this book. Only with a solid understanding of these issues will you be able to make informed decisions that result in the best solutions for your users.

2

Learning About Your Users' Information Needs

As you learned in Chapter 1, both information planning and content specifications involve analyzing the needs of your users, the tasks they want to perform, and what you must tell them. Information planning provides a strategic or high-level analysis of the information needs of the community of users you serve.

Too often, however, when planning to deliver information electronically, organizations ignore some or all of the analysis required for success. Instead, they focus on the dissemination of the information they have at hand, rather than what is needed by the user community. They focus on the technical infrastructure—deciding on the network, operating system, database structure and tools, and delivery software and hardware. The existing information and the potential technical environment must be considered carefully as part of the information design, but these issues should not dominate the design strategy. If they do, you may create a superb system to deliver information electronically, but you may also deliver the wrong information or make information inaccessible to the people who need it most.

To provide the right information in an easily accessible manner, you must take the time to understand thoroughly your users and their jobs. You need to learn

- What users think about themselves and their tasks

- The interactions between the users' world and the technology

   ■ The users' goals so you can then design effective information to meet them

This chapter provides guidelines for gathering such information and compiling it into a usable form.

Conducting your research

Developing a rich picture of your audience and their needs is not a simple task. It is not a task that can be done adequately with a single brief interview. It is a task that will take time and can profit from a gradual discovery process. Understanding your audience is a long-term and cumulative process that results in an increasingly complex picture.

How do you learn about your users' views of the information world you need to design? Formal market research methods such as surveys and focus groups may corroborate your initial design ideas, but the first sources of information must be closer to the user communities. Begin by studying how the users are supported by information today, focusing especially on cases where possibly inadequate sources of information exist. Study your users by observing them at work and asking them about the challenges and problems that occur when they try to perform tasks, solve problems, or otherwise strive to work effectively.

Consider the following guidelines when planning your research.

Rely on fact, not opinion

Marketing, research and development, training, field engineering, service and support, and others will all have opinions about the characteristics of the users. Managers and supervisors of actual end users may also have a great deal to say.

You should not entirely discount these myriad opinions, but a plan that contains more opinions than facts may be seriously flawed. You are essentially relying on hearsay, and if hearsay is not admissible in our courts of law, why should it be in your information design?

To avoid relying on hearsay, gather information about your audience and their needs firsthand. Don't cave in to other departments that have conducted their own research. Their information may be perfectly valid for that department's goals, but it probably doesn't contain all the facts you need to design an information library effectively.

Talk to the right people

Going to the users directly also does not guarantee an accurate picture. You must carefully choose who you talk to. Don't rely solely on your "friends"— those long-term customers who always serve as beta sites and who participate in every focus group. Nor should you concentrate your research in a specific area—a single industry, a single user type, a single geographic location.

Instead, develop a matrix of your potential customers (you might work with marketing and other knowledgeable colleagues to create this matrix). Then find a representative sample of individuals from each group of your users with whom to conduct your research. For example, suppose you identified three potential categories of users who use a television satellite dish. To discover the documentation needs for the installation of the product, you would concentrate your efforts with advanced users, dealers, and installers (Table 2.1).

Table 2.1: User Matrix

	Novice Users	Advanced Users	Dealers/ Installers
Install base	0	0	10
Install dish	0	5	10
Install console	0	8	10
Set up stations	3	10	10
Change stations	10	10	10

Ask the right questions

Before haphazardly interviewing potential users, develop a plan for your questioning. What do you want to find out? What is the best way to get that information? Carefully outline your strategies for gathering information.

As you create your interviewing plan, be sure to include strategies for answering the following questions:

- What personal characteristics, such as age, gender, or level of education, distinguish the users?

- What is the level of subject-matter knowledge among users?

- What experience do the users have in using information to support their tasks and achieve their goals?

- What are the users' experience using information to support their tasks and achieve their goals?

- What are the physical peculiarities of the users' workplace that may affect their ability to use information?

- What do your users do and why?

- What are their goals for their activities?

- How have they learned what they do?

- What support do they require?

Think of all the possible behaviors, habits, styles, idiosyncrasies, and work routines that you will need to design an electronic information library and include questions that will help you gather this information.

 ## *Use the right methods*

As you list the information you want to uncover through your research, you should also consider the best ways to gather that information. You have many options available:

- **Develop a written survey and send it to a selected sample of your users.** This approach allows you to obtain information from a large and diverse collection of users.

  Unfortunately, questionnaires may be the least productive way to discover the detailed information you need to understand your users' needs. A large portion of the people who receive a survey will never complete it. Surveys are also difficult to plan, execute, validate, and interpret, and they tend to produce general, broadly based information rather than the details that best help support information design.

- **Conduct telephone interviews of your audience members.** A telephone interview can be cost-effective and produce a significant amount of information in a short period of time. However, as with self-administered surveys, telephone interviews must be carefully planned if the results are to be valid. You may also find it difficult to understand your users' environment or elicit their real needs over the telephone. In our consulting, we most often find telephone interviews useful after we have conducted face-to-face interviews at the users' place of work.

- **Interview individual customers in their work environment.** Individual interviews provide a chance for you to meet with people who have very specific tasks to perform. For example, you might seek the advice of expert performers or meet with novices to discover if they will react well to information delivered through a computer.

- **Interview users in groups.** User group meetings, such as focus groups, provide excellent opportunities to meet customers en masse. The interaction among group members helps to draw out ideas and sharpen thinking. The process through which a group of users reaches consensus might tell you as much about their learning needs as the consensus itself.

- **Conduct workplace observations.** There is no better way to develop a rich picture of your users than to visit them in their own environments. People at work behave differently than people around a conference table being interviewed or contacted over the telephone. You get a feel for the workplace and the environment in which the users must function. You'll also get to know your users as individuals rather than stereotypes.

Don't limit yourself to only one method for uncovering information or to the small group of methods described here. For example, interviews are best coupled with on-site observations, because users don't always tell you what they really do. In one user study we conducted, users were quick to indicate a preference for CD-ROM delivery. However, actual observation showed they had no equipment in the workplace on which to run a CD.

Similarly, observations should be coupled with interviews. After observing behaviors, you might follow up with questions about why users performed a task in a particular manner. For example, in one study, we observed that users for no apparent reason failed to use the touchscreen provided on their equipment. In our follow-up interview, we found that users' hands were often dirty, and they had learned from experience that dirty hands transfer dirt to touchscreens, which then register the dirt as a touch.

Creating user profiles

After gathering data about your users and their needs, you need to compile that information into a meaningful form. Too often, organizations dutifully conduct user research and then leave the information in notes that they never refer to again. But data left as data is just data—meaningless numbers, statistics, and notes. There's no point to the research if you don't do something with it—make it meaningful, give it life.

We strongly suggest that you compile information about your users into profiles of audience members. Make your audience real to you by giving your profiles names and backgrounds consistent with the users who will benefit from a sound information design. Not only does such an exercise give you insight about the audience, it helps you when you later prepare information to imagine how these characters might react to your work.

The number of profiles to create depends, of course, on how your audience is divided into categories of use. However, we often find, after careful analysis, that even large initial samples consolidate to four or five useful, distinctive profiles.

As you compile your profiles, consider the following guidelines.

Categorize users by job titles

If your user groups consist of many people who perform different jobs, consider creating profiles based on those jobs—Sue, the system administrator, recently promoted from nightshift operator; Dwayne, the experienced programmer, close to retirement, who knows everything about the existing system and doesn't see a need for a new one; Terry, the manager, who travels frequently and can't oversee every action of the staff.

Describe how these people view their jobs. Consider the perceived importance of the job. Then associate specific information needs with the characteristics of both the individuals and the jobs they perform.

Categorize users by demographics

Perhaps your users are homogeneous in the job they do. Look at other factors that might distinguish them. Perhaps Sally is one of only a handful of women in a predominantly male workplace. Or Maria, who works in Spain, performs her job-related activities differently than John in California. And don't forget Dave who is colorblind.

Many demographic categories could reveal differences among your users' information needs. Consider factors such as age, gender, handicaps, geographic location, and many others when creating your user profiles.

Categorize users by attitudes

The way people approach their jobs or their information needs is also a factor in your design. Consider Joe, who is right out of college, enthusiastic, and anxious to prove himself. He may be someone who is eager to study any information available. Or look at Kevin, who repairs computers and avoids information whenever possible. Harriet may be afraid of learning a new skill because she does not want to appear stupid to her colleagues.

Also consider how users approach learning new things. Are they visual or graphic learners? Are they frightened or eager? Are they willing or hesitant? Are they anxious to appear capable or worried about failing to understand or perform effectively?

Categorize users by subject-matter knowledge and experience

The amount and kind of information you present is greatly influenced by the previous knowledge and experience of your users. Chapter 3, *Determining the Stages of Use*, provides further details about categorizing your users by their experience or stages of use.

Creating use scenarios

As you plan your information library, the most important focus of your investigation, once you have identified your users, is to understand what jobs they have to perform. By studying your users' goals for the activities you will support, you gain insight into how they conceptualize the information they need. You find out how they think about their work, what language they use to describe it, how they partition the activities of their world, and so on. With information of this kind, you can begin to plan the information topics that will support them most effectively.

To explore thoroughly the user's activities and tasks, investigate and create scenarios—detailed descriptions of goal-directed activities that users perform as part of their job activities. A scenario might describe, for example, how users perform a routine task such as receiving deliveries at the company's loading dock. The scenario describes everything that happens from the time the delivery truck arrives until the goods move from receiving into inventory. At each point in the workflow, you learn how information at that point might support the tasks.

Put the characters you have developed in your user profiles into the scenarios you create and describe how they react. By imagining their responses, you can begin to identify the information needs of the audience. For example, you will be able to decide which tasks might benefit from computer-based training (such as the routine receiving tasks) and which tasks are better handled through procedural information online (unusual tasks performed infrequently).

Consider the following guidelines when writing use scenarios.

Start with routine tasks

The first scenarios you create should concentrate on routine tasks, the normal cases that everyone knows how to do. For example, the following scenario identifies the routine tasks that a person in a motor vehicle office might perform. It also gives some indication about how the potential user feels about her job and how she learned it. The scenario should continue to provide details about the everyday tasks that Joan completes; for example, how is a form filled out? What common questions does she answer?

> As a high school student, Joan worked at the state motor vehicle office in her home town. The office handled vehicle registrations. Most of the registrations were routine—individuals registering their own cars. Every day Joan helped users fill out their forms, collected fees, and handed out license plates. Although she liked meeting so many people during her day, she empathized with how long people waited simply to pick up new plates.

Joan learned how to perform these routine tasks on-the-job from other staff members. Although an instructional manual existed, describing how to perform routine tasks, it was rarely consulted for that purpose.

Add exceptions

The next scenarios should concentrate on exceptions or unusual occurrences that happen less frequently than the routine tasks. How do your characters react in such situations? What could help them react better?

For example, continuing the motor vehicle example, the following scenario describes the user's reaction to an unusual occurrence as well as an idea Joan has for improving the process.

Occasionally, someone needed to register something besides a personal car, like the day the milk company representative appeared to register a fleet of milk delivery trucks. Joan was in a panic. They were particularly busy at that time and the waiting customers were getting impatient. Joan called Marci at the next window over but found to her dismay that she was no help. "Why don't you look at our procedure manual?" Marci advised. As Joan consulted the manual for the procedures on registering fleet vehicles, she thought about how nice it would have been to have the instructions right on her computer screen. Perhaps it wouldn't have been so obvious to her customer that she needed help.

Focus on the users' goals, rather than the tasks performed with tools

When information designers analyze the information needs of their users, they have a tendency to focus on information topics that are defined by the products or processes they support, rather than on the goals of the users. For example, if the information designer works for the software developer, he or she often focuses on the tasks associated with learning to use the software application. If the information designer is concerned about form design, he or she will focus on instructions for completing forms. As a result, the information topics designed are all focused on the designer's particular interests rather than on the users' needs. The user may need to know how to use the software application and the forms in the context of a larger task, such as signing customers up for insurance policies.

Don't get bogged down in low-level tasks

In creating scenarios, describe users' high-level goals rather than the details of the low-level tasks that support those goals. Probe to uncover higher-level goals whenever users describe lower-level goals. For example, a user may tell you that his or her goal is to stack the shelves so that they appropriately display all the products for sale. However, the higher-level goal of the stacking task involves making merchandise visible and attractive so that customers can make sound buying decisions.

A premature focus on low-level goals results in the exclusion of high-level goals. Many information libraries focus on the use of applications without a context that helps users know when and why to perform tasks. For example, the online help for a customer-service application might include topics such as "finding the customer," "entering customer data," "changing customer names and addresses," and "entering a customer complaint." Although information about performing these tasks is needed by the customer-service representative who is learning to use the application, the information is often unused because it addresses only those tasks that are simple to perform. Simple data-entry tasks are often taught to newcomers on the job by experienced users.

Too often, however, the tasks that users find difficult to perform are never included in the low-level task instructions for using the application. A group of administrators working with customer insurance policies told us that they never referred to the task-oriented manuals that the company had prepared because the instructions only covered tasks that were easy to perform. These tasks were the navigation and data-entry tasks associated with using the application. They had easily learned to perform such straightforward tasks and were adequately supported by a well-designed, task-oriented interface.

Instead of all the information about how to use the application software, these users needed information about the insurance industry. They needed to know how to choose among the various policy types that the company handled. They wanted to know how particular questions needed to be answered on an application form so that they could assist customers and sales representatives. This information, covering the technical aspects of the insurance policies, was nowhere to be found. The policy information they had did not cover the technical details of the insurance policy applications, and the computer documentation they were given did not cover the insurance industry specifics either.

Avoid defining tasks in terms that only experts will understand

It is tempting to define information topics in terms that are meaningful only for experts. For example, the authors of JoAnn's cellular phone manual include a topic called "DTMF tones." JoAnn still doesn't know what DTMF tones are or why she might want to use them.

By focusing on broader goals, information designers are more likely to identify topics that are meaningful to ordinary users. The cellular phone manual could be more useful if the designer had explained how to use the phone to store credit card numbers and use them to place long distance calls. JoAnn has yet to figure out how to perform that task, even though that was one of her primary reasons for buying the phone in the first place.

Turn the scenarios into lists of questions users are likely to need information to answer

As you write your scenarios, imagine the questions that your characters might ask in the context of their work:

- How do I…?

- What is…?

- What do I do if…?

- What is an example of…?

- When should I…?

- What will happen if…?

These questions and others will help you identify the information needs of your users. In the motor vehicle bureau example, a "How do I…" set of procedures delivered through the PC help system, on a network, or on a CD-ROM would enable the staff to easily find the procedures for performing unusual tasks. The same network or another CD might also deliver a computer-based training program for new employees learning routine tasks. If most of the motor vehicle activities are handled using software applications, the procedures might be directly linked to the screens that assist in the performance of the tasks.

Chapter 4, *Categorizing Information Needs*, provides more information about categorizing the information needs of your users from this analysis.

Further reading

Carroll, John M., ed., *Scenario-Based Design: Envisioning Work and Technology in System Development* (New York: John Wiley & Sons, 1995).

Nielsen, Jakob, *Usability Engineering* (New York: Academic Press, 1993).

Raven, Mary Elizabeth and Alicia Flanders, "Using Contextual Inquiry to Learn About Your Audiences," *The Journal of Computer Documentation*, Vol. 20, No. 1, pp. 1–13, 1996.

3

Determining the Stages of Use

After you determine what kind of users you will be addressing, you need to determine how experienced they are. The maturity of your users determines the depth of information you provide. Some users want to know everything there is to learn about a particular subject matter. Others just want to learn enough to do one small job. Focusing on the intentions of your users will help you make effective decisions about their information needs and about addressing their needs on the information network you are designing.

The Stages of Use model is an effective tool for making decisions about the most useful and appropriate information to provide to users. Developed in 1986 by Hubert and Stuart Dreyfus, this model describes a sequence of behaviors that people proceed through as they learn to use a new tool or perform a new task. It states that as users learn to perform tasks and achieve their performance goals, they move through stages from the beginner who has never performed a task or used a new tool before, to those who are comfortable performing basic tasks, and then to those who become so expert in task performance that they are able act in new, innovative ways to solve problems:

- Stage 1: Novice

- Stage 2: Advanced Beginner

- Stage 3: Competent Performer

- Stage 4: Proficient Performer

- Stage 5: Expert Performer

Since the publication of this model in *Mind Over Machine*, other researchers studying computer-assisted work models have enhanced the model through their intensive interactions with users during the design and implementation of new tools for the workplace. For example, in 1997, Dr. Hackos published an update of the model in her contribution to *The Interface Design Handbook*, "The Design of Documentation and Help." This update reflects the continued study of stages of use now taking place among usability professionals.

By examining stages of use, you can add yet another dimension to your design decisions. At each stage of use, you will find that users' needs change. At early stages, they need information that supports initial task performance and leads to immediate, although small-scale, success. At later stages, they need conceptual information that allows them to develop more complex models of how task performance is related to larger goals. They need examples and theory that allow them to enrich their understanding of the task domain so that they can develop more effective task performance, including problem diagnosis and solutions. If you are able to understand the information needs of your users both as they begin to learn about tools and task performance and as they gain expertise, you can better design the information and instructional support they need.

In this chapter, we explain the characteristics of each stage, list methods of identifying users, and describe the design implications that you should consider as you plan your online information system.

Identifying and addressing Stage 1: Novices

Novices are learning to perform a skill or use a product for the first time. This means that all users are novices at some point. In these situations, every person exhibits the following characteristics.

Novices have no previous experience

Individuals without experience with a task or tool may move through Stage 1 with difficulty. If they are sufficiently intimidated by an interface or information, they may abandon the task completely or wait until someone is available to assist them. The nervous novice user simply does not know where to begin and would prefer to be led carefully and methodically through the task.

On the other hand, individuals who have considerable knowledge and experience performing similar tasks or using similar tools will move through Stage 1 quickly, sometimes in a matter of minutes. If the tool's interface and the information provided are clear and simple to use, especially if the new environment uses known terminology or resembles a known way of working, more experienced novice users will feel comfortable quickly and will move on to Stage 2: Advanced Beginner.

Novices experience concern about their ability to succeed

Even confident, experienced users feel a twinge of fear at learning a new task. They fear the loss of the expert performance skills they have developed in the known environment. Inexperienced and less confident users may be terrified that they will not succeed. They fear they will appear incompetent to themselves, their peers, and their supervisors.

Your goal should be to design both tools and information to help novices move quickly past the fear to a feeling of success and accomplishment. Novice users need information that will increase their confidence and assist them in immediately performing a relevant task. They need successful performance to bolster their attempts at understanding. In terms of computer applications, novices need simple instructional material that leads to task performance, not descriptions of functionality. In terms of job-related tasks, novices need tasks that they can successfully complete without considerable prior knowledge of the domain. If they have considerable domain knowledge or the domain is complex, they still want to be able to accomplish something quickly and then move into more complex tasks.

Novices don't want to learn, only accomplish a goal

As novices, users come to a new task with a simple goal—to get something done and to move beyond their fear that the new task will be beyond their capabilities or the new tool will be difficult or impossible to learn. They rarely approach a new task or tool from the perspective of pure learning. They have something to accomplish and hope the tool and the information will assist them.

Novices need simple task-related instructions that allow them to perform real tasks while they are learning. For example, in the interactive guide shown in Figure 3.1, Apple designers assume that the novice user needs basic information about operating a computer. This interactive guide allows the

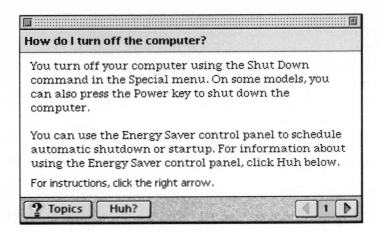

Figure 3.1: The Macintosh Guide from Apple Computer is designed to meet the needs of very new users. In this example, the user learns how to turn the computer off.

user to perform tasks in the actual operating system interface rather than a simulation of that interface. Thus, the user is accomplishing real work in the actual operating environment.

Novices don't know how to respond to mistakes

When users perform new tasks, they inevitably make mistakes—often common errors that are reasonably predictable. As part of the information provided, you should anticipate typical mistakes and include instructions for recovering from them quickly.

Even areas that are not actually mistakes should be anticipated in the likelihood that they will be perceived as mistakes. For example, in Figure 3.2, the recommended action might not solve the memory problem. However, the writers have anticipated this problem and provided further guidance.

Novices are vulnerable to confusion

During Stage 1 performance and into Stage 2, novices are particularly vulnerable to confusion. Too often they feel inundated by too much information. Many information designers tend to provide alternative methods and options for performing tasks, as in Figure 3.3, arguing that such alternatives provide freedom of choice. Unfortunately, novice users are

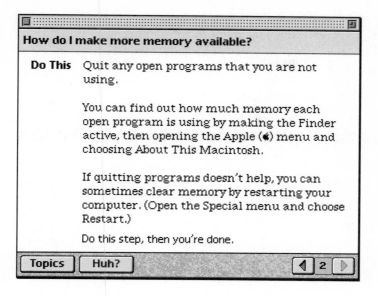

Figure 3.2: Macintosh Guide provides a recovery step if the primary action doesn't help.

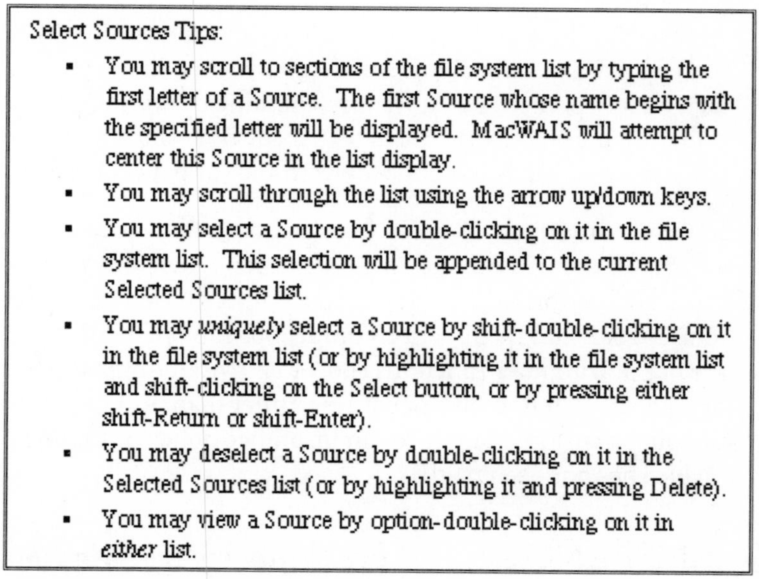

Select Sources Tips:
- You may scroll to sections of the file system list by typing the first letter of a Source. The first Source whose name begins with the specified letter will be displayed. MacWAIS will attempt to center this Source in the list display.
- You may scroll through the list using the arrow up/down keys.
- You may select a Source by double-clicking on it in the file system list. This selection will be appended to the current Selected Sources list.
- You may *uniquely* select a Source by shift-double-clicking on it in the file system list (or by highlighting it in the file system list and shift-clicking on the Select button, or by pressing either shift-Return or shift-Enter).
- You may deselect a Source by double-clicking on it in the Selected Sources list (or by highlighting it and pressing Delete).
- You may view a Source by option-double-clicking on it in *either* list.

Figure 3.3: This online manual for MacWAIS provides so many alternative ways of selecting files that novice users are likely to become confused.

unprepared for such choices, preferring to find one way to learn and perform a task, even if that way is not the most efficient. It is important, therefore, to limit the choices for novices and advanced beginners and to simplify the learning process.

Identifying and addressing Stage 2: Advanced Beginners

Once novices have gotten over their initial hesitation and have enjoyed the successful performance of a task, they are ready to become advanced beginners. At Stage 2, users move on to a process of continually learning and performing tasks. The vast majority of all users remain advanced beginners, performing the tasks they need and learning new tasks as the need arises, but never acquiring a more broad-based, conceptual understanding of the task environment. Advanced beginners exhibit the following characteristics.

Advanced beginners try tasks on their own

At Stage 2, advanced beginners are likely to explore tasks by trying them first, turning to instructional information only when they experience problems. In fact, many advanced beginners prefer asking co-workers how to perform tasks rather than using instructional text at all. Only when there is no other option will advanced beginners choose electronic (or paper) information.

In this environment, if online information is to be successful, it must be brief and highly focused on getting the work done, well illustrated with examples of successful performance, and directed entirely toward tasks that are connected to user goals and the functions of the job. Too often, information focuses on the use of computer functions (how to move among the fields in a dialog box or navigate a computer-based form) rather than how to perform real-life tasks (helping a customer apply for an insurance policy or finding out why an invoice has not been paid).

Advanced beginners have difficulty troubleshooting

Although they like to try things out before consulting support information, advanced beginners have difficulty troubleshooting problems for themselves and often get into predicaments they can't get out of. Like novices, they need help interpreting mistakes and finding quick solutions so they can get back to performing productive tasks.

However, advanced beginners are impatient with information they perceive as "nice-to-know" details, options, and explanations. For example, rather than read about the many options for performing a task, they prefer to read about one efficient way. Neither do advanced beginners read elaborate introductory material that does not appear to support performance directly. As a result, advanced beginners often prefer modular information, not extended text, to support tasks.

In Figure 3.4, you see an example of an instruction suitable for advanced beginners. The step-by-step instructions show how to perform an ordinary task in the application program. The instruction is written with minimal text for a more experienced user.

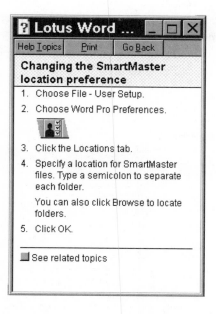

Figure 3.4: Lotus Word Pro provides very brief step-by-step instructions suitable for experienced users.

Advanced beginners want information fast

Although an electronically delivered network of information is perhaps the best means of providing job-oriented information to advanced beginners, it often fails because it is too difficult to access. For example, one group of employees was completely unsuccessful at finding the policy that told them how much paid leave they could take upon the death of a relative because the policy was titled the Bereavement Policy. The employees did not know—nor could they surmise—the meaning of the word "bereavement" as they searched through the employee handbook for the information they needed.

Instructional information, explaining how to perform standard company procedures or use application software, should be easily accessible. If the information is related to the use of an application, it should be context sensitive. When the user requests help while working with an application, the relevant help should immediately appear on the screen. Providing the advanced beginner with a table of contents from which to select the required procedural information may be too difficult a choice.

If the information needed is not related to an application, you should carefully consider how you name the procedures and organize them into tables of contents (TOCs). As much as possible, advanced beginners should be able to relate their goals to the names of the procedures in the TOCs (Figure 3.5). The TOCs should be designed with sufficient levels (primary, secondary, and tertiary) to enable advanced beginners to find the appropriate instructions within 3 minutes or less.

Figure 3.5: A complete table of contents assists users in locating the information they need to know to perform a task. When the user clicks on the task in the table of contents, the step-by-step procedure appears in a secondary window.

If advanced beginners can locate a module of information focused on task performance, they are more likely to read the information online, especially if it is sufficiently brief and does not cause reading fatigue. If they are unwilling to read text on the screen, they are often willing to print a single procedure and follow the paper instructions.

Identifying and addressing Stage 3: Competent Performers

Only a small percentage of users move beyond Stage 2. Even expert users often revert to Stage 2 when they want to learn a new procedure. But some users have the time, patience, and level of interest to become more expert in their performance of a variety of tasks. They also become interested in two aspects of task performance:

- The actions involved in solving problems

- The actions involved in performing tasks that require more complex chains of actions and decisions

Competent performers exhibit the following characteristics:

Competent performers develop conceptual models

Competent performers have sufficient experience performing a wide variety of tasks that they begin to develop a rich conceptual model of how a system works. They are beginning to be interested in having a full range of information available to them, and they are willing to read more conceptual information about the application or process they are working with. They appreciate the interrelationships among tasks to the extent that they can more easily get themselves out of trouble and correct errors.

Users at Stage 3 and above are the perfect audiences for the information offered on an intranet, the Internet, or a CD-ROM. Many organizations spend considerable resources in developing higher-level information about processes and applications. The people who originate the information are often themselves proficient or expert in their understanding of a process or application and want to share the information they have gained with less experienced users. However, only when users have the time and experience needed to reach competent performance do they begin to appreciate such detailed information. Even then, they appreciate the detail only when it has been focused to meet their learning needs.

Unfortunately, competent performers, who have a higher degree of patience for reading detailed procedural information, are often unwilling to read extended text on the computer screen. They prefer to study hard copy away from the online environment, even if they have to print the hard copy themselves. They prefer, however, to have copy that is attractive, booklike, and easy to read on paper. They do not want to read a utilitarian copy printed on computer paper in ASCII text without the illustrations in context.

If you are to provide appropriate information for competent performers and higher-level users, you must make it easy to print readable and attractive text from your network servers or CD-ROMs. Although some discrete problem-solving or troubleshooting information might be printed in modular form (one module at a time), more conceptually oriented information should be printable as a whole and retain the presentation attributes of traditional paper books.

 ### *Competent performers troubleshoot problems on their own*

Competent performers are most interested in task information to support the diagnosis and troubleshooting of common problems. They often like to work with troubleshooting tables or flow charts, selecting the appropriate symptoms from a list. They want the symptoms to lead to specific instructions for solving the problems—instructions worked out by others who have solved the same problems before.

The example in Figure 3.6 shows how competent performers might be provided with straightforward troubleshooting information that allows them to diagnose a problem and correct it.

Competent performers are not yet ready for the more complex discussions of problems and solutions that are preferred by proficient and expert users. They do not have sufficient experience with the tool or the task domain to have gained the deeper conceptual understanding that makes complex task performance and troubleshooting possible.

 ### *Competent performers seek out expert user advice*

Competent performers appreciate having access to the answers to Frequently Asked Questions (FAQs) that originate from questions to user support organizations, as shown in Figure 3.7. If the FAQs are organized into easily

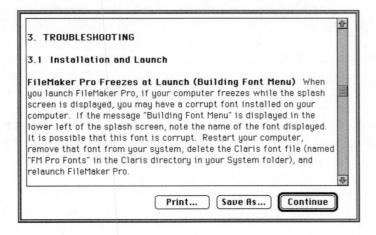

Figure 3.6: Users of FileMaker Pro are provided with advice on restarting their computers if the program does not start correctly.

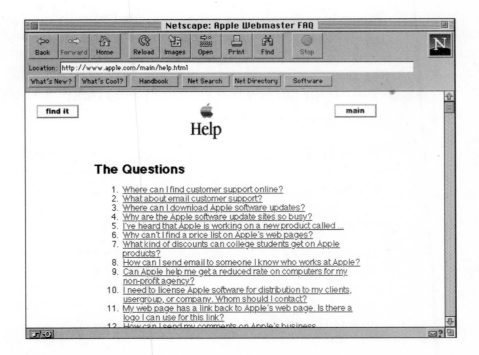

Figure 3.7: The Apple technical information FAQ (Frequently Asked Questions) Web site allows users to access answers to questions that have been asked by other users.

retrievable categories and provide specific instructions for correcting mistakes and solving the problems, Stage 3 users will be satisfied. However, if the access methods are not synchronized with the problem presentation, competent performers will be frustrated at using information networks that may contain useful information about troubleshooting and problem solving but that bury the information in inaccessible categories.

For example, in one system, users were provided with problem messages on their system screens that labeled the problems with numeric codes. Unfortunately, the information that contained the solutions was presented in alpha codes that were not related to the numeric codes. Users were frustrated in their inability to diagnose and correct what they regarded as simple problems.

Identifying and addressing Stage 4: Proficient Performers

Proficient performers have sufficient practical experience performing tasks and solving problems to be prepared for a deeper conceptual understanding of a tool or a task domain. They exhibit the following characteristics.

 Proficient performers want to understand the larger conceptual framework

Proficient performers have moved beyond simple task performance and basic troubleshooting. These users need a conceptual framework to understand how the entire system works so that they can discover solutions to complex problems by extrapolating from the framework how things are supposed to or actually work.

The potential for the electronic delivery of information is most exciting in meeting the needs of proficient performers. Little has been provided for proficient performers in the traditional information delivery mechanisms. (Paper documentation and online help are usually geared to the needs of advanced beginners.)

Unfortunately, effective information for proficient performers is more difficult for information designers and developers to acquire. Much of the knowledge for comprehensive task performance and conceptual knowledge that leads to the development of efficient and effective work flows exists only in the heads of experienced users. Effective information requires gathering the knowledge already collected by other proficient performers and expert users and transforming it into a form accessible for a proficient performer investigating a particular problem for the first time.

Such information can be captured in two ways: first, by asking subject-matter experts to write concept papers themselves; second, by using professional writers to assist the subject-matter experts in transferring their knowledge to less experienced users. The second solution may be preferred, because many subject-matter experts are not skilled communicators, and may not be especially articulate about the tasks they perform. Most of us have had the experience of asking experts how to perform complex tasks, only to have them provide incomprehensible explanations with many necessary steps left out.

Proficient performers are frustrated by oversimplified information

Users at Stage 4 are often frustrated by the simple step-by-step procedures provided them. The step-by-step procedures may be accurate, but they often are incomplete, in that they do not provide the options and conditions that proficient performers want to know about. Furthermore, proficient performers involved in solving more complex problems are also dissatisfied with the straightforward diagnosis and troubleshooting charts that were useful for competent performers. They have learned to solve all the straightforward problems that lend themselves to chartlike presentations. The problems they now experience are less amenable to simple solutions.

Because proficient performance is often automatic, based on a complex conceptual model, it is often difficult to retrieve intact. Higher-level behaviors, often inarticulate, intuitive, holistic, and immediate, are not easily broken into individual steps. In fact, one might argue that as soon as proficient performers begin to explain a process, they immediately move into an advanced beginner or competent performer level of explanation. Unfortunately, to explain complex behaviors to others requires the transformation of the behavior into a set of steps and decisions that is, of necessity, simplified.

One way to combat this problem is to focus on shortcuts that give the proficient performer information needed to optimize task skills, such as that shown in Figure 3.8. Again, the tips and tricks needed for this efficient task performance, may be in the heads of product developers who may have addressed the need for efficient performance in their original design of the processes or tools. Information gathering with product developers may lead to

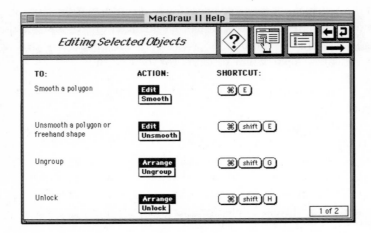

Figure 3.8: McDraw Help supports proficient performers by listing the shortcut keystrokes along with the menu options.

information about options and conditional operations not immediately obvious in the design of a task or tool.

 ## *Proficient performers correct previous poor task performance*

Proficient performers are at a point in their learning where they want to correct previous task performance that they believe is inefficient or inconsistent. Most users, when they begin to perform tasks as novices or advanced beginners, learn methods that produce the results they want but that may involve more complicated sets of actions than are necessary. Most of us have had the experience of learning to perform a task one way initially and later discovering that there is a much simpler way. Proficient performers are in a position to optimize task performance and appreciate the tips and tricks available from those who discovered them. In contrast, advanced beginners, who are often invited to use more efficient methods of performance, frequently ignore them because they lack sufficient experience to take efficiency into account.

 ## *Proficient performers learn from the experience of others*

One of the best methods of transferring proficient and expert knowledge is through scenarios—extended stories of the successful application of a procedure or the diagnosis and solution of a problem. Specific examples situated in a particular domain can be collected from subject-matter experts and made available to users of the information network. If the information network permits annotations by users to be added to the system, the scenarios may be extended by continuing contributions of tips and tricks, alternative paths and solutions, or additional insights about the task domain, thus enriching the information available. Proficient performers will also profit from online forums that allow them to exchange ideas with others at the same level of experience.

Identifying and addressing Stage 5: Expert Performers

Expert performers typically represent no more than 1 to 5 percent of users. When new processes and systems are being developed, there may be no expert, or even proficient, performers because no one has had sufficient experience to reach these stages of use. Through the trial-and-error use of a new process or tool, proficient performers and experts emerge. Their knowledge then needs to be extended to others, often most effectively through the use of electronically delivered information. Expert performers exhibit the following characteristics.

Expert performers are primary sources of knowledge and information

Experts still perform the same straightforward tasks and solve the same problems as advanced beginners and competent performers. However, they are the primary sources of knowledge and information about more complex tasks and more difficult problems. They have a comprehensive, often intuitive and inarticulate knowledge of how a process or product functions.

Expert performers continually look for better methods

Experts continue to look for new applications of processes or systems to their work environment. More than other users, they push processes and products to accommodate uses for which they were never originally intended. Because of their frequent use and in-depth practical understanding of processes and systems, they almost always know more than the original designers. As a consequence, they are most likely to seek insights from their compatriots among users and from the most knowledgeable designers.

Information networks can become effective forums for continued information exchange among experts and their less experienced colleagues. Interactive online forums (as in Figure 3.9), chat systems, and similar Web-based tools allow expert performers to exchange and debate information, leading them to innovative and efficient new solutions to problems.

Figure 3.9: The Intel newsgroup forum enables users to participate in dicussions about Intel's products and technologies.

Such forums should be monitored by information designers so that the ideas, concepts, and examples discussed might be incorporated into more structured communication systems. Information exchanged by experts might lead to opportunities to identify potential authors of additional conceptual texts or detailed use scenarios. Nuggets of information might be included in FAQ lists or in periodicals that are collected and indexed on information networks.

Responding to multiple stages in one audience

Rarely are an organization's users all at the same stage of use. Consequently, you need to determine the percentage of users at each stage and decide whether and how to accommodate their range of information needs. For example, some novice users may require instructor-led training to overcome their performance fears. Although such training might be delivered interactively through the network, it might be more cost-effectively presented in traditional training classrooms. In other cases, many of your users may have considerable experience in performing ordinary tasks but may need information on the network that allows them to optimize performance and solve complex problems.

Following are several guidelines to keep in mind as you make your decisions on the type of electronic information you will deliver to your users.

Determine the percentages of each stage of use among your user communities

Determining potential stages of use among your users provides a direction for your audience analysis. Are your users likely to be happy functioning at Stage 2, simply performing tasks that they need on the job and learning new tasks only when the need becomes critical? Are your system administrators likely to want information at Stage 3 to support problem solving? Are there computer professionals or subject-matter experts who may be interested in performing complex optimization tasks and problem solving?

Consider creating a matrix of user communities and stages of use, as shown in Table 3.1, indicating in each matrix cell the actual or potential percentage of users in each community.

Decide if your information design must support each stage of use

You may decide that you cannot support a particular stage of use in your current information design. For example, your organization may decide that novices will be trained through instructor-led classes rather than through an application or through information delivered on the intranet. Your organization may decide that, at the present time, information will be

Table 3.1: Sample Distribution of Users by Stages of Use and Job Category

Stages of Use	Clerks	Store Managers	Pricing Coordinators
Novice	40%	5%	5%
Advanced Beginner	40%	65%	75%
Competent Performer	20%	20%	20%
Proficient	0%	5%	0%
Expert	0%	5%	0%

available to meet the needs of advanced beginners rather than more advanced users, because suitable information is not yet available.

You may decide that, because most of your users are at Stages 4 and 5, you will provide them with access to an online user group where they can exchange information rather than provide them with any structured information. You may also decide that you will monitor the information exchange and prepare summaries of key points so that they can be accessed by others.

 ## *Determine how you will support each stage of use in your information design*

Decide in what way you will support each stage of use in your information design. For example, it may be useful to distinguish between procedural information for advanced beginners and conceptual and troubleshooting information for more advanced users. You may want to create modular, task-oriented procedures for advanced beginners. You may decide to support more advanced users by providing downloadable files that they can print. Remember that many users find continuous text that discusses a concept in detail much easier to read on paper than on a computer screen.

The following table characterizes information objects by stages of use. Please remember, however, that this characterization is a suggestion only. You will need to understand the needs of your own users to make decisions about the information objects most appropriate for their needs.

Stage of Use	Information Object
Novice	Task-oriented instructions
	Getting-started information
	Brief tutorials
	Error-recovery instructions
Advanced Beginner	Task-oriented instructions
	Clear purpose statements
	Examples
	Brief practice exercises
	Error-recovery instructions
Competent Performer	Advanced task instructions
	Problem diagnosis
	Problem recovery
Proficient Performer	Advanced task instructions
	Conceptual background information
	Information supporting efficient task performance
	User-group discussions
Expert Performer	Conceptual background information
	User-group discussions
	Advanced troubleshooting

Decide if you will tailor information for specific stages of use

You may want to use the concept of stages of use to label information and assist users in finding information that most effectively meets their needs. It might be advantageous, for example, to create labels such as "For Advanced

Users," "White Papers," or "Technical Notes" to discourage novices and advanced beginners and facilitate access for proficient and expert users.

 For many years, information designers have used the term "Getting Started" to label information needed by people performing a function or using an application for the first time. Be certain that the "Getting Started" label clearly identifies what the user is trying to start. Given the impossibility of using long names in many online systems, consider placing the name of the content area before the subtitle. For example, you might call a section "Travel Expenses: Getting Started" rather than "Getting started submitting your travel expenses."

In addition to labeling information according to stages of use in the introductory tables of contents in your information design, consider using labeled links inside the information objects. The labeled links should point users to related information. For example, an advanced beginner who may begin with a step-by-step, task-oriented instruction should be able to find purpose statements, alternative ways to perform tasks, examples, exercises, and conceptual background information supporting the task. The related information may be linked to the task-oriented information through the online information interface. For example, a series of labeled buttons (overview, background, example, and so on) might be placed in the context of the original task information to assist users as they progress to more advanced stages of use.

 ## Consider other media options in your approach

Users have told us that they do not want to read extended, continuous text on a computer screen. They are willing to read short passages, especially if these are available within the context of their task, but not long passages that strain both eyes and patience. Many users appear to prefer reading text on paper. However, they want to read text that is designed for ease of reading. They want text to look like traditional books, with good page layout, effective use of fonts, graphics in place, short line length, and so on.

In response, some online information designers have provided attached files that can be printed in attractive formats, including printing on both sides of a sheet (duplex) so that users can obtain a hard copy of the text that is attractive and easy to read. In such circumstances, the users can read the information online but can also choose to print the entire text or simply a portion of the text to meet their needs.

Although the problem of printing continuous, booklike text is easily solved, the problem of printing becomes more complicated when we have developed modular, linked procedural information. Many tools today do not support the printing of clusters of text and graphics that support a single content area, which may include a set of step-by-step instructions, an example, an exercise, a conceptual overview, background information, glossary definitions, and other linked information.

In most instances, users will not choose to print such clusters of information as complete sets. Rather they will choose to print an individual part of an information cluster for ease of reference while they are performing a task. However, if you find that your user community is interested in having print copies, consider structuring a cluster of information into a printable format available for downloading and printing on demand.

Further reading

Dreyfus, Hubert L. and Stuart E. Dreyfus, *Mind over Machine* (New York: The Free Press, 1986).

Ehn, Pelle, *Work-Oriented Design of Computer Artifacts* (Stockholm: Arbetslivscentrum, 1988).

Nielsen, Jakob, ed., *The Interface Design Handbook* (New York: John Wiley & Sons, 1997), in press.

4

Categorizing Information
Needs

As you move from studying your users' characteristics to understanding their performance goals, you need to categorize the individual pieces of information that will support your users in achieving their goals. For example, if your users are bank loan officers, they may need to know how to complete application forms, how to use the new loan origination system, the various loan types that the bank supports, the minimal requirements for each loan type, and more. The procedure for completing the application, procedures for using the new loan application, descriptions of loan types, and checklists of minimum requirements might all become information topics supporting the activities of the loan officer.

In Chapter 3, *Determining the Stages of Use,* you learned how to create use scenarios to identify your users' performance goals and then to draw from those scenarios the questions that users might ask in their work situations. These questions help you identify your users' needs and classify them into these categories:

- Procedural information describes the steps required to complete a specific task.

- Conceptual information provides a framework of explanations, definitions, and analysis that some users may need to complete a task.

- Reference information provides the facts and raw data that support users in performing tasks or understanding concepts.

■ Instructional information is a hybrid of procedural and conceptual information that encourages more comprehensive learning experiences for your users.

The following sections further define these information types and explain how they may fit your subject matter.

Procedural information

If you are providing support for customers who need to learn to use a product you sell or employees who need to perform tasks on the job, you will need to include procedural information in your information library. Procedural information describes the steps required to complete a specific task. The goal for this type of information is to walk the user through the successful and immediate completion of the task, not to teach the user to perform the task again without the procedures (see "Instructional information" later in this chapter).

Use the following guidelines to determine the type of information to include in procedural topics.

Include user, not system tasks

Be careful not to confuse user tasks with system tasks as you list the procedures you need to include. For example, completing a dialog box is not a user task, but a system task. The user doesn't necessarily think about completing the dialog box correctly, but rather focuses on getting real work done, often outside the context of the application software itself. The dialog box is only one part of the larger task.

Show the big picture

Many online information libraries focus on the detailed tasks that are supported by a product or tool. However, these detailed step-by-step procedures do not help the user who does not understand how the individual tasks must fit together to reach a larger goal.

For example, in the presentation software, Aldus Persuasion, users can find information that helps them export a file of presentation slides to a player format (Figure 4.1). However, this information is not helpful if they don't

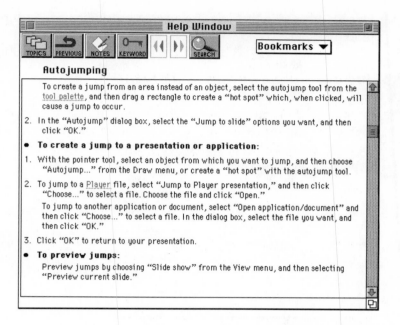

Figure 4.1: In this explanation for creating a jump in Aldus Persuasion, the user doesn't learn the full context in which the task must be performed to create a series of linked player slides.

understand that they must first create a player file before they can create a link to that file from a source file. Users need a set of information topics that carefully link the complicated sequence of steps together.

Include only procedures that are appropriate for online presentation

Procedural information that tells users how to perform the tasks they need to reach their goals lends itself to a thorough modular treatment for online delivery. Discrete topics of information that explain how to complete a travel expense form, balance an account statement, read a profit and loss report, create a work schedule, and so on are ideally suited for online presentation.

However, procedural information presented online should not be the only source for procedures that must be performed when the computer may not be running—procedures that explain how to install computer applications, perform startup activities, troubleshoot system crashes, and so on.

Plan for other ways that users might access such essential startup and recovery procedures.

Include simple purpose statements

Simple and short purpose statements help users decide whether they have found the right procedure. These statements can be written as standalone topics, as in Figure 4.2, or placed in context at the beginning of the procedural steps, as in Figure 4.3.

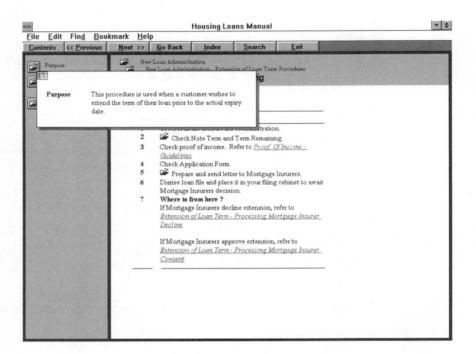

Figure 4.2: This example shows a purpose statement accessed by a button on the screen and then presented in a pop-up window as a separate topic.

If you are concerned that users will find even the simplest purpose statement to be in their way, consider putting a link to a layered, standalone statement. Users can then access the information when they are in doubt about the purpose of the steps.

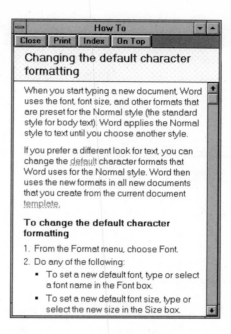

Figure 4.3: This example shows a purpose statement included at the beginning of a procedural topic. Users learn from this brief explanation why they would want to change the default character formatting.

Tell users what to do

The basic assumption behind the design of procedural information for online use is that users want only to know how to move from explanatory text back to the actual tasks as quickly as possible. Therefore, the procedural information you provide should assist users in performing their tasks quickly, effectively, and efficiently.

Present field definitions to help users complete online forms or fill in dialog boxes

A field definition describes the type of information users need to provide in a field within a dialog box, form, or table. Despite the fact that a well-designed input form should require little of this type of support, field definitions are one of the most common pieces of context-sensitive online information provided today. They are included as bubble help (PC) and balloon help (MAC). They can also be accessed through a help window or appear in a special area of the application screen.

Field definitions often provide descriptions of the field in question. For example, you might explain to users that a particular field is used to record the users' income from investments. However, field definitions also give you an opportunity to provide a very basic level of instruction with a small, succinct information topic (Figure 4.4).

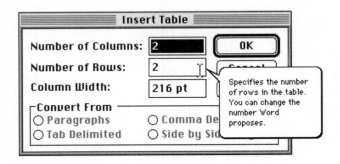

Figure 4.4: Bubble help serves as a brief information topic, defining a field within a dialog box to assist the user in providing the necessary information. Users can get quick help without having to access the formal help system.

Conceptual information

Conceptual information provides theory and background information that users may not need to complete a task. Instead, conceptual information helps many users understand the context in which procedural information fits. Users learn why they must do something in a particular manner, how to use particular information to make decisions, or how information they need might be interrelated to establish a broader context.

Although some simply stated conceptual information may assist novices or advanced beginners as they attempt to perform a new procedure or decide which procedure will suit their needs, most conceptual information is used only by Stage 3 (competent performers) and higher users. These users have enough practical experience performing tasks that they are ready to learn more about what they have been doing.

Despite the appeal to a more experienced audience, you must still carefully determine the type of information to include in a conceptual topic. You should avoid providing individual paragraphs of conceptual information without a context. Use these guidelines to help make that determination.

Tell the users only what they need to know

Often conceptual information is misrepresented as potentially useful to users. Instead of finding information that supports learning about the tasks to be performed and the goals to be accomplished, users find themselves in the depths of system definitions—descriptions of the theory behind a product's functionality, reasons for the design of the product, technical behind-the-scenes descriptions—all irrelevant to the reader. Conceptual information, although not necessarily task based, should not lose its audience focus. Just because information is available does not mean it should be included in the information you prepare for electronic delivery.

Write abstracts that explain the content and purpose of conceptual information

It has been a long time since technical and business communicators have had to consider writing abstracts for the information they deliver. When users receive paper documents, they can learn from the title, a quick look at the table of contents, and a scan of the text pages what subject the manual covers. When that same manual must be downloaded and printed or viewed by the user to learn what is in it, the process becomes more cumbersome and the time to access increases.

Many users have remarked that they find it extremely frustrating to have spent minutes or even hours to download a document only to discover it does not contain the information they need. A brief (single paragraph) abstract, such as those in Figure 4.5, that states the content, purpose, and suggested readership of a document will greatly assist the user. The online abstract should function in much the same way as the brief description you used to find on the cards in a library's card catalog. The abstract enables users to make better decisions about the usefulness of a particular text.

Provide enough information for all the stages of use in your target audience who need conceptual information

Conceptual information is primarily useful to users at Stage 3 and higher. At these stages, users are ready to learn more, to go beyond the straightforward performance of tasks to a more conceptual understanding of what they are doing and why. However, even Stage 2 and Stage 1 users may sometimes require a context for the tasks they want to perform. Such conceptual

Today's Best

Wind beneath NASCAR's wings
In GM's high-tech aerodynamics lab, race teams find out how lean they can make their machines.

They wrote what!?!
The difference between Tiger Woods, Allen Iverson and Stephon Marbury.

Top 25 breakdown
The Zone takes an inside look at Saturday's college football action.

Fowler: Bigger isn't always better
ESPN's Chris Fowler says the 16-team, five-time zone, 15-area code WAC is a good example of what's bad in college football conferences.

Figure 4.5: The short abstracts summarize the content of the ESPN news articles on this Web site. Readers can use this information to decide whether the article interests them before they access it.

information, explaining the purpose of a task, is often included in the context of the procedural text, rather than separately.

You may choose, however, to enable your users to jump from procedural information and brief conceptual statements of purpose to more conceptual information through the use of labeled links. A request for more information or a greater depth of explanation can be presented with a link to conceptual information.

Include additional conceptual information in a different layer than the primary information. That way, it doesn't get in the way of inexperienced users who don't need it, but is readily available for experienced users who want a context for their tasks or ideas about combining tasks in new ways.

 Provide information topics that help users understand why they might want to follow a particular course of action

Explanations of the importance of pursuing a course of action (or statements of the consequences of not doing so) may help users understand why the procedures must be performed as indicated. When users understand the potential consequences, they are better able to make decisions and follow effective scenarios to reach their goals.

Provide definitions of terms to increase understanding

Definitions provide information about specific terms used within the online documentation or within the specific industry or product. Definitions may be part of a glossary or programmed as a pop-up within another topic.

Just as in paper documentation, new and key terms should be defined and jargon avoided. Terminology should be used consistently throughout the information system. However, unlike paper documentation in which users must flip many pages to access a glossary item or read through a definition in the text, users can have immediate access to definitions if required but can avoid them if desired. This access is accomplished through the use of pop-up definitions.

Pop-up definitions, accessed through hypertext jumps, allow you to define all terms on a screen. However, rather than jumping to an independent glossary, thereby losing their place in the help system, users stay on the screen and see a short definition, as in Figure 4.6. This methodology allows a user to immediately learn a definition for an unknown term while remaining in the original context.

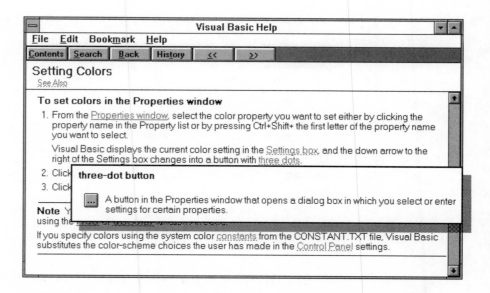

Figure 4.6: The pop-up definition for "three dots" illustrates what the three-dot button looks like and explains what it is used for.

Provide information topics that assist users in making decisions

Conceptual topics might introduce trade-offs that users need to make as they select from alternative actions to reach their goals. Examples that demonstrate the consequences of particular decision paths (as in Figure 4.7) will help users decide among options. Discussions of the criteria users should take into account as they decide on the best path of action may be presented as conceptually oriented information topics.

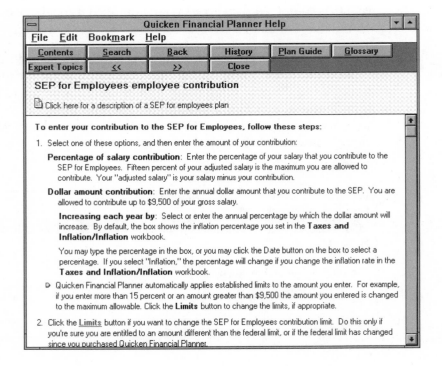

Figure 4.7: The information provided with Step 1 informs users about the input expected and the consequences associated with each possible option.

 Provide information topics that help users understand the technical theory behind a product

Technical details are often important for users who are trying to troubleshoot problems or pursue innovative ways of using products or processes. More advanced users want to know why something works the way it does. They are interested in the details behind the design. They want to know why they are doing something rather than just do it without explanation.

 ### Provide information topics that include typical scenarios users might follow to achieve a goal

Scenarios are detailed, realistic examples of how users might use a particular procedure or series of procedures to accomplish a complicated task (Figure 4.8). Scenarios help users understand and act upon complicated instructions. For example, users may be able to complete a field in their 1040 tax forms if they are given an example of a typical situation in which the field is used.

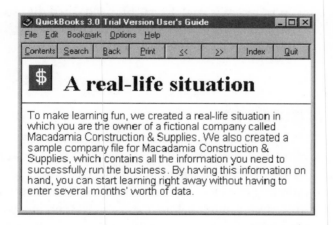

Figure 4.8: Users of Quickbooks become instant owners of a construction company so they can learn how to use the product through real-life situations.

 ### Include information about the authors, if appropriate

Where appropriate, consider including information about the authors of conceptual information. Users frequently place a high value on information that has been written by experts in the field, especially if they know something about the experts' credentials. If you have experts contributing to the development of conceptual information, it is wise to give them credit for their contributions. Some organizations even provide the users with the e-mail addresses of the experts, inviting them to send inquiries and add comments and notes to the knowledge base being developed.

However, if you do provide users with e-mail contact to the authors, be certain that the authors are alerted to the fact and that they are willing to provide timely responses to user concerns. If the responses become too time-consuming, they might refer the questions and comments to customer support.

 ### *Provide publication dates for all information in the information system*

The same frustration that accompanies the absence of a brief, descriptive abstract also occurs in the absence of a publication date. Because technical and business information on the Web is frequently updated, knowing which version is the most recent is vital. Users complain when they spend considerable time downloading a file only to discover that it is the same version that they already have.

Reference information

Reference information provides data that users need to support their decisions and tasks. Much reference information is provided in the reporting structure of database computer systems, such as reports listing sales for the month, number of customers calling customer service, new employees hired this week, and much more. This information is never meant to be learned or memorized, but rather will always be looked up when needed. It may be repeatedly consulted (as in command syntax) or used only once (as in prerequisites). Consider these guidelines when determining what reference information you might provide.

 ### *Provide information that will be used repeatedly*

Information that will be accessed frequently by different users for different reasons is best included as reference information. For example, consider programming language commands. Programmers will look for the syntax of various commands they are unfamiliar with or for a definition of the command's parameters.

Also consider the fact that when this information is a reference topic, you can access the same topic from many other topics within your system, thereby producing and maintaining the information only once.

Provide information that will be used rarely

Information that will be consulted only infrequently is often left in reference material, rather than being folded into more frequently consulted topics, where it simply gets in the way.

For example, if your users need to install a product, they may need to know how heavy it is so that they can reinforce the floors and how much heat it produces so that they can provide air conditioning. However, such information is typically consulted only during installation and would be annoying to encounter each time the user read about starting the system.

Provide discrete pieces of data that will aid in understanding and support decision making

The information library you are designing also should contain data and factual information to support decision making. You may include a collection of the company's policies, information describing the products you manufacture, descriptions of the financial or service-related products that you sell, and more. Your sources of information may include graphs, tables, datasheets, presentation slides, and other reference sources. This information as a whole helps the users make decisions from a base of information.

In most cases, the library of reference information you create will be used in a task-oriented context. If a sales representative is trying to assist a customer in choosing among insurance policies, he or she may need descriptions of each policy type. An information source that lists policy types in a decision table linked to details about each policy may provide an appropriate online job aid. The table of policy types might itself be linked to an online job aid that permits the users to search for the parameters they need in a policy (see "Parametric search" in Chapter 12).

Alternatively, the descriptive policy information may be used in the context of completing an application with the customer. If the application is online, then the descriptive information object should be linked to the computer screen displaying the application form.

Sometimes a critical piece of information will clarify a complex concept that your users are trying to apply. For example, knowing that 75 percent of customers prefer 401K savings plans, sales representatives may decide to select a 401K set of slides to introduce the company's plan to a customer.

Instructional information

Instructional information meets the needs of users who want to learn about what they are doing rather than simply complete the steps in a task. Users pursuing a learning goal often want to be able to continually and consistently perform a task, innovatively use a procedure under unique conditions, or be able to troubleshoot problems for themselves and others. Instructional information can accompany step-by-step procedures, functional descriptions, or even concepts to make them more vivid and memorable.

Users access instructional information to augment their learning of both procedures and concepts. Many users come to instructional text to "read to learn to do" (Redish, 1988). Such text supplements information provided to assist users in "reading to do" and "reading to know." Whereas procedural information simply helps the user to perform a task one time, instructional information attempts to assist the user who wants to learn how a task works and why it might be used.

Use the following guidelines when determining what to include in instructional information.

Enable users to actually complete a task while following the procedures

Apple Guide (Figure 4.9) and similar applications permit users to perform actual tasks as they interact with the help system. The guide provides step-by-step procedures that the user can perform immediately, perform with assistance, or allow the system to perform.

Use relevant, easily understood examples

Some writers have a misconception that examples are not appropriate for online documentation—the brevity of the system does not allow room for such expansion. However, as in paper documentation, examples are a good way to communicate ideas effectively and clarify difficult concepts (see Figure 4.10).

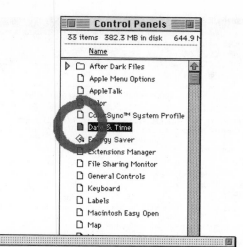

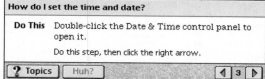

Figure 4.9: Apple Guide coaches users through a sequence of steps in individual help windows. Note that in the figure, the user is at the third step in the procedure for setting the time and date. The red coach (heavy circle) shows the user where the Date & Time panel can be found in the Control Panels folder. If users can't or don't want to complete the step themselves, Apple Guide will do it for them.

We have found that many highly experienced users do almost all their learning of new techniques by studying comprehensive examples. Users often find more information in good examples than was originally intended by the author.

Fortunately, a layered hypertext-supported design allows you to include even lengthy examples without affecting the brevity of a procedure or the simplicity of a conceptual overview. If you include a button or labeled link to an example of a procedure or a concept, a user can choose to view it or not.

Examples must be typical and relevant to the problem at hand. Too often authors will include examples that are so far-fetched that users cannot relate them to the work they are doing. We once asked a software developer why he had included a particularly esoteric example in a document. He explained, "because it could be done."

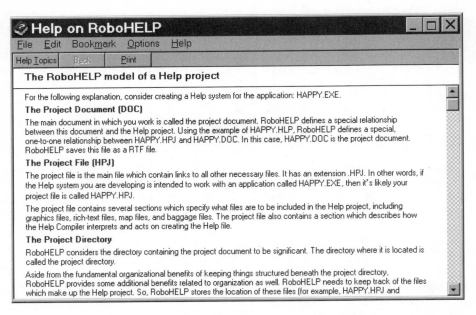

Figure 4.10: The RoboHelp help system uses the example of HAPPY.EXE to illustrate how RoboHelp names related project files.

Include simulated exercises to allow practice in a safe environment

The computer presentation of tutorials (often referred to as computer-based training or computer-assisted instruction) allows you to provide simulated environments in which users can practice procedures or experiment with data and results. They are free to explore the responses of the system without worrying about "messing up" their real data.

Using hypertext links, users can select a tutorial from within the context of a procedure they are trying to complete (Figure 4.11) or a concept they are trying to master. Alternatively, they can elect to go directly to a tutorial from a work situation and only later refer to procedural, conceptual, or reference information.

Provide positive and negative feedback

Feedback reassures users that they have performed an action correctly, and it helps users recover from mistakes. Positive feedback acknowledges a correct

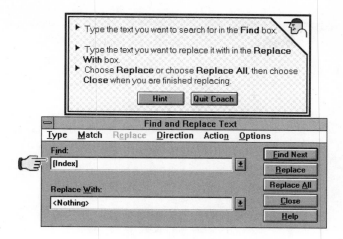

Figure 4.11: The WordPerfect tutorial allows users to practice techniques within sample documents. Once they have mastered a skill, they can then work in their real documents knowing that the WordPerfect coaches are available if needed to walk them through the skill using their real data.

choice, giving novice users confidence that they are going in the right direction.

Too often, however, instructional information focuses solely on positive reinforcement, forgetting that mistakes present an opportunity for instruction as well. Certainly negative feedback should not blame or ridicule the user, but simply point out the error and redirect effort.

Feedback is primarily available in the controlled learning environment of an online tutorial. In this environment, it is possible for the instructional designer to track errors and provide appropriate responses (see Figure 4.12). Although some designers have attempted to provide relevant feedback in the open environment of actual system use, such attempts have been largely unsuccessful. It has proven very difficult to understand the context of the users' action from a database of keystrokes.

Use demonstrations to show how a procedure works

Whereas tutorials provide users with an opportunity for interactive learning, demonstrations imply that the users are passive observers of an expert performing the tasks. In most cases, such passive demonstrations are of

Figure 4.12: The feedback statement tells users exactly what they did wrong and how to correct the problem.

limited value to the user as learner. Without participation, little real learning takes place.

However, in some cases, demonstrations can be useful illustrations of how a software application might be used. Through watching a demonstration, especially if that demonstration is supported—by an expert's voice explaining what is happening and why or on-screen annotations that provide explanations of what is going on—users are able to see what will happen if they pursue a particular course of action themselves.

 ### *Give users tools to build experience and skills*

It's one thing to train a user to complete a repetitive task and quite another to equip that user to solve a problem. A key to good instructional information is to do just that—to build users' confidence so they can face a related issue even if they weren't specifically prepared for it.

To support users' confident problem-solving behaviors, instructional information should include familiarizing users with the learning tools, including documentation, that are available to the user separate from the instruction. For example, rather than helping users out of a rough spot in a simulated procedure, refer them to the online help covering the procedure. Users learn to use the resources available to them.

Mixing information types

By no means are the four information types just described independent of one another. Most often you'll need a combination of the types for an effective online presentation. When you do so, consider the following guidelines.

Consider user needs

The majority of users of any product or service-related information are most interested in reaching specific goals. Stage 1 and 2 users prefer procedural text. They even avoid tutorials and demonstrations because they want to concentrate on getting real work done.

However, as users gain experience, they may want to add conceptual information to their reading. They may even be willing, even anxious, to pursue instructional information to support more rapid learning. They want to see examples of how other users diagnose and solve problems, and they hope that examples of good practices will help them discover the insights they need to innovate solutions to new problems. See Chapter 3 for more information about the effect of user needs on information types.

Analyze other information sources available

Once you have lists of the information needs of your users, examine the other information sources users will have at their disposal. What paper-based manuals will you provide? What classroom training? How much duplication between these items do you need or want? Decide how each will be used and the information to include in each.

For example, your paper-based library may include operating procedures, software and product manuals, descriptive information about products and services, company policies, and more. However, in many cases, you will find that the library has significant information gaps, especially in supporting high-level tasks. You may have procedural information that explains how to perform specific tasks but nothing that shows how a group of tasks performed by different departments are interrelated.

You are also likely to find that you have information that no one needs. In one investigation, we could not find anyone among the company's 80,000 field employees who had ever used the information provided in a 500-page policies and procedures manual. We advised the company to stop producing the manual and devote the resources to information that was needed and more likely to be used.

Do not repeat everything from paper-based information

Often information is provided more effectively if it is disseminated electronically. However, online information often is not intended to replace paper-based information. Your users may still require printed material to support their tasks and their learning.

There is still a time and place for paper-based information. The most obvious example is installation information. How can readers get to information about installing a product when they must first install the product to get to it? Yet we can't count the number of times we find such information simply dumped onto a CD because it was part of an original library.

However, except for information on installation and disaster recovery, you may find it more effective to deliver electronically information that you expect users want in hard copy and let them print it for themselves. Although some users complain about an increase in printing costs, this complaint is usually offset by more accessible, accurate, and timely information received and updated electronically.

Decide how you will combine information types

In combining the four information types, you can either combine the information into a single composite topic or keep each information type in separate topics, linking the related information together. Again, the choice depends on your user and the amount of information you are combining.

If the majority of your users are novices, keeping all the information they need in one topic will be most effective. However, purpose statements and reassuring feedback could simply be annoying to more advanced users. Hiding that information would be more effective if the audience is primarily at Stage 3 or higher.

Furthermore, the amount of information you are combining is a large factor. Users accessing procedures do not want to scroll through several paragraphs of background information to reach step-by-step instructions. If information will take more than a couple of sentences or require large amounts of scrolling, consider linking topics rather than combining them.

Further reading

Boggan, Scott, David Farkas, and Joe Welinske, *Developing Online Help for Windows 95* (Carmel, IN: Sams Publishing, 1996).

Brockmann, R. John, *Writing Better Computer User Documentation: From Paper to Hypertext* (New York: John Wiley & Sons, 1990).

Price, Jonathan and Henry Korman, *How to Communicate Technical Information: A Handbook of Software and Hardware Documentation* (Redwood City, CA: Benjamin/Cummings, 1993).

Redish, Janice C., "Reading to Learn to Do," *The Technical Writing Teacher*, Vol. 15, No. 3, pp. 223–233, 1988.

5

Recognizing the Implications of Design Research

After you have thought through all the design and planning steps outlined in the previous few chapters, you will have a tremendous amount of information before you. How should the fruits of your analysis come together in a sound information design? Through the chapters, we've suggested that you consider the implications of specific design data you may have uncovered. Now you need to pull all the implications together and develop a comprehensive information design that meets the needs of your audiences.

In this chapter, we help you identify and prioritize the implications of your research. We then provide four case studies that demonstrate how others made their design decisions and applied them with interesting and useful results.

Identifying design implications

The result of your information gathering will prove to be critical to the success of your information-design project. Creating user profiles and task scenarios are the most important ingredients of the design process. They are the building blocks of the information libraries you are striving to create. By now, you should be able to imagine what your users need to be successful and how they will react to the structure and design elements of your library. You have identified the factors that are most important to them in considering the following questions.

What media are required?

The first implication of your design research should focus on your selection of the best media mix for the information your users need to perform successfully and fulfill their information requirements. Is online communication the right solution? Is electronic information the only media needed?

Consider the experience and attitudes of your users. How will they feel about getting their information online? Are they intimidated by technology? Are they willing to participate in a new information paradigm? Do they still prefer the familiar world of information delivered on paper? Can that preference be overcome by providing alternatives to reading online?

Consider how your user's work environment affects the media choice. Will online information be more accessible because paper documentation must be stored out of sight and out of mind? Is electronic information more readily available in the workplace? Is the user's work environment conducive to the use of multimedia? Or is the size of a graphic displayed in the small space and poor resolution of the computer screen a serious limitation on usability?

Finally, what is the nature of the information you have to present? Are you documenting tasks that will be performed away from the computer that accesses the information? Would it be better to provide users with a job aid that sits on their physical rather than their virtual desktops?

Typically, one medium is not the total solution. You must determine the media mix that will provide your users with the best support.

How should the information system be structured?

The information structure you select should be closely tied to the way users think about the information they need. How do they categorize the information? What is most important? What is least important to their needs? Your information structure should support their mental model.

The types of information your users are most likely to use fundamentally affects the structure you design. If most of your users are novices, the most easily accessed information should be task-oriented procedures, with background information attached through hypertext links. If users are proficient performers, you may want to reverse this structure, placing conceptual and background information at the surface.

The chapters in Part 2 of this book discuss how to plan the structure of your system further.

How should information be accessed?

Given the type of information required, the users' environment, and the users' experience, what access methods should you provide? Should information be linked to a computer application through a context-sensitive system? If not, how will users get to the information they need? Will they in a table of contents or index, or use another search mechanism? Chapter 12, *Ensuring Accessibility,* provides design guidelines on access methods.

What interface design features should be included?

The way your users will interact with your system affects the features of your interface. For example, will they want to take notes or leave bookmarks for later reference? Will they want to copy information and mail it to someone else?

If your users are familiar with other information delivery systems, such as standard Windows help, consider maintaining the key interface elements of the standard designs. If they find familiar information objects, your users need not learn to navigate through new interface objects in addition to searching for the content they need.

Chapter 11, *Designing the Information Interface,* discusses guidelines to consider in this part of your design.

How will users move through the system?

Even the most experienced users of online information can become lost and frustrated with the invisibility of the information they are trying to locate. Not only will information maps and context sensitivity assist them in finding what they need, but a determinedly consistent information structure throughout your design will help them build a sound mental model. Chapter 13, *Providing Navigation Aids,* discusses these issues in more detail.

What writing style is appropriate?

The stages of use represented by your user population should have a great impact on the tone and style of your writing. Not only should you be concerned with reading level but also with the type of information required. Novices may require more assurance than more experienced users. Some experienced users find a minimalist style to be frustratingly superficial and incomplete. Chapter 14, *Composing Your Topics,* and Chapter 15, *Writing for Readability,* discuss these issues further.

What graphics are required to communicate effectively?

Your users' preferences and the types of information you are presenting dictate the graphic design elements you select and the illustrations you include. See Chapter 16, *Adding Graphics,* for a discussion of the considerations you should take into account.

What level of interactivity is required?

Given the proliferation of video games and multimedia entertainment, you may find your audience bored by your information, despite the fact that the content is not necessarily intended to be entertaining. You may discover that your audience will respond better to an interactive multimedia presentation, with more graphics and less text. Our final chapter on adding multimedia introduces basic ideas about new design elements increasingly available to information designers.

Making trade-offs

Unfortunately, the design implications you identify may not always be complementary. As with all design problems, you have many trade-offs to balance before you arrive at a solution. The implications are often at odds, forcing you to make trade-offs among a variety of design elements and conflicting user needs. You will likely have to make difficult decisions about user information needs and the information that you have at hand, whether you can develop the system within the required budgets and schedules, and how you will be able to maintain the library in the face of many demands on your time and energy. In each case, you must make the best decisions you can about the design. Remember the prime directive of information designers—if they cannot use it, it does not work.

The following guidelines will help you set your design priorities.

Put user needs first

Your primary goal, no matter what trade-offs you face, should always be to meet your users' needs first. The structure of your internal departments, the sources of information, the ways you categorize your users, or even the convenience of updating should never override a choice to support how your users think about information.

If users fail to find the information they need quickly and easily, if they don't recognize the information they find as useful to them, or if they can't follow the procedures or don't find the supporting information they need, they will reject your information library and find other means of support. Users give information designers only a few chances to demonstrate the utility of their designs. After two or three unsuccessful attempts to find information and use it effectively, users decide that a search is not worth their effort or that the information they need does not exist in the online information library. They conclude that the designers did not understand them or recognize their needs. Frequently, they will learn to call on other people for help rather than trying to use the information you have provided.

If an information design is successful, however, users will rely on it to find answers to their questions. Instead of calling for support, they will use the information at hand because it helps them complete a task and reach their goal more quickly.

Consult your users

In some cases, your research will not clearly indicate which decisions are best for your users. Don't neglect testing alternatives with members of your audience. Invite two small groups of users to try using the design elements in question—half using one alternative and half the other. See Chapter 9, *Testing Your Design and Implementation,* for more information about usability testing.

Consider available resources

Design projects will always be limited by the resources available. When balancing your trade-offs, consider your budget, schedule, and staffing to complete a project. There may be some features you simply cannot include within these constraints.

Get expert advice

If user testing does not resolve the conflict, you may want to seek the opinions of experts. Books such as this one, conferences, and online forums, all provide expert advice on what implications are most important to address. Consider reviews of other online systems—what did the reviewers prefer? What reasoning did they use to support their preferences?

The remainder of this chapter provides some of that expert advice through four case studies. These examples illustrate the designs that resulted when the following four companies were confronted with the same decisions you must make:

- SUNCORP Building Society (HowWe)

- Compaq Computer (System Reference Library)

- Microsoft (Money)

- Apple Computer (Macintosh Guide)

Although we don't know the specific issues facing each company, we point out the strengths that each system demonstrates and the reasons each system works with its intended audience.

Case Study 1: SUNCORP Building Society

SUNCORP Building Society Limited in Brisbane, Australia is one of the country's largest insurance and banking organizations. Employees of the Building Society handle a myriad of financial transactions (banking and insurance) for its customers. When SUNCORP decided to improve its electronic delivery of information, project leaders Dean Bell and Helen Smith were charged with redesigning an existing online information source that was rarely used. By all accounts, only about 10 percent of the users ever used the system to find information. The project team needed to design a more effective online information system and encourage its use.

Examples of the HowWe information library are used with the express permission of SUNCORP Building Society Limited, Brisbane, Australia.

Media choices

The sheer bulk of information about the various financial transactions handled by employees suggested CD-ROM delivery. However, Dean and Helen knew that the existing system was a detriment to the success of a new system. Employees had learned that the online information was difficult to find and had virtually stopped using it. To overcome the negative experience with electronic information, Dean and Helen thoroughly prepared the users for the introduction of the HowWe system, raising expectations that a better information design was on its way.

The combination of advanced preparation and a well-designed, thoroughly consistent library helped to ensure success. When the new information library was implemented, usage increased to 90 percent. The information designers had succeeded in overcoming user fears, producing a system that invited use.

Structure of the information system

When Dean and Helen began to design an information structure, they first considered how the users thought about the information. The structure they developed for SUNCORP's information system is based on the principle that Stage 2 users need step-by-step procedures for completing on-the-job tasks. In fact, the information library is called HowWe, emphasizing the task-oriented nature of the core material.

Dean and Helen designed HowWe specifically to serve the task-oriented information needs of a wide variety of SUNCORP employees. They organized the top level of the system according to the job activities. Employees can look for information grouped by the high-level activities they perform, including

- Collections

- Loan administration

- Reconciliations

- Payouts

- Account maintenance

- Branch operations

- Data input

Some of these tasks are further broken down. For example, some choices on the initial screen relate to the types of loans a particular employee may be handling:

- Housing

- Consumer

- Commercial

In all, users have 19 possible sources of information from which to choose.

Accessibility

Because HowWe is not tied to a specific software program, users access HowWe through the Program Manager in Windows (Figure 5.1). However, rather than simply launch the system, HowWe asks users to make an initial decision about the kind of information they want. In this way, Dean and Helen could simulate the advantages of a context-sensitive system—once in the system, users were one step closer to their information goals.

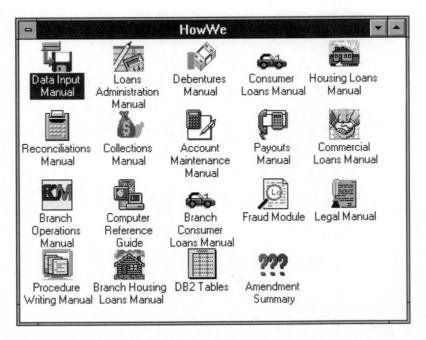

Figure 5.1: The icons in Program Manager show the wide variety of information choices that users can make as they look for information to meet their needs.

Interface design

SUNCORP's interface is a basic Windows-help interface, developed in HDK. It uses Microsoft's conventional menus, button bar, and color scheme to indicate hypertext links.Unlike standard WinHelp, however, SUNCORP uses a side bar to indicate the users location in the system and to provide links to related topics.

In addition, SUNCORP added a cartoon character, Howie, to stress the simplicity of using the system (Figure 5.2). The character appears on many screens and was part of a PR campaign to encourage employees to use the online library of task-based information.

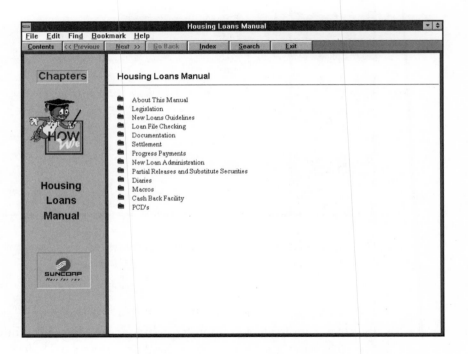

Figure 5.2: Howie adds interest to the SUNCORP interface and reminds users that the system is easy to use.

Navigation aids

Because users must move through the system looking for information, Dean and Helen recognized the potential that users might get lost. They designed several navigation aids into the interface so that users always know where they are—the manual, chapter, and subsection. By looking at the set of open book icons at the top of the procedures screen, users know that they are still in the Housing Loans Manual and in the New Loan Administration chapter (Figure 5.3).

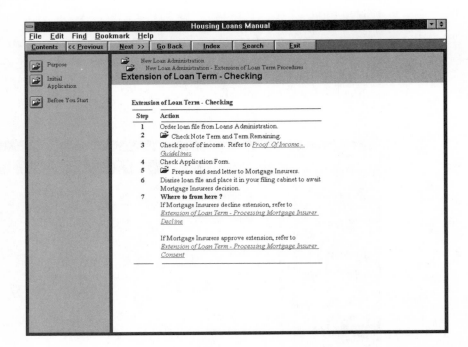

Figure 5.3: As users move through the HowWe system, they see a flowchart showing their exact location.

Users move through the HowWe system with a series of menu choices. Once they have chosen an icon from Program Manager, they move into the WinHelp-based system where they have a second set of choices to make. For example, if users are responsible for handling residential real estate loans, they double click on the Housing Loans Manual from Program Manager and see a list of 13 topics within that manual to choose from (Figure 5.4).

These lower-level topics focus on the activities and information that SUNCORP's loan administrators need to know. A loan administrator has a variety of choices from conceptual information that explains the legislation regulating housing loans to procedures for handling new loans, checking the

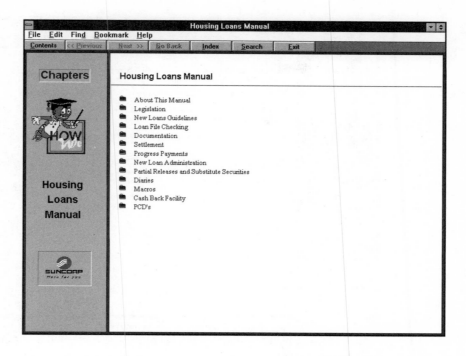

Figure 5.4: The Housing Loans Manual's main menu provides a second level of choices for the user.

loan file, reviewing loan documentation, and so on. Introductory information is provided under the topic "About This Manual," which heads the content list.

The menu-driven navigation continues throughout the system. For example, if the user selects "New Loan Administration," a list of sections related to this topic is displayed (Figure 5.5).

The user can now choose among four different types of procedures dealing with maintenance, loan extensions, surplus funds, and bank cheques. Selecting "Extension of Loan Term Procedures," takes the user to a list of topics, the third choice for someone using the Housing Loans Manual (Figure 5.6). Notice that at each step, the users make fewer choices, thus reducing the cognitive load.

The Topics screen leads the users directly from a sequence of three choices into the step-by-step procedure that explains how to check the loan file and begin to process the request for a loan extension.

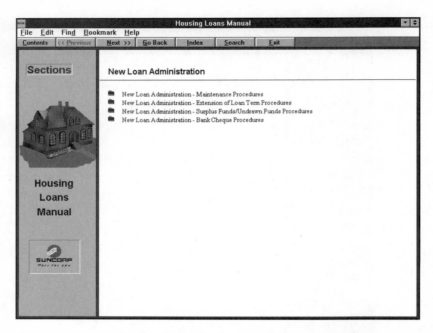

Figure 5.5: The next screen displays a list of the topics covered in the chapter on new loan administration.

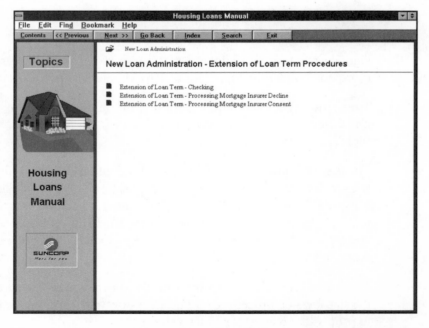

Figure 5.6: Users must choose from a list of task-oriented topics included under the high-level task of extending the term of a customer's loan.

Writing style

Once users get to a procedure screen, they find a primary window consisting of a series of action steps that explain with minimal text how to perform the task at hand.

To support the minority of users who may want background information, the secondary window contains supporting information that the users may want to consult as they proceed through the procedures. For example, in Figure 5.7, the secondary window at the left of the primary window includes several hypertext links—a statement of the purpose for performing the procedures, information about handling an initial application, and items the users might need to know, called Before You Start." If the users click on one of the open file icons in the secondary window, pop-ups appear containing supplementary information to the primary task.

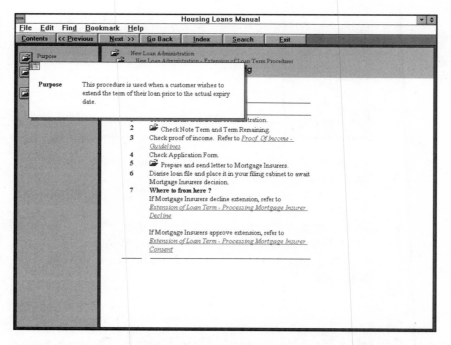

Figure 5.7: The pop-up window explains when to use the described procedure.

Dean and Helen decided to hide detailed instructions about the primary steps in pop-ups, anticipating that most users would know how to complete the primary step independently. The detailed instructions support the needs of less experienced users. Each open file icon in the Action column provides more information on completing the step. For example, if the users do not know how to prepare and send a letter to the mortgage insurers, they simply click on the open file icon and a pop-up appears with more detailed steps (Figure 5.8).

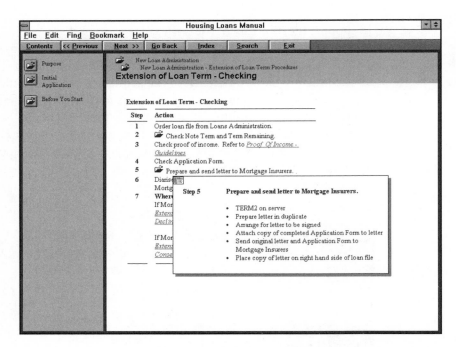

Figure 5.8: A pop-up window provides additional detailed steps to complete one of the steps in the primary window.

The underscored items, such a "Proof of Income—Guidelines" and "Extension of Loan Term—Processing Mortgage Insurer Decline," provide links to other HowWe procedures included in different chapters of the Housing Loans Manual.

Case Study 2: Compaq Systems Reference Library

In contrast to the SUNCORP library, the Compaq Systems Reference Library is designed for customers and other external users such as dealers and third-party field-maintenance organizations. The Reference Library provides information for people who want to buy new servers, add optional peripherals and other equipment, diagnose problems, repair and replace defective parts, and find ways to optimize the performance of their servers.

The Compaq information designers needed a way to leverage existing information that had been originally written for hardcopy and build a system that two distinct classes of users would find useful—beginning and experienced system server administrations and technicians. Although some of the information needed by the users would be the same, the information designers had to find ways to support beginners while not offending experienced users.

The Systems Reference Library is an excellent example of how information about multiple products might be designed for quick access and ease of use. It has been well received by system-administrator customers. They find the CDs easier to store (less bookcase space) and, therefore, more accessible to all the people in the organization who need access to the information. In addition, they find that it contains much of the information they need. They use it in conjunction with the Compaq Web site, which provides them with updates and new information between releases of the CD-ROM.

Media choices

The Systems Reference Library is packaged on a CD-ROM that is shipped with the server. Most of the information on the CD is also available from another source. For example, some of the same information appears on Compaq's Web site, allowing users to update their information by downloading copies of the files. In addition, Compaq continues to provide hardcopy versions of the documents on the CD.

Although the media choices provide considerable redundancy, Compaq has found that many advanced users do not want to read white papers and other technical information on screen. They prefer to print this information from the CD or the Web and carry it with them on a trip or take it home and read in their leisure time. Providing hardcopy, as well as online information, to these customers saves them time and keeps them happy.

Structure of the information system

Compaq's system designers believed that most of the documentation provided on the CD was well known to their audience. They felt that restructuring that documentation for online delivery would make the information harder to find for the large number of users intimately familiar with the paper counterparts. Thus, at the first level, the server library is organized according to the legacy hardcopy documents—maintenance guides, reference manuals, a parts catalog, a product catalog that describes the capabilities of the products, and detailed technical information, such as TechNotes (Figure 5.9).

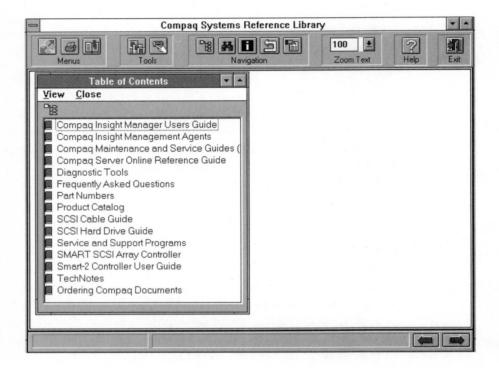

Figure 5.9: The main menu of the Systems Server Library is organized by the legacy hardcopy documents.

The users' first decision, therefore, must be about the type of information for which they are searching. The information types are loosely associated with the activities the user might be interested in pursuing. For example, someone looking for a particular part number might turn first to the parts catalog, whereas someone looking for information on replacing a part might select the maintenance guides.

Although some of the choices have self-explanatory titles, others are more obscure, making the user's choice more difficult. For example, what might a user expect to find in a technical reference manual or in a TechNote? To choose one of these titles, users must already be familiar with the title and what it contains or must search further by consulting the table of contents of each title under question.

At the next levels, however, the structure becomes increasingly specific. At the second level, the library is organized by type of equipment (Figure 5.10). The choice is much easier for all levels of users because it is likely that they know the model of the equipment they want to repair. In fact, selecting the equipment might have been an easier choice at the main menu. Users have told us that they prefer to see all the information about a particular piece of equipment grouped together, just as they would keep the hardcopy manuals together on a book shelf.

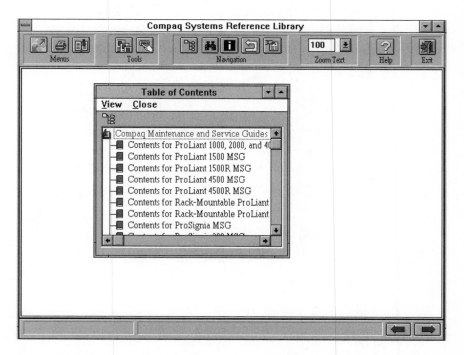

Figure 5.10: This second-level menu lists the server products for which maintenance information is available.

Regardless of the types of document chosen, this same structure is repeated. The type of equipment appears first, leading to a list of items. This repetition of structure is a strength of this particular library design. Users quickly become familiar with the structure because it is very consistent. That consistency allows them to make decisions quickly and reach the information they need.

Interface design

Compaq designers built a customized interface for their Systems Reference Library, which they tested thoroughly in formal usability testing. Although they maintained the structure of the information from their legacy documents, they did reformat it for online display. For example, product specifications have been reorganized so that are easy to read onscreen (Figure 5.11).

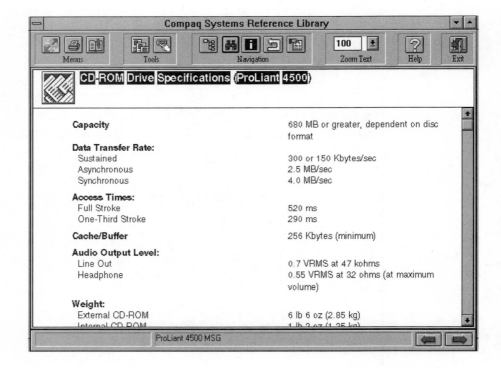

Figure 5.11: A table of CD-ROM drive specifications is organized for ease of use on screen.

Navigation aids

As in the SUNCORP system, navigation through the Compaq system is mainly menu-driven, with users choosing topics from increasingly more specific areas. The menus are short enough that they can be easily scanned for information. If the lists were longer, the designer might have grouped the items with subheadings.

Unlike SUNCORP, Compaq did not have the standard Windows navigation tools available. In their custom interface, they include a bank of five navigation buttons—table of contents, search, index, back, and history.

Graphics

The nature of the information on the CD calls for a heavy use of graphics. Compaq designers recognized that the lower resolution of the screen could create problems for online viewing of the legacy drawings. To compensate, they provided a zoom feature so that users can enlarge drawings for easier viewing.

The Parts Catalog provides yet another graphics feature that makes information quickly and easily available for users. After the users select the type of equipment for which they need parts, an exploded view of the product appears with reference numbers that contain hypertext links (Figure 5.12). When the users select a reference number, a pop-up window appears with details about the part and the correct part order number.

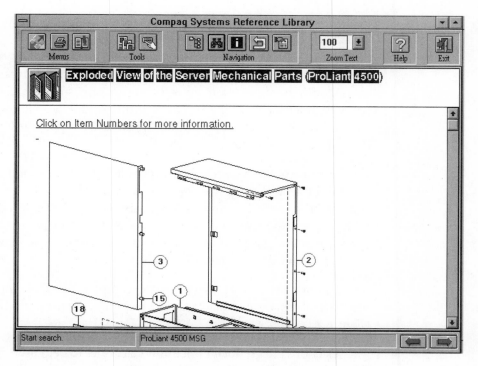

Figure 5.12: An exploded view of the server mechanical parts with reference numbers providing hypertext links to details about the part.

Case Study 3: Microsoft Money

Microsoft Money is designed for a wide variety of people who use Money to keep track of their accounts, create and monitor budgets, set up and follow their investments, and perform other personal financial record keeping tasks. The help system is shipped with the product and contains links that allow the user to move quickly between the computer application itself and the associated help topics.

Media choices

The designers of Microsoft Money anticipated that some users prefer hardcopy manuals, and others prefer to find information online. They therefore supplement the help system with a hardcopy manual. Users who use Money while on the road with a laptop computer will probably not carry the manual, relying instead on the help system to answer questions and solve problems.

Structure of the information system

The Microsoft Money help system is organized around the types of financial transactions users can maintain with the program, such as accounts, loans, and investments (Figure 5.13). The structure is very flat—in most cases only two menu choices are required from the initial help contents (main menu) to the procedure for performing the task.

The structure of the system is further clarified by brief lists of the tasks that the users will find associated with each category of information on the table of contents. For example, if users select Loans, they will find procedures for setting up a loan, entering loan payments, and creating loan reports and various types of charts. These small abstracts assist users in making the right choice and finding information quickly.

At the second menu level, users view the complete list of conceptual and task-oriented information available for the category they have selected (Figure 5.14).

The selections are grouped under four categories to help users make their selections more easily. The introduction points to conceptual information that explains what money accounts are and describes a way for users to think about

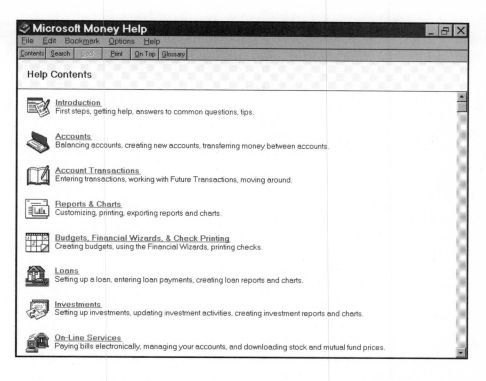

Figure 5.13: The main help menu for the Microsoft Money help system lists the different types of functions available.

naming their accounts so that they are easy to use in the future. The rest of the headings are task-oriented and grouped under three categories: "Working with different types of accounts," "Reconciling with a statement," and "Working with several accounts." The list is reasonably short, containing only 13 choices, which users will be able to scan quickly. This list should contain the most common tasks performed with accounts.

Accessibility

Microsoft Money is linked directly to a software application, helping users perform tasks and learn how the system works. As a result, specific topics can be accessed directly from a related screen in the application or through the help menu.

Novice users who want only to know how to complete a specific task can use the help button on the dialog box to get context-sensitive help. Users who

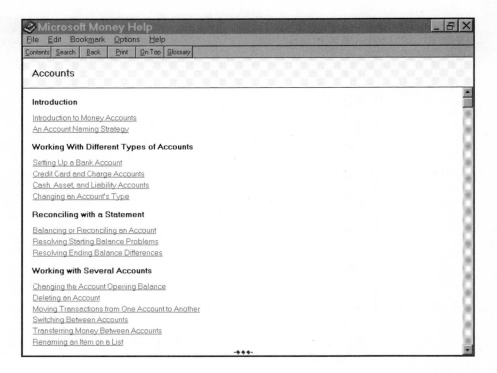

Figure 5.14: The Accounts menu appears when the user selects "Accounts" from the main help menu.

want more background can access the table of contents and go to all topics that interest them.

Included in Money's button bank is the OnTop button, which allows users to keep the help screen on top of their application so they can refer to it as a kind of coach while completing their tasks.

Interface design and navigation aids

As a Microsoft application, Money uses the Microsoft standards for interface design and navigation aids. Since many users are first exposed to Money because it is bundled with their new computer and Win95, Microsoft seems to expect that users will soon be familiar with these standards, if they aren't already.

Writing style

The writers of Money's help system recognized that most users of Money want to get something done. Step-by-step procedures are the focus of the system and typically begin all topics. In general the steps are presented separate from any supporting information, which is presented later in the topic (Figure 5.15).

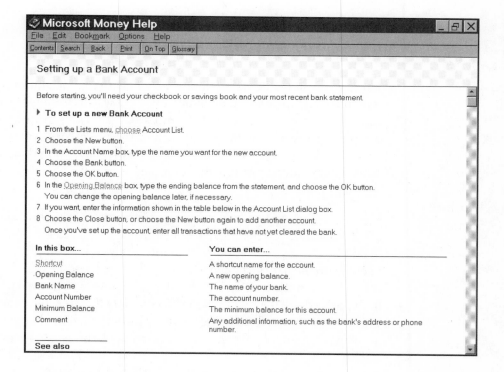

Figure 5.15: This procedure topic explains how to set up a bank account. Supporting information for Step 7 follows Step 8 so that experienced users do not have to skim through it before continuing their task.

At the end of each of Money's procedural help topics is a list of hypertext links that take users to other related topics. The related topics are clearly associated with the information provided in the help topic, helping users understand why they might want to access one of the related topics. For example, in Figure 5.15, one of the related topics, "Changing the Account Opening Balance," refers to a conditional statement included in Step 6, which suggests that the user can change the opening balance later. This topic refers to a very common mistake made by new Money users, who frequently want to change the opening balance that they originally entered when they set up a new account. The help designer has anticipated the problem and provided an immediate solution in the form of a hypertext link to the corrective procedure.

For more information, users are also referred to specific chapters of the User's Guide. References to the hardcopy user's guide also points out the relationship between the online and paper information.

Case Study 4: Macintosh Guide

The Macintosh Guide system first appeared with the Macintosh operating system 7.5 and introduced an innovative help system to support user tasks with the Macintosh operating system. The Guide assists the user in completing a task through step-by-step instructions, coach marks on the screen to indicate what menu item or data-entry field should be used, and active intervention to ensure that each step is complete before the next step appears.

Macintosh Guide provides a feature that expands its functionality beyond that of a standard help system like the one included with Microsoft's Money. Macintosh Guide enables the user to interact with the computer screens while referring to the help system, performing the steps described in the procedures. Additionally, if the user does not understand how to perform a particular step in the procedure, the help system will complete the procedure for the user. This user graduates from being a passive reader of help to being an active participant in interacting with the program with the assistance of the help system.

Accessibility

Apple designers anticipated that users would need guidance using Macintosh Guide. Thus when users invoke the Guide (from the ? menu on the top right of their screens), they first see an instruction topic that explains how to use the help system (Figure 5.16).

Three choices are then available to users:

- ■ "Topics" brings up a list of 17 choices in a first-level menu (Figure 5.17).

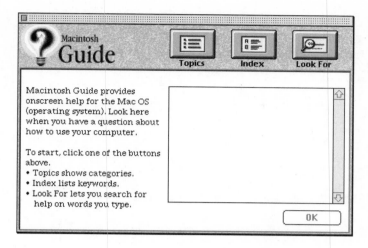

Figure 5.16: Users get immediate guidance on how to use Macintosh Guide. These instructions do not become annoying as users gain experience, however, because the buttons they describe are at the top of the screen. Users can simply click on the button they want without reading the instructions.

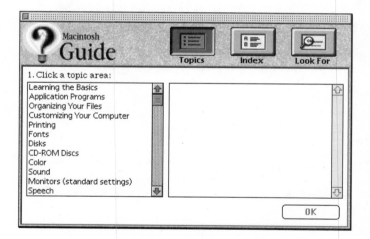

Figure 5.17: The first-level topic areas are difficult to choose from.

- ■ "Index" brings up an alphabetical list of items, controlled by a slider at the top of the choice box (Figure 5.18).

- ■ "Look For" brings up a search screen that lets the user enter one or more words and invoke a search (Figure 5.19).

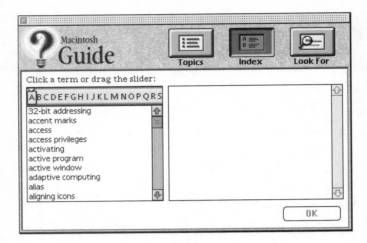

Figure 5.18: The Index screen enables users to quickly move to the right part of the alphabet without scrolling.

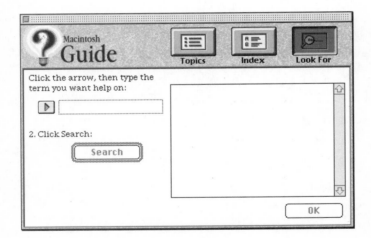

Figure 5.19: The search screen provides clear instructions to users for finding the information they need.

Navigation aids

If users choose to navigate through the topics menu, they must make a rather sophisticated set of decisions about where to locate the information needed. The topic areas are designated by words or phrases that refer to some portion of the operating system. The user must guess where among these topic areas to find the information needed. For example, if the user wants to set the date and time on the computer, will the information be found under basics, tips, system options, or one of the other areas? Contrast the limited information provided here with the more complete information provided on the Microsoft Money first-level menu. Certainly, operating system functions are more difficult to describe, especially to Stage 1 and 2 users. However, that is all the more reason to provide additional explanatory information.

To help support the decision-making process of selecting the right topic, Apple designers have split the screen so that a list of subtopics related to the primary topic appears on the right. Users don't have to access another screen of menu choices before they realize they made the wrong first choice.

The subtopics are divided into subcategories based on the interests of typical Stage 2 users and the information available. The categories vary for each primary topic, but may include the following, among others:

- "How do I" topics are task oriented, representing the activities a Stage 1 or 2 user might want to pursue, such as

  - Putting the system to sleep

  - Switching printers

  - Changing the color of an icon

  - Setting the date and time

  and so on.

- Definition topics explain key terms and objects, such as

  - Control panel

  - Keyboard layout

  - Folder

  - Stationery pad

  and others.

- The About topics cover basic concepts that the user may want to understand, such as

  - The Trackpad

- The Control Strip

There are very few About topics.

■ "Why" topics refer to questions users might ask if something is happening that they don't understand, such as

- Why is the battery draining so fast?

- Why is the pointer too fast (or too slow)?

- Why is the screen flickering?

■ "Why can't I" points to topics about items that the user expects to work but don't, such as

- Why can't I use my modem?

- Why can't I use my external monitor?

- Why can't I print with the fonts I want?

In all these categories, the information designer has tried to anticipate the types of questions users might ask. The users addressed appear to be primarily Stage 1, 2, and 3 users who are trying to accomplish tasks or correct something that has gone wrong.

Interactivity

Up to this point, Macintosh Guide looks like any well-organized help system. However, when the user selects a topic, the presentation of actions and results works quite differently. The user is provided the opportunity to perform the function indicated by the instruction or let the system perform the function instead. For example, if the user wants help with setting the time and date on the computer, three help screens appear sequentially (Figure 5.20).

The help screens take the user from the desktop through the entire task. If the user happens to have the Date & Time control panel open, the help screens begin with the first step needed to make changes in the fields. The system takes into account where the user is in the task and calls the required help screens.

Each help screen is one step in the procedure. If the user is able to perform the complete procedure using only the first step, then he or she can dismiss the rest of the help steps. Note that the first help step in Figure 5.20 contains

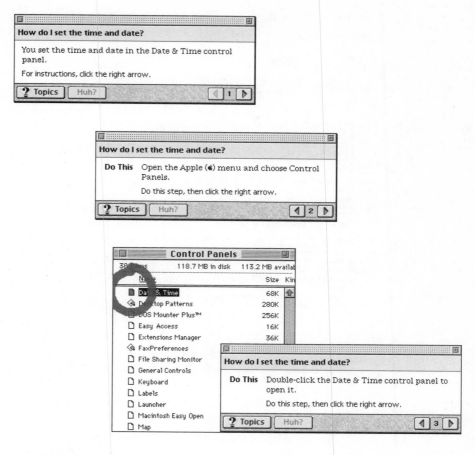

Figure 5.20: Macintosh Guide provides a sequence of help screens for the topic, "How do I set the time and date?" that guides users through the task.

sufficient information for a somewhat more experienced user to perform the task without further assistance.

When the user reaches a step that calls for selecting a menu item or opening a dialog box, the help system directs the user's attention to the menu bar or the selection menu by drawing a heavy red circle, called a coach mark, around the appropriate item. For example, if the instruction tells the user to open the File menu, the red circle appears around the word "File" in the upper left-hand corner of the screen.

Finally, if the user proceeds to the next step in the procedure without having completed the previous step, the Macintosh Guide actually performs the step for the user (Figure 5.21). This prevents novice users from overlooking the necessary steps required and later wondering why they weren't successful.

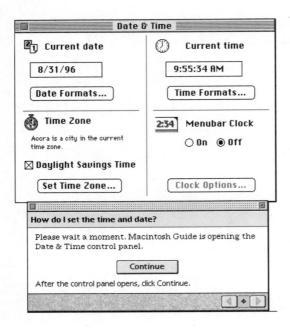

Figure 5.21: Macintosh Guide performs required steps in the sequence before continuing to the next screen.

Since Macintosh Guide was released, other systems have been enhanced to include a degree of interactivity between user and help system. For example, the Windows 95 help system provides a similar capability that allows users to click on an open icon within a procedure step (Figure 5.22). The help system proceeds to open the dialog box that is used to complete the task. However, the user is not provided information about finding the same dialog box in the future. In contrast, Macintosh Guide is especially well designed to encourage a user to learn how to perform a task without further assistance.

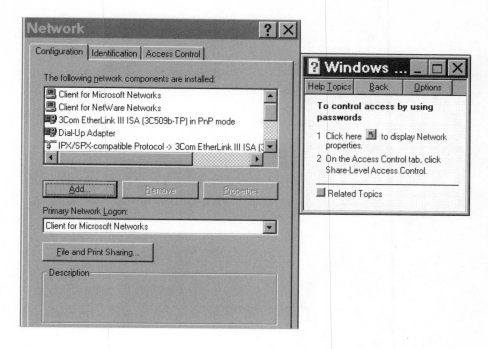

Figure 5.22: Windows 95 Help encourages users to complete steps while reading a help topic. It provides an open icon that takes users to the correct place in the system to begin work.

Further reading

Macintosh Human Interface Guidelines by Apple Computer, Inc. (Reading, MA: Addison-Wesley, 1992).

The Windows Interface Guidelines for Software Design (Redmond, WA: Microsoft Press, 1995).

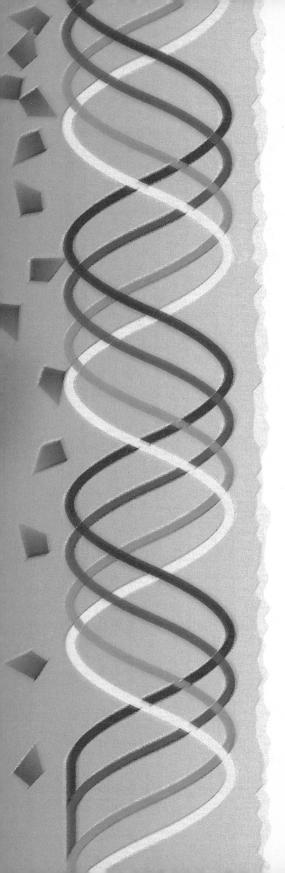

PART 2

Designing Your Online System

Both information planning and content specification involve designing the electronic library of information that will best meet the needs that you identified through analysis. Design first involves a high-level view of the information system that is the outcome of information planning. It then moves into the detailed specification of each aspect of the design during content specification. Design, however, often continues into implementation, especially when we employ rapid prototyping and usability testing to help define both the structure and the content of the information we hope to deliver.

The chapters in this part provide guidelines for translating the design implications you identified in your initial planning into detailed design specifications, including not only the design of the overall structure of the system and the topics it contains, but also of the testing you will perform, and the specifications for the tool you will use.

- Chapter 6, *Structuring Your Online System,* defines the various ways you might organize your information within your online system. It provides guidelines for knowing when to use each approach.

- Chapter 7, *Adding Hypertext Links,* provides guidelines for when to include hypertext links in your online system and for choosing a structure for those links. It also provides suggestions for ways to indicate the presence of links in the system.

■ Chapter 8, *Structuring Your Topics,* introduces the building blocks that make up any online topic. It defines each block and describes the situations in which each might be used. Finally, it describes how to combine those blocks into effective, well-structured topics.

■ Chapter 9, *Testing Your Design and Implementation,* stresses the importance of both functional and usability testing throughout the remainder of your project. It provides guidelines for how to design good test plans for both types of testing.

■ Chapter 10, *Choosing the Right Tools,* lists the factors you should consider when selecting your development and display tools. It stresses that this decision should not be made until all other design decisions have been considered.

We hope that the guidelines provided in these chapters will help you solidify your vision for your online project before you jump into its implementation. Because users are as yet unused to its presentation, online information must be highly structured and that only happens when you can follow a detailed plan, such as that described in this part.

6

Structuring Your Online System

Many people have the misconception that by virtue of the hypertext medium, online information has no structure. Nothing could be more untrue. You can and must structure the information that you put in your online system or you have effectively given your readers all the pages of a book, unnumbered and unbound, and expected them to put the pages in a logical order.

Professional communicators often hear "nobody uses the manuals anyway." Although it is true that insecure users who are afraid of learning on their own are most likely to ask others how to perform a task or solve a problem, many users prefer to learn and act independently. However, when they cannot find information (because they have none, what they have is out of date or inaccurate, or the only information they have is inaccessible), they are forced to rely on others, such as co-workers, support systems, supervisors, and help lines, to help answer questions. It is not uncommon to see groups of people gathered around a computer screen all helping someone try to solve a difficult problem because well-designed and effectively organized information is unavailable.

In usability testing, users often tell us that they will spend at least 30 minutes and sometimes more trying to locate answers to their questions on their own before they break down and call someone else. If the information is available and accessible, they are pleased. They get their jobs done more quickly, assist others in a more timely manner, learn more effectively, correct their mistakes, and get their systems up and running.

The guidelines in this chapter assist you in determining the best approach to structuring your online system.

 # Providing context sensitivity

One of your first tasks in structuring your online system is to determine if you will offer context-sensitive links. This decision greatly affects the rest of your structure:

- Context-sensitive systems are designed to anticipate where users might be when they have a question. The information designer uses the context of the application to try to anticipate the user's questions and information needs. If the user has landed at a particular part of a computer application, then the designer knows the user may need help on that part.

- In context-independent systems, the responsibility for finding information and using information effectively falls on the user's shoulders. Users interact with context-independent information just as they might paper-based information resources organized into traditional libraries. They seek information to make a decision, evaluate a product, develop a plan, differentiate among choices, perform a procedure, understand a policy, obtain a conceptual understanding of a subject, find an isolated fact to support a decision-making process, and more.

Obviously, either choice has its challenges:

- Designers of context-sensitive systems are unlikely to be 100 percent correct in their anticipation of user needs. Even when they understand their audiences reasonably well, they might only reach 60 to 80 percent accuracy. For example, most of us would find it difficult to tell the difference between a user who made the wrong choice in a dialog box and a user who simply hit a menu choice by mistake.

- Designers of context-independent information are responsible for creating the structures and providing the access tools—tables of contents, indexes, menu choices, or search mechanisms—that users need to find exactly what they are looking for and to use the information effectively and efficiently to reach their performance goals.

To determine the right approach, consider the following questions.

Is the information related to a computer application?

Context-sensitive information is available only when the user is interacting with a computer system interface for a software application or for a hardware-based system with a computer display attached. You cannot have context sensitivity if you are providing information about a function or topic that has nothing to do with a computer. For example, an auto repair online reference manual cannot be context sensitive unless the troubleshooting processes for the automobile are part of a computer system.

If the information you are providing is designed to assist the learning and performance of users of a computer-assisted application, much of the information should be linked to the application itself. Linked information increases the probability that the user will find an answer to a question or the solution to a problem. As a result, they will be less frustrated and more appreciative of the support provided.

If the information you are providing is designed to support decisions and tasks that are not computer related, the information will not be linked to any application environment. Instead, the users will have to formulate their questions and direct their inquiries to a library of information designed carefully enough to make access fast and accurate.

Can the information you provide be accessed through the computer to support and improve employee performance?

In the past, your employees relied on each other, the local experts on the staff, or, as a last resort, the technical manuals to perform tasks and make decisions. When information was not available, they improvised solutions that seemed right or were easy to perform. If the information they need is available electronically, you might design a performance-support system that would allow employees to use the computer on their desks as a source of guidance and instruction even though the tasks they perform are not computer related.

What types of information will you provide?

If all your information is conceptual (that is, functional descriptions, design decisions, and extended discussions) rather than procedural or instructional, you may find that context sensitivity is not appropriate. See Chapter 4, *Categorizing Information Needs*, for more information on this decision.

The majority of information that you might put onto a CD-ROM, a Web page, or an intranet probably falls into the category of context-independent information. However, it is important to realize that context-independent information may not be the best choice when a user is working within an application. If the application is provided by an outside vendor, application-specific information may be embedded in a context-sensitive system, but the information needed by your employees for work-related decision making will not be available within the vendor's system. Users are reluctant to leave the context of their work to find answers to their questions, whether those answers are available on paper or online.

Context-independent information may include the same information as a context-sensitive system. In fact, if both types of information are provided for a single product, the information might be created once (single sourced) and used many times. The difference lies in how the information is accessed.

How will the information be used?

In context-sensitive applications, procedural information is best presented so that users do not need to move back and forth between the information and the application. It's better to present procedural information through context-sensitive help that remains on top of the application while the user is working.

Undoubtedly, many users will approach context-independent systems with the same "in and out" approach that they expect from context-sensitive systems. Your challenge in these situations is to create an accessibility scheme that allows your users to succeed. Design for accessibility and ease of navigation is discussed in Part 3 of this book.

How will the information be marketed?

If the information is an integral part of the product, it probably should be context sensitive; however, if it is an optional feature that users pay extra for (for example, a computer-based training course), you might decide to make it context independent.

What is the source of your legacy information?

Although you may believe that online information will be more valuable to your users than information presented in a more traditional medium, you may be unable to replace existing information that is already delivered in paper documents. Reworking the information in a new form may be more costly and time-consuming than using that information as is.

However, always balance the cost of restructuring information against the benefits derived from creating structures that users will find helpful. Well-designed information may be more costly to produce the first time, but it may be easier to maintain and may reduce downstream costs of answering user questions. We often find that customer telephone support costs can be substantially reduced if we provide well-organized, usable, and streamlined information sources.

 ## What platform are you delivering on?

If your users are working on computer platforms that do not support context-sensitive information delivery, you may have no choice at this time but to create context-independent information. Consider also that particular platforms, especially those using older technologies, may severely restrict how you present information. Many older platforms do not permit multiple windows to be open simultaneously, thus restricting your use of layering as a technique to reduce depth and minimize the keystrokes and the time required for users to locate relevant information.

 ## What are your user needs?

You may find that your particular user community has special needs for either context-sensitive or context-independent information or both. Some of the users will be performing tasks that require the computer. They will keep records, search for information, analyze data, and perform a variety of tasks in their increasingly computer-centric world of work. Such users will need information presented in the context of their computer tasks.

Other users will perform tasks that have no connection to computers. They will manage business activities, sell products, perform services, interact with customers, assemble products, work with colleagues and staff, and perform all the myriad activities that support businesses, government, and social organizations. Such users also may be able to use information that is delivered to them electronically and can be usefully accessed and even used through the computer.

Who are your users?

Novice, advanced beginner, and competent users often are better served by context-sensitive information. Beginners might look for guidance when there are too many choices or when they want to perform a procedure they haven't done before. Competent users might find that a procedure isn't working the way they expected and may want information in context that will help them figure out why.

Context-sensitive systems support the "in and out" mentality of many computer users who simply want to accomplish a task and reach a goal. Goal-oriented users want a solution to their problems quickly so they can return to their tasks. They do not want to leave their work context to explore an information source; they simply want the computer to anticipate and respond to their questions.

On the other hand, proficient and expert users want information that can't be neatly put into a single context; their interests and problems cross boundaries within and among applications. They may need information that assists in planning and early decision making, activities that may precede actual work within a computer application.

Partitioning the subject matter

Once you have defined information in your library as either context sensitive or context independent, you have more decisions to make. By separating your information into discrete information objects, you will have many opportunities for multiple use. For example, if you have a topic that defines the steps in a procedure and another topic that provides an example of the procedure being performed, you may be able to use the topics more than once. In addition, you will be able to update the procedure without affecting the example and vice versa.

As you begin to decide how to partition your information objects into topics, consider the following questions:

- Are you providing information about a series of products produced by your organization for your customers?

- Are you supporting the work of colleagues and staff members inside your organization?

- Are you providing reference libraries for users with diverse information requirements?

A focus on the product means a focus on subject matter—the information itself that you are trying to disseminate to diverse people of diverse interests through electronic media.

As we work between users and subject matter, the focus of our field investigations must first be on how our users partition and group the information they are looking for. They may have a number of ways of structuring information:

- By product type

- By service performed

- By user organization

- By tasks to be performed

and many others.

Following are several guidelines to keep in mind as you make your decisions.

 ### *Is the information related to the products that you sell to customers?*

If your users think of the information you provide in terms of the products they own, consider using product designations as a primary organizing structure for your information. You might provide information divided by large categories of equipment, as does the company that sells agricultural and construction equipment. The groups using this information do not overlap and do not need access to one another's information sources. You might further partition the information according to individual equipment model names or numbers. Then all the information associated with a particular product will be grouped together in one place.

For example, consider the information provided by a computer manufacturer to its diverse user communities. We might discover that users who already own computers made by this manufacturer first conceptualize their information needs in terms of the machines themselves. The user might look for a grouping of information according to laptop, desktop, and server models. Once the primary grouping is located, the user might then look for a particular model of computer by number or by name (as in Figure 6.1).

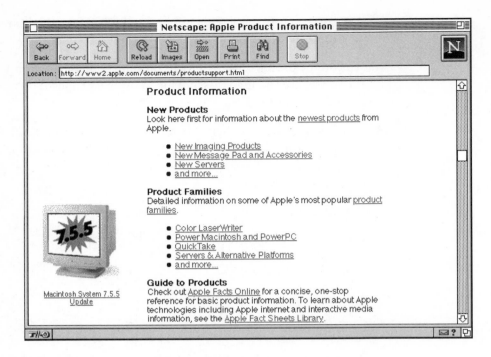

Figure 6.1: The Apple Web site is organized by product.

Within the choices of computer models, users found information about parts, troubleshooting, repairs, and more. Users reported that they found the information easily accessible and that the organization allowed them to find the information they needed and ignore information about other irrelevant machines.

Another computer manufacturer was less successful at organizing information. The designers of the information CD-ROM decided that a more formal logical structure would be appropriate. They placed several hundred manuals on the CD-ROM alphabetically by title. As a result, information related to specific products (hardware, operating systems, networks, and others) was not grouped together. Users commented that the information they needed was nearly impossible to find because they thought first of the products and then of the various information types associated with the products. One user commented to us that at least when he received paper manuals, he could group them together by product on his bookshelf.

For some companies, product groupings are not associated with types of hardware or software applications. Insurance companies, for example, are likely to have information associated with policy types, such as life insurance, health insurance, liability insurance, and so on. The loan department of a bank might divide its information according to type of loans.

 ### *Is the information related to the services you provide for your customers?*

Organizations that provide services to their customers may find that their customers relate most to a services structure. If you provide information related to the services you perform for customers, consider that your users may think of information in those terms. You may have an advertising agency that purchases advertising space, creates video productions, handles slide presentations, and so on. If your users think of your services in these categories, you may find it most useful to respond to the structural expectations your users already have (see Figure 6.2).

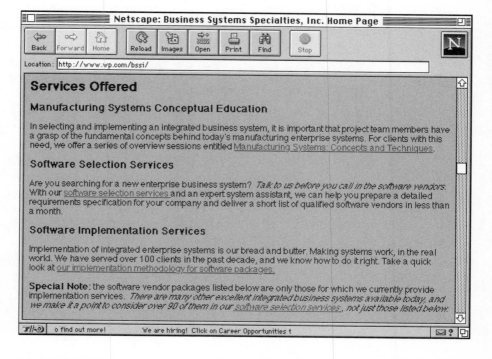

Figure 6.2: This Web page is structured by the services the company offers to its customers.

If you produce service-oriented products, such as software applications or courseware, you may find that the services addressed by the products provide the best way to organize your information. For example, Seminars in Usable Design, our seminar consulting company, organizes its information according to courses offered, such as

- Managing Online Projects

- User-Centered Interface Design

- Online Documentation

- Web Pages

- Downsizing your Documents

and so on (Figure 6.3).

Figure 6.3: The home page for the Seminars in Usable Design Web site organizes information by the courses offered.

For designers, once again the key question is how information will be used. Sometimes a partitioning of information according to departmental structures seems appropriate. However, such partitions may result in users who do not recognize the broader context of the tasks they perform in relationship to a continuum of tasks performed by a variety of departments.

Is the information related to the services you perform within your organization?

For many organizations providing internal libraries of information, the service areas within the organization become the most useful ways of partitioning and grouping information. Areas needing information might include marketing and sales, accounting, human resources, customer service, manufacturing, maintenance, benefits, and many others.

Some organizations focus on their internal structures, dividing information according to departmental structure. One such organization partitions information among departments engaged in administering pension funds, health insurance, beneficiary programs, and others. Many universities group information by department for easy access by students (Figure 6.4).

Is the information related to the activities performed by your users?

You may want to consider how your users organize themselves into professional or functional areas. Your users may think of themselves as distributors, dealers, system administrators, operators, salespeople, technicians, field engineers, and more. If your users are looking for information to support their particular job functions, consider partitioning and grouping your information to meet their needs.

If you select user organizations that are not well understood by your customers or employees, however, you run the risk of confusing everyone and making information extremely difficult to find. One organization decided to organize the information on its Web site according to the way the marketing department characterized its customers. Some customers were distributors, some end users, some administrators in large organizations that purchased directly. The distributors were organized into at least a dozen categories, as were the end users. Unfortunately, all of the categories were virtually unknown to the people who needed to find the information. The categories were only informative to a few people inside the company who thought of users in terms of their contractual relationships.

Figure 6.4: The University of Wyoming Web page groups information by the departments of the university, including Student Services, information Services, Academics, and so on.

 ## *Is the information related to the tasks that your users need to perform?*

User tasks are often at second or even third levels in the design of libraries of information that span product lines, services provided, or services performed. At the task level, users are looking for specific information that supports the activities they need to perform to accomplish their goals. If your users are handling invoices, they may want to know how to add vendor information to a vendor database, how to enter new invoices into the system, or how to release invoices for payment. These tasks might be organized under a category called "accounts payable." The category will enable a group of users to find information related specifically to the functions they perform or the departments in which they are located. Within the larger category, the users are then likely to look for information related to specific tasks.

Information may still be partitioned according to broad categories of tasks performed by specific groups of users. For example, one operating system developer organizes information according to tasks such as system administration, operations, and services. Although all of these tasks might be performed by a single talented individual in smaller customer organizations, in larger customers the tasks are partitioned among specialized user groups.

Care must be taken by designers following task organizations to ensure that they do not partition tasks according to the functions performed by the hardware or the software, by computer applications or by machines, instead of according to the users' understanding of the tasks. One manufacturer of operating systems decided for convenience of updating, to organize information according to platform-specific administrative tasks and administrative tasks that were performed across many platforms. The resulting information groups were easier for the designers to maintain because the platform-independent tasks changed with considerably less frequency than the platform-specific tasks.

The system administrators for whom the information was intended, unfortunately, did not partition tasks in this way. In fact, they were completely oblivious to the relationship between tasks and platforms. They were unable to locate information they needed quickly because they had to search in two places at random, rather than in one place.

Organizing your topics

Once you have chosen a high-level design for your information, you need to group your information into that structure. The organizational structures that you design for information must be shaped by how the users of that information think about what they do and hope to do. You must look beyond formal logic to information design situated in the users' view of the world.

A number of structures are possible for outlining online information, depending on the users' needs. You may want to use a sequence that reflects the order of the tasks to reach a particular goal. You may want to use a sequence that reflects the frequency with which particular tasks are performed. You may want to use an unstructured sequence such as alphabetical or numerical order, which may be the simplest way for users to locate information topics.

The following sections discuss possible approaches and list considerations for deciding which approach is best.

Alphabetical

Alphabetical ordering is perhaps the simplest structure you might use for your information. Alphabetical order is used for telephone books, dictionaries, encyclopedias, and indexes organized in much the same way. Because alphabetical structures are so ubiquitous, your users will already know how to use them.

We once used an alphabetical structure to organize a set of tasks performed by a local administrator of a small business phone system. All the tasks supported goals for changing the configurations of individual telephone sets. For example, the phone administrator might want to set one employee's phone with music on hold and another's phone to allow long distance calls to the remote office in Bangladesh. The administrator might want to restrict the phone in the lobby to local calls only.

After our user and needs analysis was complete, we decided that the tasks related to configuring individual phone sets could be performed in any order at any time. We couldn't anticipate when the administrator might want to perform a particular task. As a result, we used names for the tasks that the users would understand and organized the tasks in alphabetical order. We also used an alphabetical order for the tasks on the telephone user's quick reference card (conference calls, calls on hold, and so on).

However, familiarity alone does not justify your use of an alphabetical structure. Alphabetical order is not appropriate for most information libraries. The work that users need to perform is rarely random. In most cases, you will find that you need to group information into useful and recognizable structures. For example, an early version of Microsoft Word manuals was organized alphabetically by command. All but the most experienced user complained. Novice users didn't know the command they needed, only what they wanted to do, so the organization was useless.

If you are contemplating an alphabetical structure at some level in your information design, consider the following issues.

How many topics are you listing?

Although users understand how to refer to an alphabetical list, a long list becomes unwieldy, especially if the list scrolls through numerous screens of information.

If you have a long alphabetical list, consider providing a tool to help your users reach the part of the alphabet they need (Figure 6.5). Many online indexes are headed by a small alphabet. When users choose the letter they want, the list scrolls to the entries beginning with that letter. You might also use a combination box that lets users type the first few letters of the word they want. The list scrolls to the word closest to the one typed.

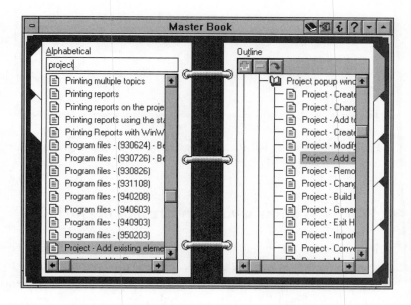

Figure 6.5: This reference information is presented alphabetically. However, the designers provide a search mechanism in which users begin typing the word in the list they would like to find and the display scrolls to that part of the list.

Can information in the alphabetical list be grouped?

If you have a long list of information, consider ways to the information before alphabetizing. For example, you might group information by functional area and then alphabetize within each area. When we organized the information for a small business phone system (Figure 6.6), we first divided the tasks into two broad categories—tasks performed on individual phone sets and tasks performed on all the phones in the system at once. We knew that the administrators were more likely to perform tasks on individual phones and would use these tasks more frequently. System-wide tasks were less likely to be performed. Once the two task divisions were established, we could list the tasks alphabetically for easy access.

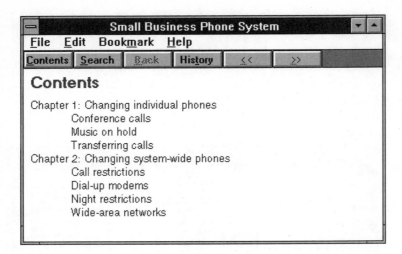

Figure 6.6: These alphabetical listings have first been grouped according to the type of task the user needs to perform.

Will users know what they are looking for?

Like an index, an alphabetical organization is only effective if users know what they are looking for. For example, suppose programmers need to look up the syntax of a command (Figure 6.7); if they know which command they need, they can find it quickly with an alphabetical ordering. However, what if the programmers only know that they need a command that performs a loop, but do not know its specific name? How will they find the right command in an alphabetical list of command names? They might be better served by a list grouped according to functions with an alphabetical order at a second level of detail.

Are information topics uniquely named?

Topics that are similarly titled are not appropriate for an alphabetical listing. For example, if your information on printers has a majority of topics starting with "Print" or "Printing," users will find it difficult to scan an alphabetical list for the specific topic they need. They will be forced to read each topic carefully to distinguish the differences among them. An alphabetical organization is only effective if the names of topics are sufficiently unique.

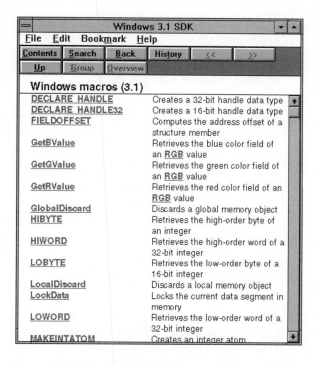

Figure 6.7: This alphabetical listing of Windows 3.1 macros provides additional information that helps users decide which macro to choose to get more information through the hyperlink. Without this information, novice users would have no way to determine which macro they wanted as there are no other groupings within the list.

Is information reference oriented?

Reference oriented topics are typically titled using noun strings, rather than gerunds or infinitives. For example, you may have a high-level set of information organized according to the names of the users' departments, such as the Home Loan Department, the Car Loan Department, and so on. You may have 15 products that users will want to use and maintain. The high-level organization of the product names might be best listed alphabetically. If you believe that the information you have to organize requires a random order that is easy to access, choose an alphabetical list of information topics.

Sequential

Like alphabetical organizations, sequential organizations are also well understood by most users. Again, however, this fact needs to be coupled with the following analysis to truly determine the appropriateness of such a structure.

Is the information time based?

Sequential organizations are often best suited for task-oriented information because such information has an implied order. Users need to complete Step 1 before moving on to Step 2. However, conceptual information may also be built around a loosely sequenced structure. To present concepts, you may decide to build ideas in a certain order, leading the user on a path to understanding. For example, if you are explaining the relationship of desktop publishing to word processing, you may want to list the similarities first to help orient the users before you move on to the differences.

Are users aware of the required sequence?

The sequence of information may not be obvious to users because they do not realize that the tasks have an implied order. For example, some users may not understand that this book is ordered in process-oriented sequence—you should conduct front-end analyses before you structure your library, and you should structure your library before you begin writing topics.

When information is sequenced in a manner unfamiliar to your users, you need to work hard to make the sequence obvious. Information becomes more difficult to find when users don't know where to look. They don't know where their specific concern falls into the logical sequence.

In Figure 6.8, the information designer created a sequence of tasks and labeled the tasks according to their place in the sequence.

How will you prevent users from jumping into the middle of the presentation?

The danger in using a sequenced structure to your information is that your users are likely to jump into the middle of a sequence. You need to determine if such an event could be harmful. For example, do you expect that users will recognize that the information is part of a sequence when they simply need information on one part of the sequence? Or do you believe that users could mistakenly begin in the middle of a process?

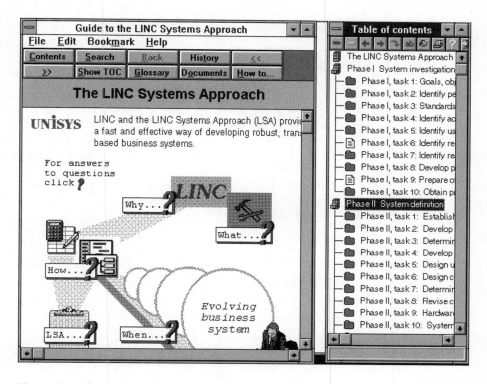

Figure 6.8: The LINC task sequence is displayed clearly and labeled effectively in the table of contents window.

Depending on the potential problems introduced by jumping into the middle of the sequence, you may need to consider the following:

- Clearly label the information as being part of a sequence (Figure 6.9).

- Put information that is dependent on other information being read first in a pop-up on the primary information screen. Users can't access the pop-up without having read the primary information.

- Prevent users from jumping into the sequence by not including any links, including TOC and index entries, to the subtopics. All links will take users to the head of the sequence.

Logical

"Logical" approaches to online organization run the gamut from effective to seemingly arbitrary. As a result, many so-called logical organizations of

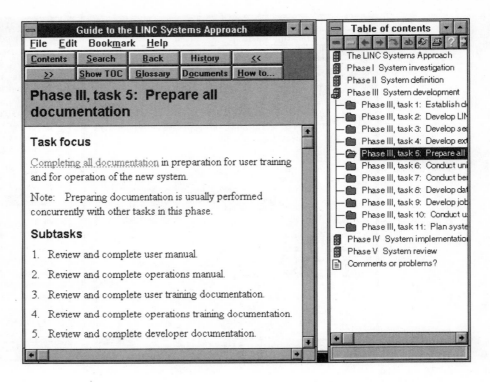

Figure 6.9: LINC users always know what step they are on in the sequence because it is indicated both in the table of contents and the nonscrolling head of the primary help window.

information ill serve the needs of the people who need to use the information to perform tasks, understand their responsibilities, or look beyond their narrow job functions to the well-being of their organizations or activities as a whole.

If you choose to implement a logical structure, carefully consider the following questions.

Is the structure apparent to the users?

A focus on subject matter related to products and services must itself be informed by an understanding of the user communities that you serve. Too often, information designers look myopically at the information at hand and give it a seemingly logical structure. The logic is often driven by the nature of the subject matter itself—a partitioning and grouping of topics and subtopics that comes from the internal logic of the subject.

For example, if we look at classical descriptive biology, we find animals organized by the details of their anatomy. The birding guides we use to identify birds in the field are organized by anatomical structure, rather than by the habitats in which we might ordinarily find them or by easily identifiable characteristics such as color or form. For some reason, known only to the ornithologists, loons and grebes come at the beginning of most birding guides, widely separated from the ducks with which they associate. The logic may make perfect sense to the ornithologist or the geneticist, but it is not at all apparent to the untutored users.

In the CD-ROM that allows users to order copies of articles from the Harvard Business Review (HBR), the list of articles is organized according to the HBR issue in which the articles appeared (Figure 6.10). That organization is not apparent, however, unless the users carefully analyze the dates of the articles. In fact, the users are more likely to refer to the articles by subject matter or author, rather than publication date. The chronological sequence is

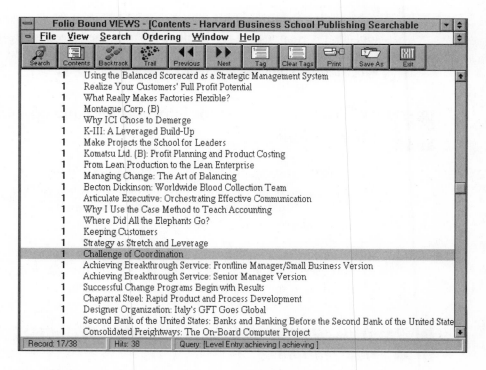

Figure 6.10: Even if users know the title of the article they are looking for, they have no chance of finding it in this unstructured list.

meaningful to the information designers but makes the information almost completely inaccessible to potential users, who must scroll through the entire list to find a particular article.

 ### *Does the application structure suggest an organization?*

The traditional organization of information supporting users of software applications is often determined by the structure of the application. Information designers order the help according to a computer screen or a menu. Such documentation typically provides lists of screens by name or number, accompanied by lists of the information elements (called fields) that are associated with each screen.

Such a structure might be effective if the information is strictly used as a reference by experienced users who already know how to use the application. Unfortunately, organization by system element is almost useless for novices and advanced beginners. These users do not know how the application supports the tasks they want to perform. Although the screens might be the tools that users must use to complete the task, users need information that supports their use of the tool to reach their goals. They often do not know which screen of information to use.

 ### *Will users access certain information more often than other information?*

If you believe you can predict which information will be accessed most frequently, you might make this information the most visible in your system. For example, you might include a fast path to information about the ten most common tasks performed by your users.

Such a structure, however, has a potential for failure. Have you taken into account users who only access the system for the less common problems? What if the ten most common tasks were to change?

 ### *Will certain users have access only to certain types of information?*

Your audience analysis might reveal a variety of stages of use and user job categories that might suggest a logical structure. For example, you might group all task-oriented information separately from conceptual information, as the information designers for Microsoft Word help have done in their design of "How Do I" and "Tell Me About" topics shown in Figure 6.11.

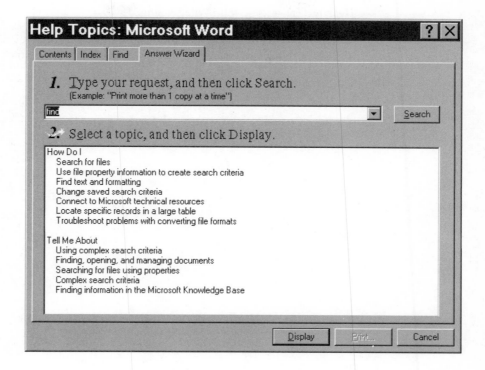

Figure 6.11: Microsoft Word help designers separated task-oriented material ("How Do I") from conceptual material ("Tell Me About").

Of course, such a structure works only if users know what kind of information they need. They might be confused about what constitutes a definition or may need to discover if troubleshooting information is included in the task-oriented topics.

Further reading

Bailey, Robert W., *Human Performance Engineering: Designing High Quality Professional User Interfaces for Computer Products, Applications, and Systems*, 3rd edition (Saddle River, NJ: Prentice Hall, 1996).

Boggan, Scott, David Farkas, and Joe Welinske, *Developing Online Help for Windows 95* (Carmel, IN: Sams Publishing, 1996).

Brockmann, R. John, *Writing Better Computer User Documentation: From Paper to Hypertext* (New York: John Wiley & Sons, 1990).

Petrauskas, Bruno, "Online Reference System Design and Development," *Perspectives on Software Documentation: Inquiries and Innovations*, ed. Thomas T. Barker (Amityville, NY: Baywood Publishing Company, 1991).

7

Adding Hypertext Links

One of the most difficult areas for new help designers to handle successfully is the design of hypertext links from one topic to another. It's relatively simple to add pop-up definitions (although tempting to add too many) or to activate table of contents links, but planning how users will move through the online information is much more difficult. Because links provide navigational options to your users, too many might allow them to become lost; too few might keep them from finding the information they need.

Furthermore, the wrong links add even more confusion. For example, in the past several years the most enthusiastically touted use of hypertext links has been based on an encyclopedia model. In this model, users enter the information system at a particular piece of information. From that original focal point, they move through related topics of interest, exploring several different, but related, topics using an idiosyncratic path.

The result is a picture of someone browsing through the online information world, moving gleefully from a map of Africa to a description of the Zambesi River to a dissertation on forest elephants in Ghana to a discussion of endangered forests in India to an editorial on the impending extinction of tigers in the wild and so on.

Unless you are in the encyclopedia business, however, this model of hypermedia inviting the reader ever onward through links with dubious connections bears little resemblance to the way people need technical information in support of business tasks. The idiosyncratic browsing envisioned by the original definitions of hypermedia is simply too time-consuming and undirected for the business world.

Fortunately, the addition of windows technology to the hypertext world provides the information designer with a more useful model to superimpose—new opportunities to increase the usefulness of information and assist users in remaining focused. By combining the presentation of specialized supporting information in layered windows surrounding a central topic, you can assist your users in investigating many aspects of a complex subject matter within one context.

For example, a technician using a hypertext-based information system might first enter the system by selecting the product to be repaired from a well-organized list of all products included in the system. The product link might lead to a picture of the product with labeled links to diagnostics, troubleshooting charts, and technical descriptions (Figure 7.1).

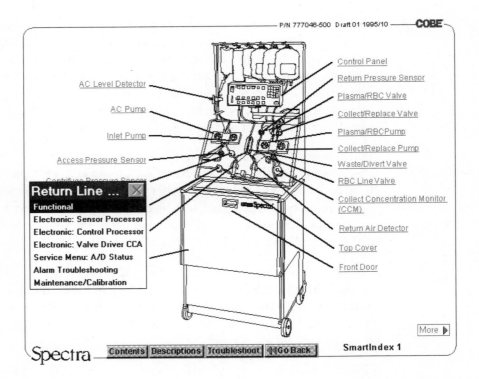

Figure 7.1: Technicians for the COBE Spectra machine can access all the information they need from this graphical main menu. By clicking on a labeled part of the machine, they see a pop-up menu from which they can access troubleshooting and maintenance information, as well as electronic schematics.

The technician may select a troubleshooting chart, which helps pinpoint the problem with some aspect of the product, such as a power supply. An audio link might provide the sound of a properly operating power supply. By linking back to the picture of the product, the technician uses graphic hypertext links to move into the machine and find the illustration of the power supply. Another set of labeled links gives the technician the ability to order the part from a window that provides a part description, the part number, and an automated modem link to the manufacturer's parts-ordering system. Another labeled link provides suggestions on other parts that may need to be ordered at the same time. Yet another link leads the technician to the instruction set for removing and replacing the part in question.

Throughout such a windows-supported set of links, the user remains in the context of the product and the information needed to perform the repair quickly and efficiently. This user does not want to browse through interesting information about other products, but wants to remain focused. A well-constructed system of links can provide this focus by anticipating the user's series of questions surrounding a single task scenario.

This chapter provides guidance on when to use links within a layered, windows-based model and how to implement the links effectively.

Determining when to use links

First, it's important to understand why you might add links to your online system. Why give your users optional paths through the system? Isn't it better that they follow an optimal path that you have predetermined? Won't users overlook critical information because they missed a browse sequence or failed to follow up a link?

Actually, users will find their own way through information whether we like it or not. They have a habit, even with hardcopy books, of skipping information that seems irrelevant to their immediate needs or skimming information that looks too long or too complicated. Hypertext links acknowledge the idiosyncratic reading habits of our users while attempting to guide them through online information that lacks the signposts that they have always relied on in books. Use the following guidelines when deciding when to provide links.

Use links to address different audiences

If you expect many different audiences or audience levels to access your information library, links can help direct information to the appropriate audiences. For example, if you are addressing both expert and novice users, how do you provide sufficient explanation of steps for the novice while allowing a quick path for the expert? Hypertext links allow you to hide the extra information in related topics or through pop-ups (Figure 7.2).

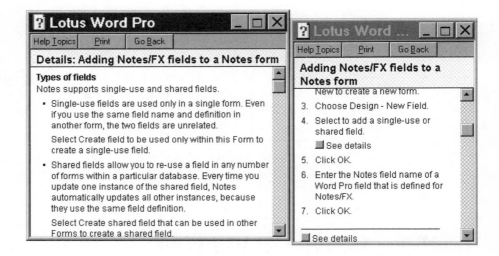

Figure 7.2: Lotus WordPro provides detailed information in secondary windows. If users don't understand how to complete step 4, they can click the labeled link for more information. However, if they do understand, they are not forced to skim through all the details.

The extra information that you hide might be as simple as definitions of technical terms or feedback statements for the novice user. Or the hidden information may be more complex, such as detailed information about special instances when variations of a basic procedure must be used.

 ## *Use links to point to related information*

Despite your best design and intention, users will often access a topic and find that the information is not quite what they had hoped. Rather than requiring that they start their search over from the beginning, you can use hypertext links to point them in another direction (Figure 7.3). Try to anticipate why users might access a particular topic. For example, a topic titled "Installing an audio CD-ROM" might be inadvertently accessed by a user interested in installing an informational CD-ROM. A related topic might point the users to the other type of installation rather than requiring that they return to the table of contents or the search screen and begin again.

Related-information links may also educate the users about issues that they didn't even think were related to the topic at hand. For example, you might link a topic on printing a document to one on ensuring that you have the right printer fonts. Users who are having problems printing might never have thought that fonts were part of the problem without that related-information link.

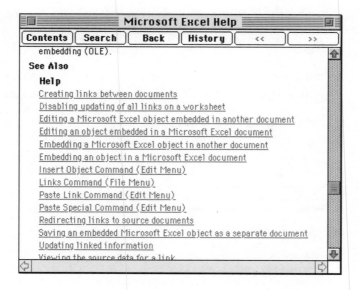

Figure 7.3:   Excel Help lists topics that are related ("See Also") to the primary topic.

 Use links as cross-references

Like related-information links, cross-reference links point users to other sections of the online system for more information about an aspect of the current topic. Typically, however, you expect users to read related information in conjunction with the topic at hand, whereas they may choose to read cross-references at another time.

For example, if a user is reading about company policy on travel expenses, you may want to provide a cross reference to entertainment expenses. The user can choose to read about entertainment expenses immediately or simply note that the topic exists for future reference.

 ## *Use links to define browse paths*

You might use links to control movement through your system rather than relying on your users to use navigational buttons, such as forward and back. For example, you might provide the first few steps of a long procedure and then require that users click a link to indicate they are ready to move on to the next set of steps. Such a link might take many forms:

- You might provide a link that encourages a page turn (a dog-eared page at the bottom right or bottom left page corner, for example) to indicate that the information on this topic continues through more pages.

- You might label a button "More," indicating that you have more to say on this topic than will fit in the first screen of information.

- You might use page numbers to indicate a browse sequence (Figure 7.4).

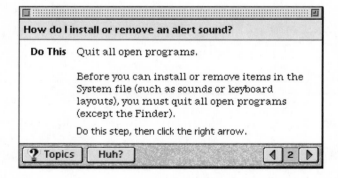

Figure 7.4: In Apple Guide, each screen in the procedure is a separate step. In the lower right-hand corner is a page number that indicates the user is on page 1, 2, or 3, and so on. When the forward arrow is active, more steps are to come. When the forward arrow is grayed, the user is on the last step of the sequence.

Use links to control topic size and appearance

Inexperienced online users sometimes don't realize that a topic continues because they don't see or recognize the scroll bars or directional arrows on the screen. As a result, you should minimize the amount of scrolling that you require from your user. To do this, break information into more than one topic and use well-labeled links to create browse paths.

Use links for common topics

When including information that will be relevant to many different topics, such as definitions or high-level overviews, write separate topics or pop-ups rather than burying the information within a topic. All related topics can then reference the same topic through a link, meaning that you don't have to maintain the same information in more than one place.

In addition, designing common information, such as glossary definitions, examples, overviews, and others, means that information can be written (and updated) once but used many times.

Use links to display graphics

In some situations, graphics may be difficult to display or your users may want to refer to a graphic in a secondary window while reading the related text in the primary window. If you provide a link to the graphic, they then have the option to view the graphic side by side with the text (Figure 7.5). If their systems are slow in displaying graphics, they can decide to wait for a graphic to display or continue reading without viewing the graphic.

In general, however, we recommend that graphics be included in context because users can clearly understand the interrelationship between text and graphics. Only if display space or speed is a special concern should you consider including graphics exclusively through links.

Use links to zoom in on graphics

For complicated graphics, such as engineering drawings in which users need to see detail, use graphic links to provide closeups. Start with a high-level view of the graphic with minimal detail. Then allow users to click on the area of the graphic that interests them to see further detail (Figure 7.6). You can add more and more detail the farther you allow them to zoom in.

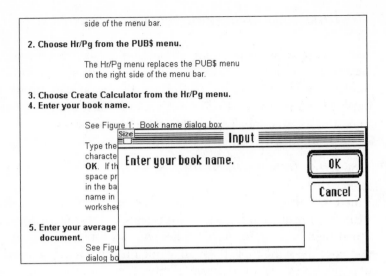

Figure 7.5: In the example, the screen shot is located in a separate figure file. The user can open and view the figure or simply note the "Figure 1" reference in the text.

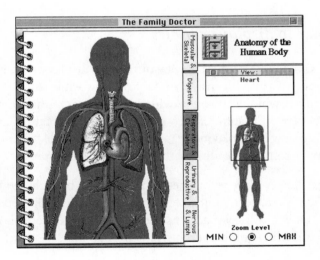

Figure 7.6: The user of The Family Doctor can select a section of the small graphic on the right and zoom in for a closer view of the details.

If you want the detail to remain in the context of its position in the original graphic, you might also decide to use a pop-up to display the detail rather than replace the entire screen.

Use links to call other support

In more complex online systems, you may want to provide many different types of support. You can call this support through your links. For example, to illustrate the steps of a procedure, the users might call a video or simulation of the steps being performed; they might call a lesson of a computer-based tutorial (CBT) to practice; or they might call an application program to actually perform the steps while the instructions are still on the screen.

Many online systems allow you to link your users to other information systems, application software, and CBTs, even to sources outside their immediate environment. For example, a service CD-ROM provided by Apple Computer to its dealers and repair organizations allows users to find a part they need and automatically dial the modem to order the part. A system designed by information designers at Unisys Corporation permits users to open templates of their documents directly from their procedurally based CD-ROM.

 Many Web applications permit users to send e-mail messages to the company with requests for information. Others permit users to place orders for merchandise through secured access to credit card-based order forms. Web pages also permit users to jump to other Web pages to obtain related or cross-reference information.

Choosing the type of link

The primary decision you need to make in choosing a link type is whether to move the user to another location in the system (jumps or unidirectional links) or to display the additional information in an overlaying or secondary window (pop-ups or bidirectional links). A secondary window can later be dismissed, leaving users where they started. Consider the following guidelines when deciding the type of link that will best serve your users' needs.

 ### *Consider the type of information you want to provide*

Because pop-ups typically cannot be indexed or defined on a browse path, you cannot be sure that users will read them, and users will have no way to access them independently from the table of contents or through a search. Therefore, do not put primary pieces of information, such as instructional steps, in pop-ups. Instead, include information that users will only need once or may want to use for additional information.

Consider the amount of information you want to provide

Pop-up topics that overlie the primary topic should be kept short, that is, one or two sentences (Figure 7.7). If you are providing more information than that, use a jump. Topics appearing in secondary windows alongside the primary topic may be longer because they are intended to contain independent content.

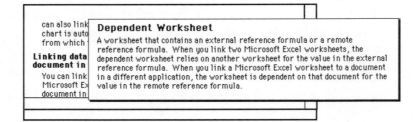

Figure 7.7: Definitions are commonly included as pop-ups on top of primary topics.

Consider navigational issues

The primary advantage to using pop-ups is that they keep the user in the context of the primary topic and reduce navigation problems. Use pop-ups to keep the user from getting lost navigating among topics.

Use expansion links

Another way to maintain the context while providing additional information is through an expansion or stretch link rather than a pop-up link. With an expansion link, the topic screen actually changes to include an additional sentence or paragraph within the existing text. For example, an expansion link is typically used in a table of contents to provide views of second- or third-level headings. The users click on an item in a list of primary headings, and the screen expands to display the second-level headings and so on.

Similarly, expansion links can be used in procedural text to provide more-detailed instructions to help a less experienced user. For example, you may have provided short descriptive sentences to explain each step in a procedure, including the amount of information appropriate for an experienced user. However, a less experienced user may need further explanation of how to perform the step. Expansion links (labeled, of course) between steps can provide additional descriptions of how to perform the steps (Figure 7.8). The original context of the full set of steps is not lost, because the user can close the expansion and return to the original presentation of the procedure.

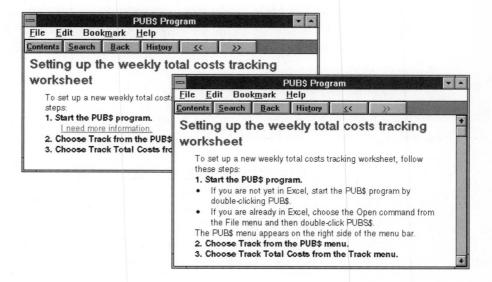

Figure 7.8: Users who need additional information to complete Step 1 choose the expansion link "I need more information." The step then expands as shown in the screen in the foreground.

Avoid links that produce changes between primary and secondary windows

Unless you have carefully considered the impact and design for the problems that will occur, avoid links in secondary windows that change the information in the primary window. If you change the primary window, the users' original context will be lost.

For example, some systems provide related topics or hypertext jumps within secondary windows that result in new topics appearing in the secondary window. The users understand that the action they take in the secondary window will affect the topic displayed there. Their focus of attention is on the secondary window, and they easily observe the topic change.

However, other system designs use links in the secondary window to change the topic in the primary window. In one such system, a table of contents in the primary window subtly changes to another table of contents when the users choose one of the related topics links in the secondary window. The result is pure confusion. Because the users are focusing on the secondary window and because some links result in the expected changes to the secondary window, they completely fail to notice the change in the primary window. In fact, the change to the primary window is almost imperceptible because one table of contents is instantaneously replaced by another table of contents that looks remarkably similar.

Choosing a link structure

A movie made popular the quote, "If you build it, they will come." This quote also applies to links—if you provide them, the user will try them. This presents a danger that users will randomly try links until they become hopelessly lost. Your task is to help your users stay on track by carefully structuring a series of links presented in context through pop-ups, expansion links, and secondary windows or by judiciously providing jumps to additional topics.

Before you ever write the content of your topics, you should know how the topics will interconnect:

- **In a linear structure, the topics are linked one right after the other.** Users are forced to proceed through the topics in a predefined path. Such a structure can also be made cyclical by linking the last topic to the first.

- **In a hierarchical structure, subordinate topics are linked to the primary topic.** If users choose, they can get information about the subordinate topics, but they must return to the primary topic to continue.

- **In a webbed or network structure, related topics are linked together.** For example, one topic might define a particular command while another topic explains how to execute this command. The two topics can be connected via a cross-reference hypertext link.

The webbed structure provides the most flexibility in an online system, but most navigational problems appear to occur in webs, rather than in the other structures. Webs are difficult to plan. For example, there must be sufficient hyperlinks to take the user to relevant information without leading to undesired information or to the possibility of inadvertently bypassing critical information. Users move from topic to topic in a nonconsecutive order; however, they also need to be allowed to browse through topics, similar to page turning, without becoming disoriented because of sudden jumps to unrelated topics.

In contrast, the linear and hierarchical approaches seem to improve the user's ability to find and retrieve information. Studies show that users retain the most information when using such structures. Unfortunately, users' stated preferences contradict these findings—they prefer the more complex structures.

To determine the best linking structure for your situation, consider the following guidelines.

Reinforce the information structure

In Chapter 6, *Structuring Your Online System*, we discussed how to structure your online system as a whole by designing and describing how information will be grouped and interrelated. Your links should reinforce the structure you have chosen. For example, if you have separated conceptual, procedural, and instructional information, you should provide links among the three so users have easy access. If you differentiate between information for advanced beginners and information for experts, you should retain that distinction throughout your information design.

The detailed structure of your information should remain consistent so that users are able to learn and reuse the organizational patterns you have established. We have seen many online information systems that have no easily discernible, repeatable structure. A lack of structure is common when legacy hardcopy documents are simply downloaded into the information system. All the diverse original structures are maintained in electronic form.

In contrast, a well-designed online information system is conceived as a whole, with repeatable structures and a thoughtfully structured web of interconnections that enable users to learn and use the patterns to direct their search for answers. Even if you are working with legacy documents, design a consistent pattern of links to ease navigation and help users predict the types of information they may expect to find.

Meet the users' goals

Links should help users meet their goals of finding specific information. They should not distract the user from the topic at hand. For most online documentation sets you will design, assume that the primary user of your network of links is not the explorer but the person looking for specific solutions to problems. If users truly want to explore the system, they have other means available—such as searches, indexes, and tables of contents.

Layer information appropriately for the user

If you have multiple levels of users accessing the system, you should probably structure the information by type of user. Use links to move within the appropriate level of information. For example, if your primary user is a competent performer who doesn't require instruction about how to use the interface, you might provide interface use instructions through a link for the more novice user.

If you are able to provide a way for your users to indicate their level of experience and interest, you may want to design a system that provides different topics and different paths through the topics depending on the users' choice. For example, users might want to decide if they want complete or abbreviated versions of the information. Choosing abbreviated information would lead a user to a subset of the available information.

Limit the number of links per topic

Too many links may only confuse and distract the user. For example, many early online help systems provided links to pop-up definitions for every instance of every word in the glossary. The result was a sea of green text (the WinHelp standard color for indicating that a word is associated with a link). The green text interfered with readability, just as any distracting, randomly applied highlight color would.

Other designs have given users lists of 20 or more related topics for every topic in the system. To the users, it appears that everything is linked to everything else, which it may indeed be. Too many links often means that the designer hasn't thought carefully about the links at all.

A useful guideline might be to limit the number of links to no more than five per topic. If you find yourself exceeding the limit in too many instances, consider carefully whether all the links you are providing are really helpful to your users or simply leading to confusion.

Provide sufficient links to relevant additional information

Despite the last recommendation, be sure that users have easy access to all information they need. Don't hesitate to break the previous guideline occasionally if necessary.

Avoid excessive branching

Even though we strongly advocate a layered approach to presenting more details and more explanation in online information, too much branching can make information difficult for the users. One of the worst examples of online information design we have run across took the reader through eight levels of menus just to get to an obscure overview. Readers then had to go through another four levels to get to actual procedural information.

Regardless of structure, most experts agree that users should not have to go through more than three jumps to find the information they need. Users will be frustrated by continually seeing tables of contents rather than real subject matter. Make it easy for the users to find what they are looking for by limiting the number of menus they must go through before they reach actual topics.

One of our favorite examples of a deep structure that caused users considerable frustration was the help provided for Lotus 1-2-3 users switching to Microsoft Excel in an early online help system. After moving through seven levels of menu choices, the user reached a help topic that said simply, "Consult the manual for information on this topic."

We have seen help designers demonstrate the ease of use of their system by showing how simple it is to reach a topic or a set of related topics with only four or five jumps. They forget that they already know which choices to make at each step in their progress through the system. At each jump, new users are faced with a potentially confusing series of choices, further complicating their ability to find the information they need.

Construct a map of the link patterns you are designing

As you identify the link patterns you will include in your system, construct a map of your design (Figure 7.9). If you can't easily map your system, it is probably too complex for your users to figure out.

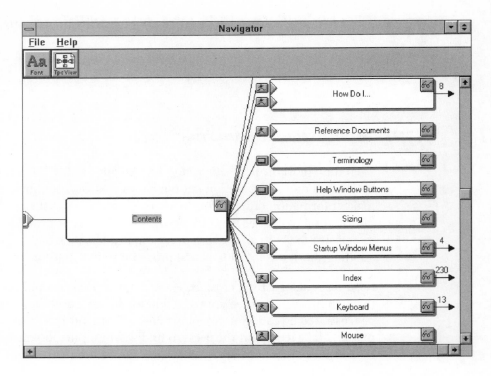

Figure 7.9: The example shows a system map with the links from the table of contents to the first-level topics.

Avoid arbitrary links

In many poorly designed online documentation systems, the choice of hypertext jumps appears to be completely haphazard. It seems as if the designer simply decided in the middle of writing a topic that the user might want to jump somewhere else, or the designer subscribed to the notion that users want the freedom to go wherever they want from any point in the online document to any other point. The designer may simply want to be accommodating, promoting the notion of a user-defined web of information linking seemingly unrelated parts of a text. Unfortunately, such accommodation introduces more confusion than assistance.

Remember that users do not have the same conceptual model of the information in the system that you do as the designer. You aren't likely to be confused by the links you design because you have a map in your head of all the information and its internal relationships. The users begin with no conceptual model at all, and only gradually build a model from repeated use of the information system. Link only to those topics that directly contribute to what you believe your users are trying to learn to do.

Avoid dead ends

As a general rule, users should never reach a topic from which they have nowhere to go except by returning to the main menu or exiting the information system.

Ensure ease of navigation

The links you provide should not complicate navigation. Users should be able to click on a link to move forward or to backtrack to the original topic. Provide Back and History buttons to allow easy backtracking. Also include a related topic that returns the user to the original topic from the linked topic.

If you are using pop-up links, ensure that they can be closed easily. For example, don't require users to click a Close button. Allow them simply to click anywhere to dismiss the pop-up.

If users do get lost, they need a way to jump immediately back to the main menu rather than work back up through the hierarchy of previous jumps. Although you should try to ensure that users can always retrace their steps, sometimes it's easier to allow them to return to the main menu and start over. Refer to Chapter 12, *Providing Navigation Aids*, for further guidelines in the area of navigation.

Indicating the availability of links

Unless users understand that links are available, they will not use them. Follow these guidelines to indicate the presence of links.

Consider industry standards

Help systems have established standards to indicate the presence of links. Typical WinHelp standards recommend using a color and dashed line to indicate which words are linked to pop-up definitions and using a color and underscores to indicate which words or phrases have a jump associated with them (Figure 7.10).

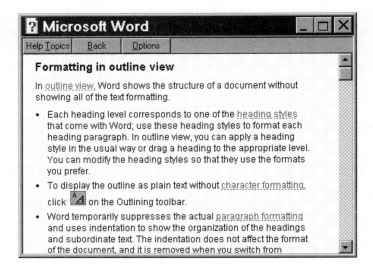

Figure 7.10: This example from Microsoft Word Help shows the standard dotted underscore that indicates a pop-up definition link.

Although this system is not perfect, consider your audience before deviating from it. Are they familiar with the established conventions? Will you be trying to teach them new tricks?

Other link indicators are being used more frequently in current practice in part to avoid the distraction of too much green and underlining. Designers often place a small icon in the context of a sentence or alongside a linked item to indicate the availability of a link (Figure 7.11). The icons also can be varied so that the link is labeled, indicating the type of information that users should expect when they click on the link.

Make links recognizable

Whether or not you choose to use industry standards, ensure that your conventions make links recognizable. Use color, emphasis techniques, icons, or other noticeable characteristics, but don't rely on users noticing subtle changes, such as the cursor changing from a pointer to a hand.

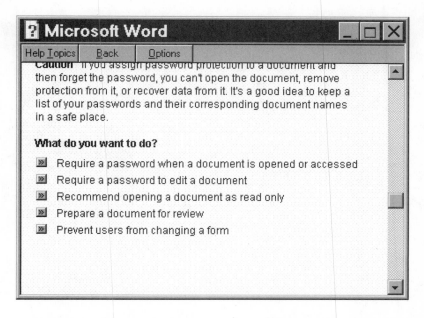

Figure 7.11: In this example, links to "How to" topics are indicated by a small button with an arrowhead, rather than by traditional underscores.

 ### *Distinguish between link types*

If you are linking to pop-ups, graphics, and other topics, consider indicating through the look of the link what kind of information users can expect. However, don't expect users to pick up on subtle clues, including color differences. Instead, consider using icons or other methods to clearly indicate the distinctions among link types (Figure 7.12).

 ### *Consider the physical size of the links*

Establish a reasonable size for your links, especially graphic hotspots. For example, they should be at least as wide as the cursor. Do not put graphic hotspots so close together that it's easy for the user to inadvertently select the wrong one. Maintain enough space around hotspots so that they're both easy to see and select. Conversely, avoid buttons that are so large that the users do not recognize them as buttons but assume they are simply part of the graphic design.

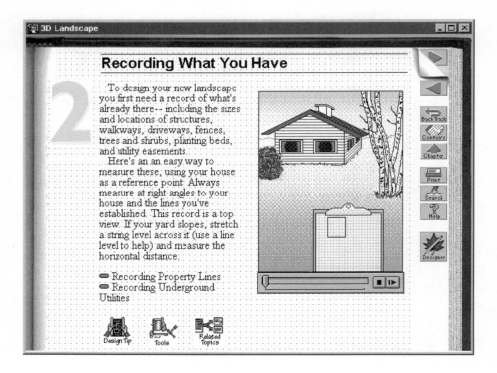

Figure 7.12: The icons at the bottom of this online book page inform users exactly what type of information they will see if they choose the link.

 Many viewers allow users to change the size of the displayed text. Be sure to test the size of the hotspot with multiple text sizes.

Instruct users what to do

Don't expect all users, especially novices, to understand the conventions that you have chosen. Consider providing a topic on how to recognize a link, select it, and backtrack. If you have structured your system to control what appears in the first few topics, consider explicitly telling the users to click a particular link so they learn what it does. For example, if users go first to a table of contents, include instructions to click on the title of the topic in which they are interested.

Definition links

Perhaps the most common use of pop-up links is to provide definitions of terms in the text that the user might not know. If the help designer has decided that a particular term is likely to be new to a number of users, the designer will highlight the term to indicate a definition is available. By clicking on the unknown term, the user moves to a linked topic that contains a definition of the term.

Consider the following guidelines when creating definition links.

Select terms that are likely to be new to your user

To avoid topics with too many highlighted terms, consider your users' needs when choosing terms to define. Rely on your user analysis to point out terms that might be unfamiliar to many of your users.

Avoid providing definition links for every instance of a term

Some development tools provide a way to automatically program links for the terms in your glossary. Do not use automated glossary links unless you plan to confirm each choice. The automated systems do not recognize that the same term may appear multiple times in a single topic or that the same term is used in a slightly different manner in a particular context and the definition doesn't quite apply.

Provide another way for users to access definitions

Rather than requiring that users encounter a term in a topic to link to its definition, provide a way for them to see a list of all defined terms. A glossary of terms might be accessed through a menu item or a glossary button in the interface.

Provide a means for users to quickly move through a long list of terms and definitions. Many glossary interfaces display an interactive alphabet, allowing users to jump to part of the alphabetized list of terms. Others allow the users to type a word or part of a word while the list of terms scrolls to the correct position.

Definition links

 Link to different definitions of the same term if the context is different

If you use the same term in several different contexts, consider providing different definitions. For example, Apple Balloon Help defines items differently when they are grayed out and cannot be selected than when the user can select the item (Figure 7.13).

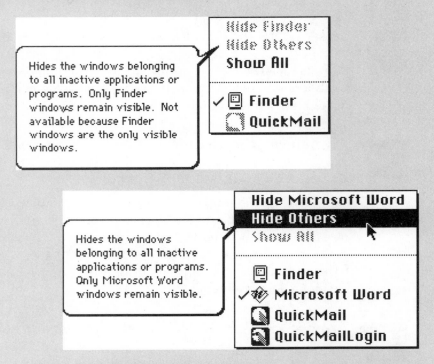

Figure 7.13: The Apple Balloon Help changes for the same Hide Others menu option depending on the conditions that exist on the computer.

 Don't nest other definitions

When defining a term, use words in the definition that are familiar to your users. Don't send them on a wild goose chase through the glossary by using equally unfamiliar terms in the definition.

Definition links

Repeat the term being defined in the definition window

Always repeat the term being defined as the heading of the pop-up definition. Then users can recall the term they are looking up without referring back to the text.

Ensure that the pop-up window does not obscure the original linked term

If you have sufficient screen space, place the pop-up window so that it falls immediately under the selected term. If definitions cannot always fall directly below the term being defined, program your pop-up window placement so that it does not obscure the term.

Further reading

Brockmann, R. John, *Writing Better Computer User Documentation: From Paper to Hypertext* (New York: John Wiley & Sons, 1990).

Deaton, Mary and Cheryl Lockett Zubak, *Designing Windows 95 Help: A Guide to Creating Online Documents* (Indianapolis, IN: Que Corporation, 1996).

Horton, William, *Designing and Writing Online Documentation*, 2nd edition (New York: John Wiley & Sons, 1995).

Price, Jonathan and Henry Korman, *How to Communicate Technical Information: A Handbook of Software and Hardware Documentation* (Redwood City, CA: Benjamin/Cummings, 1993).

Shneiderman, Ben and Greg Kearsley, *Hypertext Hands On!: An Introduction to a New Way of Organizing and Accessing Information* (Reading, MA: Addison-Wesley, 1989).

8 Structuring Your Topics

In Chapter 6, *Structuring Your Online System,* and Chapter 7, *Adding Hypertext Links,* we discussed how to create a well-structured system by categorizing the information you need to present and planning links between information topics. The result is a detailed system map showing the interrelationships of all the topics in your information library.

Nevertheless, the best-planned structures become irrelevant without well-structured information behind them. The text and graphics in each topic must support the information structure you have designed. For example, if you've decided on a task-based structure and then write only about the concepts supporting a task, neglecting the how-to's, you have failed to support your structure. Users may find a topic describing the task they're interested in, but they won't find the information they expect and need.

In addition to outlining the general structure of the information library as a whole, your content specification must establish the structure of individual topics. What kind of information will topics contain and in what sequence? For example, you might decide that each topic will describe a procedure and that all procedures will start with an explanation of why the procedure must be completed, followed by numbered steps for completing the procedure. You might further decide that each step will provide feedback that allows the user to verify that the step has been completed correctly. When you specify the detailed structure for each type of information topic you plan, then the topics created will be consistent and the structure and content predictable. Users will know what to expect once they reach the topic of their choice.

In this chapter, we provide guidelines to plan the flow of information within your topics and then choose building blocks for structuring each topic.

Planning information flow

A major difference between writing for paper and writing for online is that online information is often divided into short individual topics. Procedural information, reference information, statements of purpose, examples, and other self-contained information types support a modular, action-oriented approach.

Furthermore, because the topics are linked through hypertext jumps and users have the option to read them in any order, topics need no formal transitional language to link them together. Instead, each online topic is presumed to stand alone. The glue holding the topics together is the logical structure behind the topics. This structure presents a web of related topics that the user experiences as a browse sequence or as a set of layered information surrounding and supporting a primary topic.

The design of the individual topic provides a second and essential glue that mirrors the sequential, hierarchical, or weblike structures underlying your library design. Absolute consistency in the internal structures of the information topics, affected by the nature of the topic itself, reinforces the higher structures and builds confidence in the users. When they open a topic of a particular type, they know what to expect. They can move with confidence through hypertext jumps because they know that the web of paths available will always lead to topics structured in exactly the same way. There are no surprises.

To achieve this degree of design consistency requires first that you establish a standard design for every information type you have to present. You achieve the standard design through the organization of the topic itself. The internal organization of each information type is then maintained rigorously throughout your design, providing a predictable structure for your users. To use an analogy to object-oriented programming, each information type must function as an object class, always behaving (through layout, language, and graphics) in exactly the same way.

The following guidelines suggest how to begin the process of building an information flow from the consistent application of details rather than through the tradition of expository prose in which information is connected with transitional language.

Plan the design of each information type

In Chapter 4, *Categorizing Information Needs,* we describe the core information types you are likely to be working with—procedural, conceptual, reference, and instructional. Your particular design may require some other special information types. In any case, your next design step is to establish a structure for each of the types that you have decided to work with. This structure provides a standard that you can communicate to every writer contributing topics for the information library.

The design of each information type should include

- The informational building blocks described in the rest of this chapter

- The physical format of each information type so that it is immediately recognizable by the user

- The structure of links that will surround an individual information type with supporting and related information

For example, a procedural topic may include

- The set of building blocks that will be included (as applicable) in each procedural topic

- The appearance of each of those building blocks on the screen

- The links that every procedural topic will include

- The relationship (through a browse sequence, a table of contents, navigational buttons, and buttons supporting hypertext jumps and pop-ups) of the topic to every associated topic in the library

Ensure that each information type contains only the building blocks that you have assigned to that type

Users should be able find all the information they expect in one location in your information library. Each topic should include only the building blocks it is supposed to have and no others. For example, a procedural topic should not include conceptual information or examples unless the procedural topic has been defined to include these building blocks. In fact, we often see a clutter of extra information included under the ubiquitous and undefined "Note." Notes appear to function as a catchall for fuzzily defined information.

Consider carefully how the building blocks should be ordered within the information type

Because of the size limitations of many computer screens, the sequence of building blocks within a particular information type must be carefully considered. Be sure to place the most important building blocks first so that they are always visible as soon as the topic is displayed. For example, every topic, no matter its type, should begin with a title. Even a pop-up glossary definition should repeat the word that is being defined. The title labels the topic and orients the user, often serving as a brief purpose statement.

Hide secondary information until it is needed

As much as possible, try to predict the path that the majority of your users might take to land on a particular topic. Make the topics that users encounter first in a sequence of jumps the primary information topic of that type. For example, if users are looking for how-to information, make the procedural topic the first topic that the users find from the table of contents or other navigational device. Then create secondary topics through jumps and pop-ups to support the primary topic.

Include the information that the majority of your users will need in the primary topic. Hide in secondary topics information of interest to a minority of users. These underlying topics might include your conceptual information types, reference types, definitions, examples, exercises, and more.

You can hide information types by using pop-up links, links to other topics, or expansion links. See Chapter 7, *Adding Hypertext Links,* for more information on links.

Choosing your building blocks

After deciding what information types you will include in your information structure, whether procedural, conceptual, reference, instructional, or other, you next need to choose the building blocks that you will assemble to create the information type. Note that different information types may include the same basic building blocks.

The building blocks outlined in this section encompass most of the blocks that have been identified by other researchers into information design such as David Farkas and Robert Horn. The 12 building blocks we present here are

- Action

- Condition

- Data

- Definition

- Demonstration

- Description

- Feedback

- Illustration

- Interaction

- Navigation

- Option

- Purpose

The following guidelines are designed to help you decide on the building blocks you will need in your information library.

 ## *Will you explain step-by-step instructions?*

Step-by-step instructions are the most common building block you will use in any information library designed to support novices and advanced beginners. Because these two initial stages of use represent the great majority of our user communities, almost every information library that most information designers will be asked to plan will be largely driven by step-by-step instructions. In fact, the action building block is likely to be the primary topic in many information libraries.

Step-by-step instructions are ordinarily constructed using numbered lists. Each sentence should begin with an imperative ("Press the Return key" or "Type the customer's name") and provide explicit instructions to perform a task, as shown in Figure 8.1.

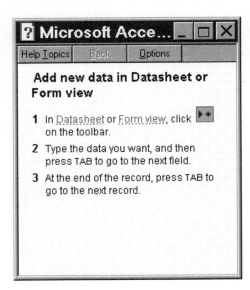

Figure 8.1: Users of Microsoft Access are provided explicit instructions for adding new data in a Datasheet or Form.

 ### Will you list the conditions associated with an action?

Conditional blocks establish the requirements that must be in place before an action can be taken. This might take the form of prequisites before an entire action is completed, or it might be an "If" clause starting a single step (Figure 8.2).

 ### Will you present data and other factual information that users need to support actions and decisions?

Data blocks are the building blocks of reference information. All information libraries will include many data blocks and are likely to draw on data that is produced through the reporting coming from corporate databases. Factual blocks might include such elements as syntax diagrams to support users who are creating software, product specifications (Figure 8.3), configuration requirements for setting up hardware (for example, electrical and air conditioning requirements), and many others.

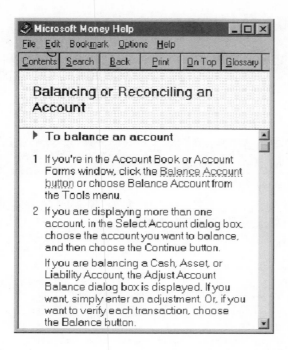

Figure 8.2: Steps 1 and 2 in this procedure start with the conditions that should be true for the user to complete the step.

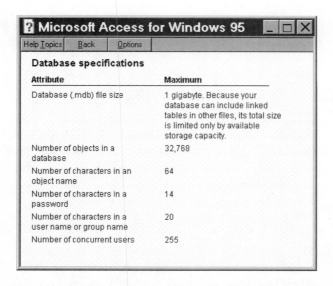

Figure 8.3: This data block provides specifications for the maximum size of a database created in Microsoft Access.

Will you define key terms?

A definition block provides a definition of key terms used in an instruction or concept. A glossary of terms (Figure 8.4) is an information type that contains only definition blocks.

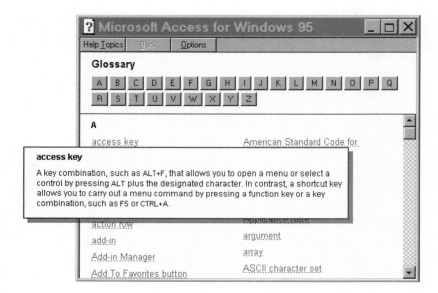

Figure 8.4: The term "access key" is defined in this glossary of terms. The same definition may also be used as a pop-up within other help topics that use the term.

Will you demonstrate a procedure?

Unlike interactive blocks, demonstration blocks require no more than passive observation from the user. Demonstrations might include video segments, animations, or simulations of a task showing the actions required (Figure 8.5) or the result of the actions.

Will you provide descriptions that introduce or explain concepts?

Descriptive blocks are the basic building blocks of conceptual topics and cover a myriad of subject matter. Descriptive blocks might include explanations of why a machine operates the way it does (a theory of operation), how the

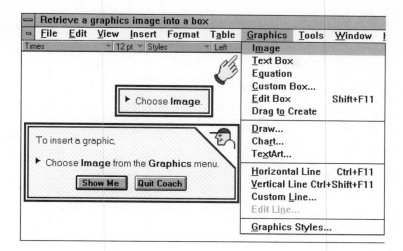

Figure 8.5: The WordPerfect coach provides a ShowMe button that demonstrates the required action rather than requiring the user to complete the step.

elements of a software application might be used together to produce a particular result (Figure 8.6), why a company has decided to take a particular course of action (a policy statement), the statement of a rule, and so on. Descriptive blocks provide the underlying explanations that help more experienced users understand why they need to do something.

Descriptive blocks may also describe products. In many information libraries, you will include descriptions of the products and services your company supports.

 ## *Will you explain the results of an action or event?*

Feedback blocks describe the effects or consequences of an action or event (Figure 8.7). They can be used by users who want to verify that they have followed an instruction correctly. They may also be used to set up expectations for a particular procedure—what will happen if these steps are followed.

A feedback block might, for example, be included at the beginning of an example to illustrate what the final result looks like before you explain how it was achieved.

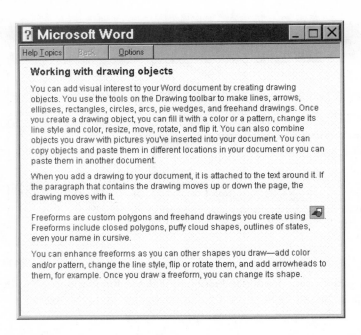

Figure 8.6: This descriptive block introduces users to drawing objects in Microsoft Word. It lists the tools and features available, defines terms, and explains what happens when you include a drawing in your document.

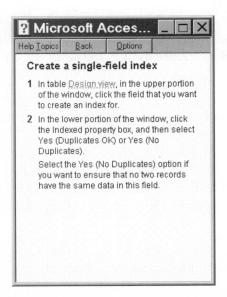

Figure 8.7: The text following Step 2 explains the consequences of selecting Yes (No Duplicates) in the Indexed property box.

Will you provide illustrations or real-life examples of a procedure or concept?

Examples illustrate the purpose, steps, conditions, or other information discussed in the primary information topic. Examples may include graphics (Figure 8.8), scenarios, reference information (such as code examples), or even elaborated descriptions.

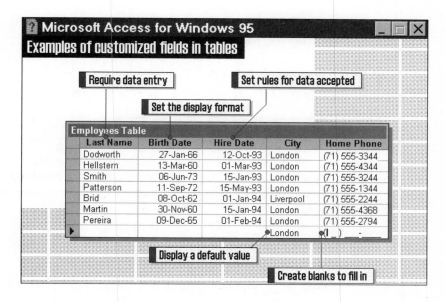

Figure 8.8: This illustration block identifies the potential for customized fields within a database.

Will you require interaction from the user?

An interactive block, such as an exercise in a computer-based training segment, requires that the user actually act before the next topic will appear. Users may need to press a button to continue, perform an action, or answer a question correctly (Figure 8.9).

Will you explain how to move through the system?

Navigation blocks provide instructions on how to proceed through the system itself. The navigation block might take the form of a secondary table of

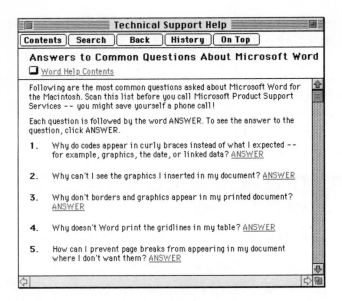

Figure 8.9: Rather than scrolling through all the questions and answers, users are asked to select which answers they want to read by clicking "ANSWER." This small degree of interactivity gives users more control over what they read.

contents or a map of the structure of the information. It might also include brief navigational text as part of an information topic.

Help on Help topics typically provide navigational blocks as they explain the help interface to the user.

 ### *Will you provide purpose statements to support an action or decision?*

Purpose-statement building blocks explain the context in which users perform tasks (Figure 8.10). Because users generally come to step-by-step instructions with a particular goal in mind, the purpose statement orients the user. Purpose statements help users verify that they have indeed found the right task.

The title of a task often functions as a sufficient purpose statement for many straightforward tasks. Other tasks require more elaborate purpose statements to help users confirm that this task is indeed the one they have been searching for.

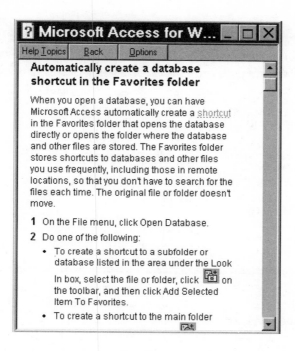

Figure 8.10: The purpose statement in this example explains to users why they might want to complete the task described in the rest of the topic.

 ### *Will you provide optional ways of performing a step or a task?*

Option blocks list alternatives to the prescribed method of performing a task. As you learned in Chapter 3, *Determining the Stages of Use,* options are not particularly welcomed by novices and advanced beginners, who prefer to learn one way of reaching their goal rather than many. However, more experienced users are often looking for more efficient methods for doing things they already know how to do. For these audiences, you might want to provide option blocks.

Option blocks include such elements as shortcuts (Figure 8.11) or even descriptions of actions that might be taken but are not necessary. You might, for example, construct an option block by explaining that the users might adjust the way their screen appears but need not do so.

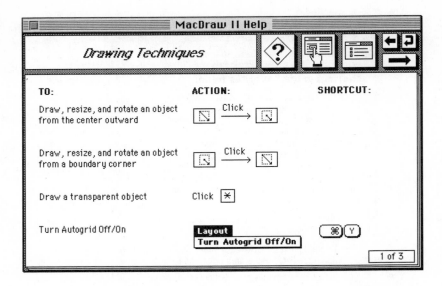

Figure 8.11: Users have the option of using the Layout menu or a shortcut key stroke to turn the autogrid on and off.

Constructing an information topic from building blocks

To determine which building blocks are appropriate for your users and their goals and how they should be assigned to various information topics, consider the following questions.

Are your users primarily novices?

Novices and advanced beginners want to get their work done. They do not want to spend time learning about the subject or understanding its nuances. When writing primarily for novices and advanced beginners, focus on action, purpose, feedback, definition, and illustration building blocks in your procedural topics (Figure 8.12). Avoid descriptive, conditional (unless absolutely necessary), and option blocks that are more suitable for more experienced users. For instructional topics (computer-based training or tutorials), couple action blocks with feedback, interactions, demonstrations, and examples.

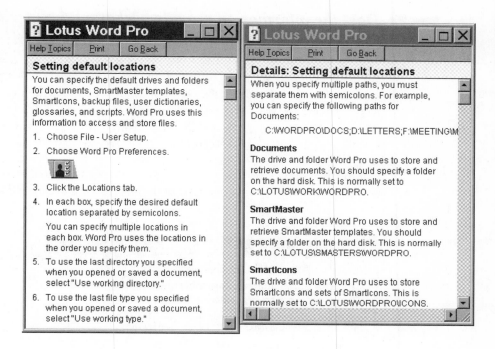

Figure 8.12: Lotus WordPro supports novice users by providing specific information in a secondary window about each of the locations they must enter in Step 4. The primary and secondary windows combine a purpose statement, action blocks, and definition blocks to fully address the novice user.

 ## *Are users experienced?*

Proficient and expert users do not always require the explicit instructions provided by action blocks. Rather, they prefer to learn about the conceptual theory and find their own shortcuts. When writing for these audiences, use descriptive, illustration, conditional, option, and data blocks liberally. Include examples in the form of scenarios describing what other experts have done, and include advice from those experts constructed of conditional, descriptive, and option blocks.

Because experienced users prefer to make their own choices and follow their own paths through a task or a decision, you might use option blocks to list all the alternatives available and conditional blocks to explain the complications that may be caused by a particular action.

Does the information provide background material that provides a context?

When designing conceptual topics to support users who are trying to perform complex, highly integrated tasks, troubleshoot problems, find new approaches, or solve complex problems, you will most obviously select descriptive blocks (Figure 8.13). However, you should also strongly consider combining these blocks with illustrations and data for a more comprehensive discussion.

Conditional blocks are also useful in providing a conceptual framework, especially when you must describe prerequisites for a task or a decision.

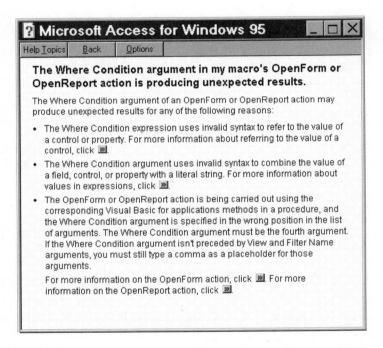

Figure 8.13: This troubleshooting topic provides background information about the conditions that might have caused the problem.

 ## *Does the user need to make a decision?*

When they must make a decision on how to act in a particular situation, users need descriptive information, conditions, options, illustrations, and more to support their decision-making process (Figure 8.14).

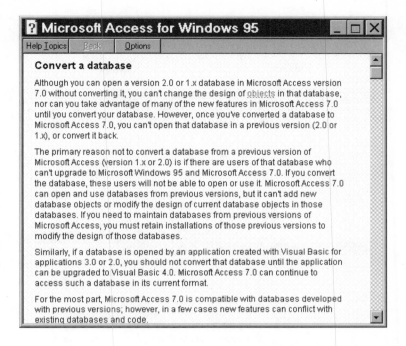

Figure 8.14: This topic provides detailed information for users considering whether to convert their existing databases from a previous version of Microsoft Access. It provides descriptive information that explains users options and the consequences of each option.

 ## *Does the information describe how to complete a task?*

When describing a task in a procedural topic, you will select primarily action blocks. However, you may want to provide a very brief purpose block describing the reason for the procedure or a conditional block explaining what should already have occurred or may occur.

For extremely cautious novice users, you might also include feedback blocks showing the expected result after each action step.

 ## *Do users need to learn the information being presented or simply perform an action?*

If you are building instructional topics, you may want to include many building blocks, but especially actions, illustrations, interactions, demonstrations, and feedback. When users choose the wrong answer or take the wrong action step during an interactive session, consider providing action blocks that suggest what might be done rather than explicitly stating what the correct choice or action is. Better yet, allow them to go down the wrong path and see the results of their actions (Figure 8.15).

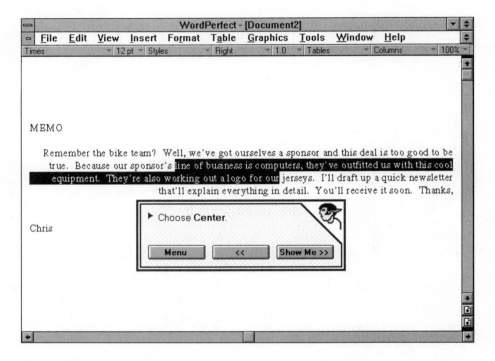

Figure 8.15: The WordPerfect tutorial allows users to perform the wrong actions and see the results. In this example, the user chose Right justification rather than Center.

Further reading

Boggan, Scott, David Farkas, and Joe Welinske, *Developing Online Help for Windows 95* (Carmel, IN: Sams Publishing, 1996).

Brockmann, R. John, *Writing Better Computer User Documentation: From Paper to Hypertext* (New York: John Wiley & Sons, 1990).

Deaton, Mary and Cheryl Lockett Zubak, *Designing Windows 95 Help: A Guide to Creating Online Documents* (Indianapolis, IN: Que Corporation, 1996).

Horn, Robert, *Mapping Hypertext* (Lexington, MA: The Lexington Institute, 1989).

Price, Jonathan and Henry Korman, *How to Communicate Technical Information: A Handbook of Software and Hardware Documentation* (Redwood City, CA: Benjamin/Cummings, 1993).

9

Testing Your Design and Implementation

As you plan, design, and implement your online information system, you need to plan for several iterations of both functional and usability testing. Online information, like software applications and hardware products, needs to be tested to be certain that it

- Works properly

- Does what it was designed to do

- Is effective

- Is usable

Sufficient time must be reserved for testing in the development life cycle. Without adequate testing, it is unlikely that the information system will work properly. By testing, you come closer to achieving a successful system design than you ever will without testing. Considering the investment you are making in development and the promise you have held out about increased and easier access to information, the need for testing is obvious.

Testing functionality

Nothing is more annoying to users than to get an error in the very document in which they hope to find information to keep them from making errors. To

175

avoid that situation, you must thoroughly test your online system before releasing it.

When you test functionality, you should approach the task with the intent of finding errors, not hoping to avoid them. In fact, your test is most successful if indeed you do find an error, because that's one less that the user will find for you.

To be most effective and successful in your testing, follow these guidelines.

Create a test plan

Before you begin development of your online system, you should have a plan for how you intend to test it. The primary reason for early planning is to ensure that you allow enough time to do the testing.

Your test plan should outline how often and when you will test, who will conduct the tests, what you will test, how you will respond to the results, and how you will know you are done testing.

Exercise every link, button, and menu choice

At a minimum, your test should make certain that every link, button, and menu choice is properly programmed. This means not only that users do not receive error messages when they choose a hotspot, but also that the topic displayed is the correct one. That is, you can't rely on your tool's automatic link-checking facility, because it can't tell if you programmed the right link, only that a link is programmed and exists.

Because most development tools provide a way to generate a list of links and their locations within your files (as shown in Figure 9.1), you should be able to systematically test every programmed link within the system. However, it's another matter to guarantee that everything that should have been programmed was. Compare your system to your original planning documents to ensure that you've done what you set out to do.

Test both the functionality within the information system and the links between application software (context-sensitive links) and the online help. Once again, the correct information should appear as designed.

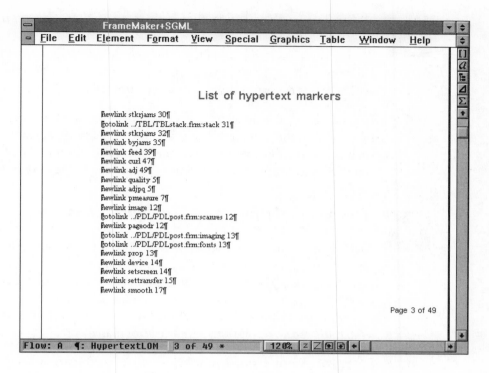

Figure 9.1: FrameMaker + SGML lists the links in your document so you can easily test them.

 Use someone outside of the development team to perform the test

By the time your system is ready for functional testing, your development team is far too close to the product to test it effectively. They know how to do everything correctly and even subconsciously correct for things that don't work quite right.

To provide for a fresh look and thorough testing, your test team should be separate from the development team. Expect that the development team may not appreciate that new perspective. Over the development period, they have come to view the system as their own, and they resent the implication that it may be less than perfect.

Allow enough time to test and respond to the results

Testing is useless if you don't leave enough time to respond to the results. Unfortunately, as development time stretches beyond your original estimates, testing seems easiest to shorten or even eliminate.

In general, you should allow at least as much time as you've taken to program the system in the first place to test and fix problems. For a complex design, such as one in which you programmed a custom interface rather than using a standard one, testing time could be twice as long as the development time.

Test on all platforms and configurations

Just because your system works perfectly on your development computer doesn't mean that it will work perfectly on your users' computers. Test your system on every possible configuration that you have available to make certain that your system works as expected. Test especially on systems that can handle the information library but are at the low end of workable functionality. Watch for speed, resolution, and directory management issues.

 Be sure to test your HTML (hypertext markup language) code on all Net browsers that you expect your users to have.

Anticipate nonstandard access

Don't just test the correct way of doing things, anticipate the unique ways that users may try to use or interpret your system. For example, in testing their CD-ROM, one company found that inexperienced users didn't understand the standard Windows Help index functionality. In one case, a user typed the word "ballet," a word that did not appear in the index. Not realizing that the topic with the closest match was highlighted, she hit Return and couldn't understand why she was taken to a glossary item for the word "background." If you have a high percentage of very novice users, you may have to make adjustments to the standard interface features to help them avoid misinterpreting their results. In this instance, the real problem was that the index search took the users directly to a help topic instead of providing them with a list of the help topics most relevant to their search request.

Know when to stop testing

Although the ideal is to release a system that works perfectly on all platforms, practically speaking, that time never comes. How do you know when you've tested enough? When you're out of time or money? Because, in this case, the testing burden shifts from you to your users, this is probably not the ideal criterion.

Many quality assurance organizations define the time to stop according to the number and severity of the errors found. As you find the number and severity of errors decreasing on an increasingly steep curve, you may decide that the rate of errors uncovered has declined sufficiently to justify ending the test.

Establish acceptable error ratios before you begin testing. For example, although it's probably not acceptable to have any linking errors, how many copyedit errors will you allow? When your rate of finding copyedit errors decreases to one every 3 hours, you are probably ready to release the system.

Evaluating usability

Usability testing refers to tests that measure whether potential users of the information are able to find what they need with reasonable effort and within a reasonable time. Through such testing, you can answer the following questions:

- Will users be able to understand how the information system works?

- Will users be able to find information easily, using tables of contents, index searches, full-text searches, and other navigation aids you have provided?

- Will users understand at first view how you have structured the information?

- Are users able to turn their goal statements into explicit search routines when they first see the interface you have provided?

- Does the structure make sense to users so that they know where to find the information they need?

- Have you used terminology that users are familiar with? Does the language make sense to them?

Usability testing is not a demonstration of the proposed design to potential users. Demonstrations rarely help improve the details of designs and often lead to misleading positive feedback. Users may be impressed by seeing the features of a system even though they will find it unusable once they try to use it themselves.

Usability testing means that users are on their own, trying to answer their own typical questions and use information to perform tasks. They are not aided by developers and others who already know how the system is supposed to work. By their mistakes, real users help you discover what is not intuitive, neither learnable by the novice nor obvious to the experienced.

Without usability testing, users may find information inaccessible and incomprehensible. Given the wide range of user background and abilities and the thousands of design decisions you have had to make, the likelihood that all your decisions are correct is really quite low. Design guidelines, like the ones presented in this book, go only so far in ensuring success. We know too little to guess correctly about how people search for information they need.

The following guidelines provide only a rudimentary view of usability testing. Be certain to consult the several excellent and comprehensive books on usability testing listed at the end of this chapter before you embark on a testing program.

Plan iterative testing throughout the development life cycle

User testing, early and often, helps give your product a competitive edge. It helps to ensure that your product will be well received by your users because they can find and then understand the information they need. Testing iteratively throughout the development cycle also means that you have ample time to fix design problems and later refine smaller issues.

You will find many opportunities during the development life cycle to perform usability tests, including early in development when changes to your design are easiest to institute and least expensive. In fact, you can perform usability tests long before any information has been put online at all. Usability testing at several points in the information development life cycle, as shown in the following table, will help you determine if the design you have created meets your users' needs.

The first opportunity for testing is during the design phase, when you are defining the system. At this phase, you may want to produce storyboards that show how the information will be organized and how the interface will look and behave. During the design phase, you can ask potential users to maneuver through paper prototypes of the help screen, Web pages, or tables of contents.

Table 9.1: Testing as a Part of Every Phase of the Development Life Cycle.

Information planning	Content Specification	Implementation	Testing/ Production	Evaluation
Conduct early paper-and pencil tests of library designs	Conduct early paper-and-pencil tests of your ideas for organizational patters in the publications, terminology, instructional text designs, graphic designs	Conduct tests of early prototypes instructions and reference text	Conduct formal user testing of completed product	Conduct evaluative tests of completed publications
Conduct tests of previous and competitive products and publications		Conduct tests of early and later publication drafts	Conduct functional testing	Conduct user site studies
Test index ideas		Test indexes		

Throughout the development of your information system, you should continue to test aspects of your implementation with your potential users. You may test as soon as you have a prototype of the interface available. You may test once you have designed initial access screens or tables of contents to ensure that users can sort through the information structure you have provided. You may want to test your search mechanisms to make certain that they are easy to use. Any number of elements of the design are candidates for usability testing. Throughout the process, the goal is to discover how well users understand and are able to use the functions available to them.

Define your testing goals

Determine which aspects of your system require focused investigation and which require only general evaluation. Where do you anticipate that users may stumble?

You may want to evaluate the system on any of the following criteria:

- Accuracy

- Appearance

- Access time

- Clarity of writing

- Completeness

- Entry points

- Pertinence

- Readability

- Task orientation/support

Be careful not to test the help interface if you are using a standard help system such as Windows Help and have no ability or interest in modifying the interface. There's nothing you can do about usability problems if you cannot redesign the interface or the help functionality.

Define your expectations

If you don't know what you're looking for, you usually won't find it. Defining your expectations helps you focus your observations. For example, do you expect users to find information within three mouse clicks? Design your test to count mouse clicks when a user is looking for information. In all cases, make sure that your expectations are measurable and well defined, and that they coincide with the expectations of your users as well.

Setting goals for your usability tests is critical to determining when your system is sufficiently usable to be placed into operation. Until you meet your testing goals, defined by the metrics in your test plan, you will need to correct problems and improve your design.

Recruit the right test participants

The people you test should have knowledge of the content, have experience with the media, and be members of the target audience. Use different groups of these people at different times in the development cycle. For example, after writing the information, use subject-matter experts to test the accuracy of the information.

Most critical for usability are the tests you perform with people who will actually have to use the information system you design. These are the people who will ultimately decide if your system is a success. It is not sufficient to test only supervisors or super users who may know more about the subject or about system design than the average user.

Prioritize your potential list of participants in order of most to least important. Start with the most important users—those who have a critical need for the information. Start with a small, homogeneous group of critical users, often no more than four to six.

Always test a small group of similar users, not just one or two. One or two users may have idiosyncratic problems that will not be representative of their group's needs. By the time you have seen four to six people make the same mistakes, however, you know you have a usability problem that must be corrected.

If you have time, test more than one group, depending upon the priority of their need to find information. For example, you may want to test a group of clerks from the accounting department and a group of customer service telephone representatives. Their needs are likely to be quite different. Testing one group may not help you determine if you are creating a usable system for other groups.

 ## Create test scenarios

usability testing:During your early analysis, you learned about the information needs of your users. These information needs were often stated in terms of learning and performing goals, questions of "What is that?" or "How do I do this?" The questions your users discussed during the needs analysis become the questions that guide the scenarios you will want to submit to usability testing.

Here is a typical scenario for a usability test of an online information system:

> "You are a system administrator for your company's client/server system. You are responsible for repairing desktop computers and file servers that are part of the local area network. You discover that the front door on your server has broken, and you need to replace it. Find the part number of the door using the Internet system, order the part, and then find the instructions for removing and replacing the door."

With a scenario like this one, you can watch users, one at a time, try to find the information they need. You will know where they get lost, when the information structure is not obvious, when the word used for the door is not what the users expect it to be, when the information on the part number is in an entirely different part of the system than the instructions for removing and replacing the part and there are no hypertext links joining them. Such is the possible outcome of a well-designed usability test—a clear direction for improving and perfecting the information system.

Conduct a pilot of each test

To ensure that you are testing the right things, perform a pilot test and analyze the results before proceeding. The pilot test is intended to work out any potential problems with the test itself. For example, you may find that your instructions for the scenarios are unclear and cause users to become unnecessarily confused. You may discover that you must correct a functional bug in the part of the system you are testing before submitting the system to unsuspecting users. You may have equipment problems that must be corrected.

The pilot test is critical to the successful implementation of the test. Once the problems with the pilot are corrected, you are ready to move on to the group of subjects you have recruited.

Make careful observations

Usability testing requires close observation of the participants. You watch exactly what they do to try to find the information they need. In addition, you ask them to talk aloud so that you have some idea of what they are thinking as they search for information. Their attempts to interpret what they see and make sense of what they do will provide you with critical insights into the shortcomings of your design.

To guarantee that you capture the details of your users' thoughts and actions, we recommend that you use two observers. One observer records everything that happens, everything the user does, and all the system responses. The second observer serves as the test administrator, introducing the user to the test environment, ensuring that the system is operating correctly, asking the users to explain their actions if they forget to talk aloud, and more. Neither observer helps the users find the requested information or navigate through the system. The users are on their own, just as they would be on the job.

Debrief the users at the end of each test session

At the end of each individual test session, you may find it useful to ask for user response to the experience that they have just had. You may want to know how they would rate the design compared to other information systems they have used. You might ask them to compare using the system with using paper documentation. Keep the questions open-ended so that the users can help you evaluate the success of the design or pinpoint improvements that must be made.

Analyze your results

As you review the performance of each test subject and after you have tested all the subjects, you need to analyze the results of the test. Both observers should go through the observation notes and highlight problems that occurred, especially if those problems occurred for more than one test subject.

Make a list of the problems you have observed (we recommend using sticky notes to put problems onto a white board). Then group the problems into categories such as problems with the keyword search, problems with the initial screen, and so on.

Once you have the problems grouped, prioritize the problems in terms of the difficulties they might cause the users. You will want to correct the most severe problems first. You may not have time to correct all of the problems you find, so leave the least important (to the user) until last.

Decide on changes you will make to the design and implementation of your system

Once you have analyzed and prioritized the problems, you need to assemble the development team and decide upon solutions. Some of the solutions will be straightforward. For example, if the users cannot find the words they know in the keyword search, you may want to add synonyms. If users cannot find information through a table of contents, consider using different headings that better illustrate what they are looking for.

Sometimes, however, you may be able to fix specific problems such as adding a word to the keyword search, without fixing the underlying problem. Perhaps your entire index needs rethinking. You may have to add synonyms to the index throughout, not just in the particular case that showed up in the usability test.

You may discover that your entire information design proves incomprehensible to your users. Everyone you test has difficulty locating information and often gives up. It is not unusual to find on a first usability test that you have a lot wrong with your organizational scheme. If this happens, you may have to start over rather than try to patch the problems with small changes.

Remember, however, that a problem with the organization of the information library may reflect the fact that you retained the original structure of your hardcopy books rather than designing a new structure for an online library. Consider the more comprehensive global changes you need to make in your design from the hints you gain during usability testing.

The possibility that your initial design may fail to meet users' needs underscores the importance of testing early. If you start to test when all you have is the layout of the initial screens that present the structure of your information system to your users, you will find it easier to make massive changes than if you wait until you have tagged all your information and designed a special interface.

Go back for more information if necessary

If you find inconclusive or mixed results, don't hesitate to add more subjects or to modify the test to more closely examine the area of confusion. You need to have conclusive results on which to act. Sometimes you'll find it useful to add another usability test with a different group of users to see if the same problems occur again.

Allow enough time to test and respond to results

Perhaps even more than with functional testing, it's important to leave sufficient time to respond to the results of usability testing. The later the testing, the more difficult this becomes if you haven't caught the more important problems early on.

Retest solutions or changes

Don't assume that the problems you observed the first time you test are the only problems in your design. Once you've fixed the first issues, you may find further issues that couldn't be found until the first ones were resolved. Or you may introduce new problems with your solutions. Retest the system until the users achieve the performance goals you have set for them.

Further reading

Dumas, Joseph S. and Janice C. Redish, *A Practical Guide to Usability Testing* (NJ: Ablex Publishing Company, 1993).

Nielsen, Jakob, *Usability Engineering,* (Cambridge, MA: Academic Press, 1993).

Nielsen, Jakob and Robert L. Mack, eds., *Usability Inspection Methods* (New York: John Wiley & Sons, 1994).

Rubin, Jeffrey, *Handbook of Usability Testing* (New York: John Wiley& Sons, 1994).

Wiklund, Michael E., ed. *Usability in Practice* (Cambridge, MA: Academic Press, 1994).

10

Choosing the Right Tools

Only after you have determined the design implications of your research should you begin to consider which development and display tools to use. The tools should meet the needs of your information and your users, not vice versa. Too often we find that organizations select and purchase a tool before they have established the functional and usability goals of the information system they are developing. Too late, they try to force the information into forms that the tool can handle, thereby distorting the information for the users and often increasing the cost of information development.

Just because a display tool meets the technical and functional requirements of hardware, software, and network communications does not mean that it will be usable. Some years ago, we encountered a display tool that was the first choice of the programming professionals in the organization. It was compatible with system hardware and software, and could easily be made to work with the network system in place.

Unfortunately, users found the tool almost impossible to use. The tool produced an exact facsimile of the original paper documents with graphics, table of contents, and index as originally printed. However, it provided only minimal capacity for hypertext links. Consequently, the index of the original document could not be used to find the references in the text. The index referred, of course, to information by the page numbering of the original text. Although the page numbers remained on the facsimile pages of the document, they could not be located except by turning the on-screen pages. Any search for a page number ended up on the wrong page, because the system counted as pages all the front matter of the text plus invisible pages created during the conversion process.

The only other search mechanism available was full-text search, which was limited to exact words or phrases in the documents. Every instance of every word or phrase requested was then displayed in order of its appearance in the entire online library. The user could not limit the search even to a single document. The tool proved disastrous and the entire library had to be removed from electronic circulation.

In another case, a tool was selected that would not include graphics or tables as they originally appeared in the text. This tool limitation not only made reading and comprehension difficult for the users but also added considerable additional work for the information developers. Every graphic had to be removed individually from the text and saved in a separate file. Then a graphic reference had to be coded with a hypertext link so that the user could display the graphic on request. When the graphic window was open, the user could not display the text simultaneously but had to toggle between the two. You can imagine how such a system decreased the usability of the information.

Such cases of tools that make online information unusable abound. Often the people who select the tool fail to consult with either the users or the developers of the information. Even when users are consulted, they often approve a display system that they later find unusable because they do not understand the limitations or the capabilities of well-designed systems.

No tool available will be perfect for every information environment. Few tools will do everything that the information developer or the users might wish. As you specify and evaluate the tools you will need to develop and display information online, you will need to make trade-offs. One tool will do A, B, and C well; another will do B, C, and D well. The key to making a good selection is to write a detailed specification and prioritize the capabilities in terms of those that you must have and those that would be nice to have.

With such a list, you will be able to weigh the capabilities of the various tools you evaluate and make the best decision you can make under the circumstances and potential limitations you must take into account. This chapter provides guidelines for creating this list and choosing a tool.

Writing a specification

Based on the requirements for your online system, you should write a specification for the characteristics and features that your chosen tool must support. The following sections outline information that you should include in your specification.

User needs

First and foremost, your chosen tool must support the system features that you have determined are crucial for your users. In your specification, repeat the design features you have established in your planning documents, as prompted in the following guidelines. Then, as you choose the tool, look not only at whether the tool supports the features, but also at how you will have to create and implement them.

Include your interface requirements

Describe the look and feel, such as layout and colors, of the interface you have designed for your system. Some tools have restrictions on the way text or graphics are displayed. Others limit the number of colors you can use. Ensure that your tool will support the design you have created.

Describe the system's organization

Describe the type of branching and links you plan to include. Does the tool support these plans? Also, consider how many branches and links you intend to include. Can the tool support that many without performance suffering? Finally, consider how branches and links are shown in the tool. Is this compatible with your design?

List the ways users will access the system

Although most tools will allow some level of searching and will automatically generate tables of contents and indexes, the functionality of these features may be limited. If you desire specific responses from these features, you need to find a tool that supports them. Look at the defaults available and the degree of customization allowed by the tool. What limitations are placed on access features?

Discuss your security requirements

In some cases, you may not want all users to access all the information in your system. For example, you may want to limit access to administrative information about changing passwords or managerial information about accounting procedures. Ensure that the tool you choose supports the levels of restriction you require.

Describe how users will move through the system

Discuss the navigation buttons you intend to provide. Do you expect the tool to provide these buttons as defaults or options? How does the tool allow movement through the system? For example, can you build visual maps of the information structure and allow users to link from a point on the map to the relevant information?

Describe the type of feedback you will provide

If you expect to provide error messages or other information to users when they have a problem in an online application, describe those messages here. What types of default messages are offered by the tool? Are they useful and acceptable? Can they be overridden if necessary?

List the ways users can interact with the information system

Describe the types of interaction you envision your users will have with the information system. What kind of input must be evaluated by the system? Will users be able to provide keyboard input or is everything mouse driven? Will they enter text and if so, to what degree must their entries exactly match a specific format? That is, is capitalization important? Are wildcard characters supported? Will you need to track mouse clicks? Can your tool do that automatically or will you need to explicitly program it?

Describe the ways users can control the system

The amount of control you give to your users depends on their sophistication. You may want to provide the following controls:

- **Sound, animation, or video controls.** Explain how users should be allowed to control volume and playback. Should controls be present on screen or accessed through a menu or button?

- **Text annotations.** Will users be able to add notes and comments of their own to the text? How will their annotations be preserved when the information topics are updated?

- **Text modifications.** Will users be able to modify the online file for their own use without changing it for everyone? Will they be able to copy information from an online file and use it in a document they are creating?

List any special effects you intend to include

If you envision using any special effects such as zoom (for text and graphics) or dissolve (for presentations), list them in the specification to ensure that the display tool supports them. Also look at how you control those effects. Can you change the speed or pattern?

Describe how users will be able to print files

Some tools allow users to print only a single topic at a time, others only entire documents. Other tools allow users to print a range of contiguous topics at one time, and still others allow for printing topics from throughout the system.

If you are providing a great deal of conceptual and reference information, you may want to provide special PostScript files or other file types that allow your users to print documents that look like regular paper manuals. If you provide special print files, how will users find them? Will they be accessible from the online viewer? Will they have to be accessed separately?

What if users want to download the online files to their own PCs and save them for their own use? Will this be possible with the tool you select?

Compatibility

Beyond meeting your functional requirements, the tool must also be compatible with all the hardware, software, network communications, and file types that you are using. Use the following guidelines when evaluating a toll in this area.

List your minimum hardware requirements

Include computer type, processing speed, and required memory. Discuss any special sound or video requirements. Also list the requirements you have for peripherals—for example, monitor resolution required, CD-ROM drive speed, printer driver, and mouse type.

Besides listing minimum requirements, consider specifying ideal requirements. Although your system may run on a 286 processor, if a user wants an answer this week, you may want to recommend a Pentium. Especially test how your multimedia effects, if any, run on slower machines or lower resolutions.

List your minimum software requirements

Describe the minimum system configuration of your users' computers. Specify the operating system or systems, viewer, and any other software required to use the online system. What items must be installed before your system will work? What items may be incompatible or cause other problems? For example, screen savers can cause problems with Internet access.

As with hardware, also specify your ideal requirements for the software configuration.

List the file types that must be supported

Establish the types of text, graphics, animation, sound, and video files that must be supported by the tool you choose. In addition, specify the types of files you may want to export to another piece of software; for example, graphics files that users might modify in an art package or text files for printing.

If you will be supporting different file types for display and printing, discuss the capabilities you require for your tool. For example, do you want to single-source the files and simply apply a new format depending on the destination of the information?

Also consider font files. Will you provide fonts on your CD to properly view the file as designed? What will your tool do if the proper font can't be found? Does your tool support international fonts if required?

Discuss your compression plans

If you hope to deliver on anything smaller than a CD-ROM or if you intend to have users download files using modem or other slow-speed connections, you will probably need to compress information. Specify how much compression you will require and ensure that your tool supports the scheme chosen.

Specify your printing needs

If you will allow your users to print portions of the online information system, specify the print drivers and printers that your tool must support. Also consider whether you want the printed document to look identical to that on the screen or if you want to format it differently.

List your productivity requirements for the final system

The tool you choose should not slow down the performance of your online system. Include specifications for responsiveness. For example, how long should it take to retrieve a topic or list of topics?

Consider how the tool's productivity may change with file size. How many information objects will you have and how might that affect speed of access? How large will your information objects be?

Plan for updates

If there is one truth in electronic information delivery, it's that the field is constantly changing. The tool you choose today will be different in six months, the company may be out of business, or a better tool will be on the market. Include in your specification your plans for accommodating tool updates.

As you choose a tool, research how it has been upgraded in the past. How often is it upgraded? Is it typically backward compatible? What has been the upgrade schedule? What is the quality of the upgrade—is there often a flurry of patches to fix bugs after a release?

If you find a compatible tool that meets your users' and your developers' needs and also fits your budget, go for it. Don't wait until next month or next year. Yes, new and improved tools will become available as soon as you have made your decision, but that will always be the case and you need to get started.

Conversion requirements

An important consideration in choosing a tool is your plan for handling information that already exists in your organization, known as legacy documents. How much existing information needs to be included versus how much new information do you intend to create? Problems with the format and design of legacy documentation has been a major cause of cost overruns in the development of online information systems.

In fact, probably the most costly aspect of implementing your online information will be the cost of converting your legacy information into a form compatible with the display tool you have selected. Too often we find that the conversion costs for legacy information are underestimated because the difficulties are not thoroughly evaluated. Many people, especially financial managers, seem to believe that conversion and development costs will be trivial in comparison with the money to be saved by eliminating paper. However, at least one organization we know, faced with development costs three times higher than anticipated, doubts that they will be able to recoup their investment over the life of the system.

The planning you do and the information you develop about the tools available will help you arrive at an accurate and honest assessment of the cost of moving your information online. Use the following guidelines to help you in making that assessment.

Describe characteristics of your legacy documents

Do you have documents that were created in a wide variety of word processing, desktop publishing, graphics, presentation, and spreadsheet programs? When they were created, did everyone use standard templates so that all the formatting within an application was handled in the same way? Or were individual authors allowed to "do their own thing," formatting information in any way they pleased? We generally find that little discipline has been exercised in the original development of legacy systems, resulting in a wide variety of files that will be difficult to convert and will each have different conversion problems.

Check the validity of the files that you do have. Are heading levels, numbered lists, bulleted lists, and other design elements tagged according to company templates? Have individual writers deviated from the prescribed templates? For example, if you have documents prepared in Microsoft Word, move your cursor through the file and watch the style designation at the bottom of the screen. Are all headings in the text labeled heading 1, heading 2, or something similar? Do you notice plus signs next to the style name? If so, the style has been changed from the standard, and you need a tool that will ignore these changes.

If you have many documents that were not prepared according to your format standards or if you had no format standards at all, you may have to reformat the documents before you convert them for online viewing. Many current tools translate existing tags to tags that are built into the tool for display on screen. If the original tags are inconsistent, incorrect, or nonexistent, you have no way of knowing how they will be translated or whether they will convert to online formats at all.

In many cases, legacy documents will have to be reformatted to be used online or the files will have to be corrected manually after the conversion to eliminate bugs in the viewer version of the file.

 ### Decide if, when, and how you will add hypertext links to legacy documents

Some development tools allow you to add hypertext links into the source files. When you convert the file to its online form, the links will also be converted. In other cases, you will have to add links within the online development tool after the file is converted.

If you choose to add links to source files, be certain that every type of link converts into the online tool. In too many instances, we find that 90 percent, but not 100 percent, of the links convert, requiring time-consuming manual debugging.

Author needs

After you have taken all other needs into account in the specification of the display tool, you should choose a tool that is the easiest for you and your development team to use. Several companies we have known, full of technical, knowledgeable people, have had cost overruns of 500 percent in the development of an online information system. They have had to abandon expensive systems not only once, but two or three times, because the tools were rejected by the developers as too difficult to use. Consider the following guidelines to choose a tool best for the authoring and development teams.

Describe who will do the development

Indicate how you plan to produce the information objects you have defined for your online library. How much will you do yourself rather than using outside vendors or relying upon automated techniques? As a rule of thumb, single time functions are better outsourced.

Describe the workflow and support expected

Describe how you expect to complete the project. Will you require rapid prototyping early in the project? Do you intend to use the same development tool for the prototype? How many drafts will you complete? How much editing do you expect to do within the tool, as opposed to on the paper storyboards?

What are your expectations for testing and debugging? Does the development tool provide assistance such as test macros for these functions? For example, find out if the online compiler generates a report when it identifies missing hypertext links.

Describe development logistics

Consider the number of people who will be authoring the system. How many people can use the tool at one time? How is the integrity of each individual file maintained if many people are able to interact with it?

List peripheral products that you might require

Look at the tools provided within the tool. What kind of editor is supplied? Is there a spell checker? Can you define styles easily? Can you create animation within the tool? Can you use a programming language to enhance the look of the viewer? Can you modify the search system? Program your own buttons? Redesign the interface? Are these things easy to do or difficult? Do they require separate programs or add-ons to the original product?

Describe your expectations for training

If you will be learning a new tool, include in your specification your training requirements. How much time can you commit to training? Will training be delivered at your site? Can training be customized for your needs? Is follow-on or more advanced training available? Are there local trainers who might be called upon for consulting later in the project life cycle?

Ensure that the tool provides adequate documentation and support. Is the documentation usable? Is it online? If so, does the vendor seem to understand the requirements of good online documentation and help?

You might try to find information in the help system in answer to a basic question. Can you find the information? How long did it take? Is the information complete and accurate? Can you understand what it says? Does the vendor provide paper as well as online documentation?

How is support handled? Is there a charge for support after an initial getting-started period? Is support available 7 days a week, 24 hours a day? What do other users of the tool say about the responsiveness and effectiveness of the support people?

Be sure to look at support available in addition to the vendor. Is there a local user group, bulletin board, or chat group? Can you attend a users' conference? Are there local consultants who have been certified by the vendor?

Describe your tracking needs

Consider how the tool helps you keep track of your topics and links. How are topics numbered and stored? What happens when you want to add another topic to a compiled version? Do the topic IDs change?

Can you obtain a listing of all the topics and all the links in the system? What happens to the links if you remove a topic?

 ### *List the statistics you will need*

Look at the statistics provided by the product. For example, can it help you track which topics are accessed most frequently? Can you find out how much time your users spend using the online information system? Can you tell not only how often a topic has been accessed but also by whom?

 ### *Plan for updates*

Discuss the future of your online system. How will you update it? How does the tool handle changes? Are links maintained? What about user annotations and bookmarks?

 ### *Describe how information will be stored*

Will you keep all the files on a server to be accessed through an internal network? How will the files be stored? Do you need a documentation database that stores the source files, permits controls on access, provides data about system use, and allows you to reconfigure the system if necessary? Once information is put into the database, can it be extracted easily and in its original format? What access system is available to keep developers from changing files inappropriately or inadvertently?

Cost

Of course, the bottom line in choosing a tool is often cost. Be sure to include your budget in your specification and include each of the following considerations.

 ### *Consider the cost of the tool*

The cost of the tool not only includes the copies you buy for your own development purposes, it may also include licensing fees for each copy of the viewer that you distribute. In addition, look at what upgrades of the tool have cost in the past so that you can include upgrade costs in your estimate.

Consider the cost of hardware

If you don't have the hardware required to use the tool or if users cannot adequately display the information online, you may have another considerable cost for upgrading. Remember to evaluate memory requirements as well as processor speed.

 If you are hoping to deliver on CD-ROM, especially if some of your users do not have intranet or Web access, can you count on them having CD-ROM drives? Are the drives on their desktop computers or available only at some central location? Will they have to use someone else's computer to access the CD-ROM? If they don't have CD-ROM drives, will you supply them at no or reduced cost?

Consider the cost of training

Include in this consideration not only the costs of training classes and phone support, but the cost of your learning curve. How much extra time will your staff need before they are competent with the tool? Will many people within your organization be required to change the way they develop information? Will they need training as well?

Choosing among tools

Most likely, no one tool will provide all the ideal features you have identified for your system, and you will be forced to make difficult choices. Consider developing a list of priorities and a weighting system to evaluate the pluses and minuses of each tool you have considered. A weighting system will make your decision making more systematic, if not easier.

Use a decision table, such as one shown in Table 10.1, to help you in your decision making.

When analyzing your table and making your tool decision, consider the following guidelines.

Table 10.1: Decision Table Comparing the Performance of Four Tools In Relation to the Features Important to the Designer

Functionality	Tool 1	Tool 2	Tool 3	Tool 4
Automatic rules checking to ensure correct use of SGML	Yes	Yes	Yes	Yes
Real-time parser to validate SGML markup	Yes	Yes	Yes	Yes
Provides multiple views of document for navigation	Yes	Yes	Yes	Yes
Provides graphical representation of DTD structure	Yes	No	No	No
Easy table creation	Yes	Yes	Yes	No
Creates hypertext links automatically	Yes	Yes	Yes	Yes
Ease of use	Excellent	Good	Good	Fair
Features an intuitive interface	No	No	No	No
Provides bookmark features	Yes	Yes	Yes	Yes
Spellchecking, thesaurus, and search by word or SGML tag for word processing	Yes	Yes	Yes	Yes
Allows user to preview and print fully SGML formatted draft documents	Yes	No	No	No
Provide training	Yes	Yes	Yes	Yes
Customer support	Yes	Yes	Yes	Yes

Distinguish between wants and needs

After writing your specification, go back and identify which needs absolutely have to be met and which ones are negotiable.

Prioritize wants and needs

Within each category, list the specifications in order of priority. Ensure that the top priorities in each category are met.

As you evaluate your choices, we strongly recommend that you make your users' needs the highest priority, rather than your development needs or the requirements of your technical infrastructure. It is usually more cost-effective in the long run for you to accommodate your users by doing extra work on development or by spending money on infrastructure improvements than to accept results that will decrease or virtually eliminate use of the information library you have made a substantial investment to create.

Balance cost with features

Especially for optional features, weigh the cost difference between a tool that offers the feature and one that doesn't. Will you have more users simply because of one feature or is anyone even likely to notice its absence?

Don't take the vendor's word

Although we don't intend to be cynical, vendors will make claims about their capabilities that simply don't turn out to be true. As you research tools, don't rely solely on the vendor's literature and sales presentation. Instead, find out what other people are using. Use chat groups on the Internet to solicit the voice of experience. Request demo copies of the product and try it yourself.

Request a trial of the product functionality

Once you have narrowed your choices, ask the vendors in competition for your account to convert some of your legacy files. Better yet, have them show you how to do the conversion yourself. Track the amount of time required, noting that you will probably become faster as you gain experience. Consider the amount of debugging and manual corrections you have to make to the legacy files. What will be the time and cost if you multiply one file by the hundreds you will have to convert?

Consider personal preferences

If you don't like a particular operating system or platform and you don't have to use it, consider your own preferences and the personal preferences of your staff. People are more likely to learn the tools in which they have the most interest. Of course, reaching consensus among your staff members may be difficult if there is real contention over tools. Someone will ultimately have to make the decision. Beware of becoming victim to a tool that is available but that everyone on your staff will dislike intensely.

Further reading

Deaton, Mary and Cheryl Lockett Zubak, *Designing Windows 95 Help: A Guide to Creating Online Documents* (Indianapolis, IN: Que Corporation, 1996).

Horton, William, *The Checklist* (Boulder, CO: William Horton Consulting, 1994).

Zubak, Cheryl Lockett, "Choosing a Windows Help Authoring Tool," *WinHelp 96 Conference Proceedings* (Seattle, WA: 1996).

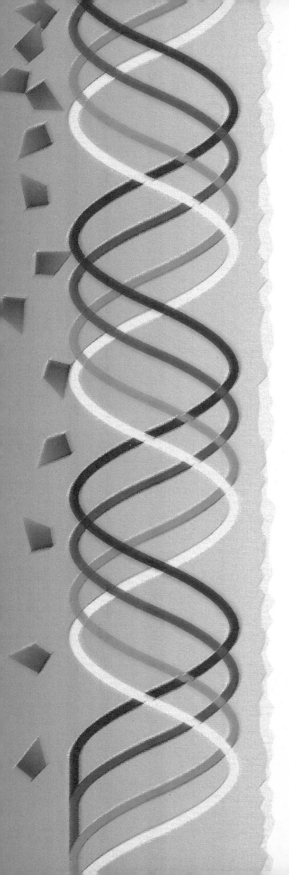

PART 3

Implementing Your Design

By now you're probably very eager to get started with the "meat" of your online system. You've completed all your planning stages and have a great system mapped out. We encourage that enthusiasm, but also provide a caution—don't forget your foundation. The work you've done so far was not simply an exercise; it should always be in front of you, influencing every decision you make about the specific features of your system.

The chapters in this part provide many guidelines to consider as you create your system, but all these guidelines may not be appropriate for your particular situation. Consider each in light of the discoveries and plans you've made so far.

- Chapter 11, *Designing the Information Interface,* provides guidelines for designing the look and feel of the online system. The chapter discusses design issues related both to the overall screen layout as well as the appearance of the text within that layout.

- Chapter 12, *Ensuring Accessibility,* discusses the importance of providing multiple entry points into the online text. It introduces the various ways users may access the information for which they are looking, including context-sensitive links to application software, external links to applications, tables of contents, indexes, full-text searches, and keyword searches.

- Chapter 13, *Providing Navigation Aids,* explains how to provide tools that assist users of online documentation in moving within the text once they have found their initial starting point. The chapter discusses such navigational tools as bookmarks, history buttons, and browse sequences (paging forward and backward). It also stresses the importance of providing clear markers, such as graphic maps or dynamic tables of content of the system, to give users the ability to identify where they are and how to get where they need to go.

- Chapter 14, *Composing Your Topics,* provides guidelines for writing each of the four information types identified in Part 1—procedural, conceptual, reference, and instructional.

- Chapter 15, *Writing for Readability,* summarizes the generally accepted standards for good writing and emphasizes the importance of creating a project-specific style guide to ensure standards are followed.

- Chapter 16, *Adding Graphics,* lists the possible situations in which you might want to include graphics in your system. It provides guidelines for how to control the appearance of the graphics and cautions you to pay attention to the constraints of your users' systems.

- Chapter 17, *Moving Forward with Multimedia,* lightly touches on the use of animation, video, and audio within your online system. As in Chapter 16, it provides suggestions for when each media is appropriate and cautions about the constraints you must also consider.

We recognize that these guidelines do not go in depth on any particular issue, but we hope that they provide a good introduction to the multitude of issues that surround the design of a good online system. We strongly refer you to the more detailed books and courses on particular subjects that interest you so that you might continue to develop as an online information developer.

11

Designing the
Information Interface

As a display medium, the computer screen is very different from the printed page. Consequently, choices appropriate for paper documents may be inappropriate for online documents. Unfortunately, many organizations have tried to reduce the cost of moving information from paper to electronic delivery by maintaining the format of the printed page. They have argued that users who refer both to paper and electronic media prefer consistency. Customer service organizations have argued most persuasively that they need to be able to identify the "page" of information to which the users are referring. If the on-screen pages are exact duplicates of the paper pages, the original page numbering system can be maintained for reference purposes.

However, many users complain that information formatted for the printed page makes on-screen viewing unpleasant and difficult. Type is too small, line length too long, pages require frequent scrolling, tables and illustrations are inaccessible, and the relationship to tables of contents is often obscure. We know, for example, that

- Online displays are smaller than the printed page. One printed page may require from three to six screens to be displayed online.

- Online displays are generally viewed in landscape orientation (horizontal distance is greater than vertical distance) whereas printed pages are portrait (vertical distance is greater than horizontal distance).

- Generally, the distance between the screen and the reader is greater than that between the printed page and the reader.

- The viewing angle is often vertical and above or below eye level rather than the "natural" orientation slightly above the horizontal that people use when they read from paper.

- The resolution of a typical screen is inferior to that of paper, making small fonts difficult to decipher and obscuring the details of many graphic images.

- Many monitors exhibit slight screen flickering, which makes extensive reading difficult.

These factors contribute to the observation that reading from computer screens is generally slower than reading from paper. This chapter presents guidelines to compensate for these differences.

Text

The most obvious change to make between paper and online display is the appearance of the text. We know that reading is slowed online because type that works well on paper is often too small and contains features that are difficult to see online. Use the following guidelines when designing text for online presentation.

 ### *Select readable on-screen fonts*

Many fonts that are appropriate for paper do not work well on a computer screen. The decreased resolution of the screen display renders subtle font characteristics invisible. Font sizes that are appropriate for the contrasts of black type on white paper are too small for on-screen reading.

Avoid stylized, cursive, or decorative typefaces. Instead use sans serif typefaces like Ariel, Avant Garde, and Helvetica for most on-screen displays. Unless you can count on high-resolution displays, avoid many of the standard serif fonts such as Palatino, Times Roman, and Garamond. If you do select a serif font, avoid fonts that have thin lines in their design; the thin lines may disappear on the screen.

Look carefully at the punctuation. Are periods and commas so small that they are no longer visible on the poorest resolution monitor that you must work with?

Use larger font sizes for on-screen display

Use a larger point size than you would typically select for paper. We recommend that for most on-screen displays you select a sans serif font at 11 to 12 points. If you anticipate having many middle-aged to older users, consider even larger fonts.

If your users are viewing your documents with a Web browser, you will not be able to control the font they use. You might note, however, in a preface to the document, which font and size will work best. If you are especially concerned about the appearance of a text, such as a highly graphic piece, consider using PDF files for your Web page rather than HTML files.

Avoid too many font changes

The most conservative choice for fonts is to use the same font for all text with changes in size, weight (bold or semibold), color, and italics to emphasize information. Some designers want to indicate information differences by changing fonts, as shown in Figure 11.1. However, you can use other techniques, such as placement on the help screen, to indicate these differences.

Keep line lengths short

Line lengths of two and a half to three alphabets, although suitable for paper, are inappropriate for on-screen reading. Long line lengths on screen often require that users turn their heads to see both the beginning and end of a line (if the online text window is opened to its maximum width) or scroll from one end of the line to the other (if the viewer does not automatically wrap text). Consider using a line length of one to one and half alphabets instead.

Many displays allow the users to change the width of the help screen to meet their own information needs. Some systems, such as WinHelp, dynamically resize the width of the text as the width of the window changes. Consider using tables to keep control of the display margins for your text.

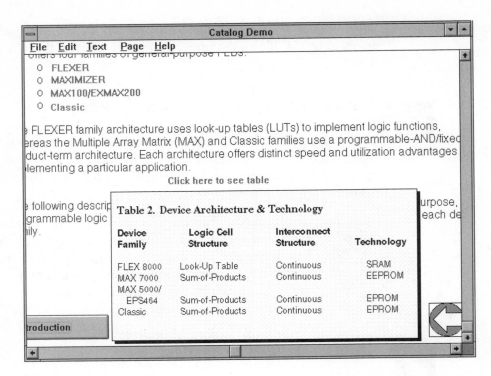

Figure 11.1: This help screen uses too many fonts in attempting to distinguish between elements. Note the different fonts used in the text, link, table caption, column heads, and table cells.

Distinguish important elements from normal text

Highlight key terms, user actions, and hyperlinks to clearly distinguish them from regular text. However, do not use too many different fonts. To emphasize words, you might use bold, underscores of various types, color changes, and font changes (for example, from sans serif to serif). Minimize the use of italic fonts on screen; they are often difficult to read (Figure 11.2).

Avoid excessive emphasis techniques

Inexperienced communicators often decide that more emphasis is better than less. A word that the writer wants the reader to notice may be printed in bold, enhanced with color, underscored, and enclosed in quotation marks. All the emphasis techniques scream, "Pay attention to me."

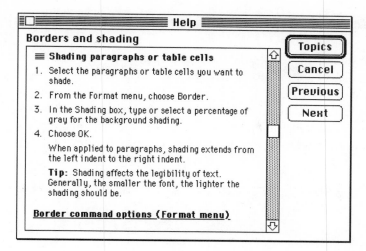

Figure 11.2: This help screen uses bold to call attention to the Tip and first-level heading, and underlining to distinguish the second-level heading. Because the rest of the text lacks any other emphasis techniques, these features draw the reader's eyes, which is exactly what the designer intended.

The same problem occurs when you decide to use a font change to indicate that a word belongs to a specific category of words. For example, some writers print all command names in large capital letters. Unfortunately, in most type fonts, words in all capital letters appear very large and dominate the text. The text readability is reduced because the users' eye movements are halted every time they encounter the emphasized text. In many cases, such text is actually no more important than any other text on the page.

We strongly recommend that emphasis techniques be used sparingly and with deliberation rather than be handled in terms of a rule that is applied to every case.

Layout

The physical appearance of the type and graphics on the screen will enhance the usability of the text as much as font variations. The combination of areas containing type of graphics and areas left blank (white space) assists users in differentiating among information types. Purpose statements, action steps, feedback, cautions and warnings, and so on all can be differentiated by placement and separation from one another.

Be consistent in the format and design of display screens

Ensure that each topic containing the same category of information has a consistent appearance, with the same fonts, margins, indents, placement of graphics (Figure 11.3), and so on. Every time your users encounter a procedure, it should look like every other procedure. When they access an overview, it should look like an overview. The look of the text and graphics is a very powerful tool for increasing the users' comprehension of the purpose of the text.

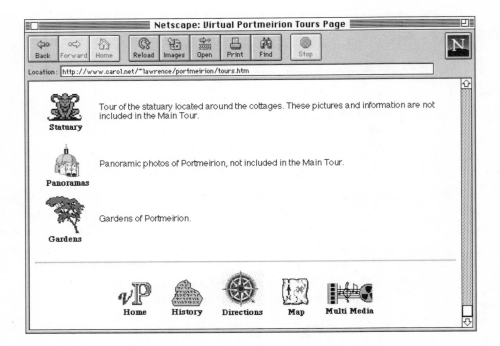

Figure 11.3: Most Web pages provide a standard set of buttons at the bottom of each topic. Users have learned to look in this location for these navigational aids.

Create standards for your information interface

The layout of the screen objects surrounding the topic is as important as the layout of the topic itself. The placement of navigation buttons, scroll bars, close buttons, and others must be consistent across all displays. If you are using primary, secondary, and pop-up windows in systems that permit multiple information windows to be open at the same time, the designs of each window type must also be consistent. For example, if you are going to include an Example button on each primary window, the button should be present whether or not you have an example for the topic. If the button cannot be used, it should be grayed, not removed.

If you have created your own layout for the online information screen, write standards to be used throughout the information library. Users find it disconcerting to look at screens in multiple, and often ineffective, formats.

Follow industry standards when applicable

Microsoft publishes guidelines for using Windows Help. The standard windows help layout will be familiar to many PC users. Apple provides standards for the design of help systems that use Apple Guide as a tool. If you decide to use Apple Guide, your version of the guide should closely resemble the standard.

If you follow the standards, your users will know what each of the help screen buttons do and how they might navigate easily from topic to topic.

If you decide to use an industry standard for the look of your information interface, ensure that it follows the standard in all respects. Minor deviations from a standard can cause confusion and frustration for users who bring prior experience to the task of using the information system.

Establish conventions for the use of each element

Just as you would create a standard for the design of a graphic user interface, you should also create a standard for the layout of your help screens. Apple, for example, always uses a horizontal rule between the topic title and the text (Figure 11.4). The title always appears in a larger bold font than the instructional text. The instructions for navigating through the help topics

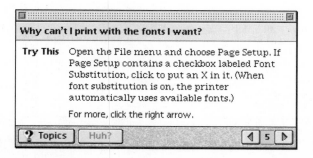

Figure 11.4: The Apple Guide standards ensure that all the topics look alike.

always appear at the bottom of the instructional text and are displayed in a font that is different than the standard text font.

Use negative space

Provide enough negative, or white space, to balance areas of positive space displaying text or graphics (Figure 11.5). Add sufficient white space so that the screen looks uncluttered. For example, in designing your screen, use white

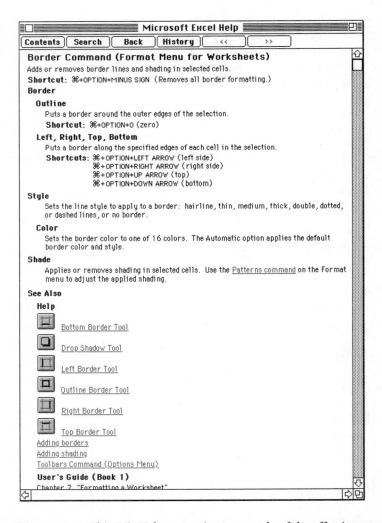

Figure 11.5: This WinHelp screen is an example of the effective use of white space between information types. Notice the various indents make headings easy to scan and to call attention to the shortcuts.

space between headings and paragraphs to clearly distinguish titles from purpose statements, purpose statements from steps, and so on.

White space provides the most effective means of grouping headings with text, text elements together, graphics with text, and so on. Adding additional vertical space, however, may require more scrolling. In general, users prefer not to scroll through long screens of text to find desired information. When designing your online screens, you must balance these conflicting concepts and determine the best trade-offs for your design.

Avoid horizontal scrolling

Horizontal scrolling severely interferes with the readability of the text. The users are able to read only part of a line of text at a time because the end (or the beginning) of a line scrolls off the screen. Provide at least one standard screen size that will not require horizontal scrolling. In general, avoid systems that do not dynamically rewrap text lines as the window size changes.

Make the interface easy to remember

By keeping the topic interface simple and consistent, you will ensure that users will find it easy to navigate. For example, the Apple Guide interface always includes four buttons at the bottom of the help topic (Figure 11.6).

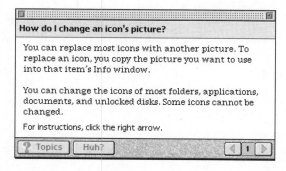

Figure 11.6: The Apple Guide interface is simple for users to understand and use.

The leftmost button returns the user to the main menu. The Huh? button takes users to an additional explanation of some aspect of the current topic that may be confusing to them. The Forward button always moves users ahead one topic; the Back button always back to the previous topic. The Number button tells users which step of the procedure they are currently viewing. The standard interface helps the user understand immediately how to navigate.

Window placement

In addition to the general look and feel of your system, its placement on the screen and the placement of its secondary windows and pop-ups can be very important.

Do not obscure important information

If your online documentation is associated with an application, design the document so that the part of the application window that is covered contains the least valuable part of the program. The document screen should not cover the entire window. Preferably, it should cover only one fourth or one third of the window.

Within the online documentation itself, do not obscure primary topics with secondary windows. Users should be able to refer to the original context at any time.

Place pop-ups in the center of the action

Because pop-ups are meant to be read quickly and then dismissed, place them prominently in the window so they aren't overlooked. As much as possible, place pop-ups near the information they supplement. For example, place definitions directly below the word being defined (Figure 11.7), or instructions next to the field to which they relate.

Size secondary windows to fit the information

In some systems, you can use a default window size for pop-ups and secondary windows. Placement will look more planned and be more controlled, however, if you size each window to fit the information it contains.

Use cascading windows

If you will allow your users to have multiple windows of information open at the same time, cascade the windows so users can easily bring any one to the top for immediate reference.

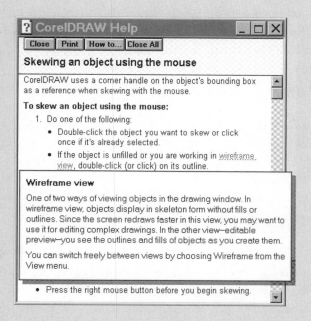

Figure 11.7: Pop-up definitions should be placed in close proximity to the words referenced.

Incorporating color

Using color in your information topics makes the information more attractive while it helps highlight significant information. Too many colors, however, can make information more confusing because the colors send a variety of messages. The more colors you plan to use, the more careful you must be in choosing these colors.

Use color sparingly

If used sparingly, color is an attention grabber. However, too many colors are distracting and potentially confusing. Each color needs a purpose. If there are too many, users spend more time trying to decipher the purpose behind the color than reading the information they need.

Limit your colors in your interface to three. Note that this recommendation does not refer to incorporating full-color graphics. See Chapter 16, *Adding Graphics,* for more information about color.

Consider limitations of the hardware

Be sure to research the minimum hardware configuration your users have available. How many colors do their monitors support, if any? Sixteen or 256 colors or only a gray scale? How will color map from one system to another? Will you provide a custom palette?

Consider limitations of users

Keep in mind that a small percentage of the population is colorblind. Do not depend solely on color to convey important information. In particular, avoid red/green and blue/yellow combinations close together. However, if the colors you use are saturated (bright primary colors), they will maintain sufficient contrast even on a grayscale monitor.

Consider as well the emotional responses that can be triggered by various colors. For example, if you are trying to reassure your users, don't provide feedback information in red. Take into account that colors have different meanings in different cultures. Red is used for warnings in the West but signifies happiness in the East.

Choosing an effective metaphor

A metaphor uses real-life objects and situations as the primary interface. If the metaphor is effective and users understand its significance, they can use the metaphor to make sense of the interface. For example, in the commonly used book metaphor , users understand that to continue reading a topic, they simply "turn the page." A link that looks like the dog-eared page of a book helps them recognize how to accomplish this feat.

Good metaphors improve usability because they allow users to associate the unfamiliar application interface with a familiar situation. However, the wrong metaphors have a great potential to destroy any semblance of usability. When choosing a metaphor, keep in mind the following guidelines.

Choose from the users' experience

A metaphor is an effective communication tool only if users have the background to understand it. If the object or situation you choose as your metaphor isn't well known to the user, you effectively add a level of difficulty—first, they have to learn about the "every day" situation, and then they have to associate it with the unfamiliar interface.

Carefully consider your users' backgrounds. What experience do they have to draw on? If your users are familiar with books, a screen view that resembles a bookshelf (Figure 11.8) or the pages of a book may be the best choice.

Figure 11.8: The bookshelf interface designed for HDK draws on the users' common experiences with a hardcopy library. When they select a book from the shelf, users see an open book with a table of contents.

Ensure that the metaphor fits the task

A metaphor should sit in the background providing subconscious help to your users as they navigate the system. Users should not spend time wondering about the relationship between the metaphor and their current task. For example, although an artist's palette metaphor might provide a recognizable background for your users, is it really effective if they are learning to hook a patient up to a heart monitor?

Explain the metaphor

Don't rely on the interface design alone to communicate the metaphor to users. Be sure to provide a topic in which you explain the metaphor. Also include textual clues within topics.

More elaborate metaphors are quite common in computer-based training systems. Use your opening sequence to set the stage for your metaphor. For example, a lá Mission Impossible, run a video or animation sequence in which the users' orders are given via a self-destructing tape. Then use spy-oriented backgrounds, buttons, bullets, and so forth throughout to maintain the metaphor.

Remember that metaphors need to have some significance to the concepts being taught. A "cute" design works the first time but not the fifteenth time.

Don't overdo it

Metaphors should not be the focus of your online system. Too often information developers get caught up in the "Hollywoodization" of online presentations. Keep the metaphor simple.

Simplicity also keeps you from having to test for varying monitor sizes, screen resolution, and so on.

Don't force the metaphor

You probably will not find the perfect metaphor that applies globally throughout your system. Don't force its use in situations where the metaphor simply does not work. By doing so, you will be grasping at straws to find an obscure connection between your system and the metaphor that no users will understand. For example, will the fish picture really signify "scaling" to most users. What about the cue ball, which looks like a white circle, signifying "print queue management?"

Don't forget the metaphor

At the same time, however, don't simply drop the metaphor in the middle of the instructional material because it no longer fits. Users will notice that it's gone.

If you have taught the user to anticipate the metaphor, its sudden disappearance will be disconcerting. We have observed users continue to click on objects in the interface that have provided them with feedback or entertainment in the past.

Test metaphors

Metaphors are very difficult to design. What seems obvious to you in a moment of creative ingenuity may be meaningless to your users. You absolutely must test your metaphors with your target audience to find if they grasp its significance to the learning experience you are trying to create. See Chapter 9, *Testing Your Design and Implementation,* for guidelines on testing.

Consider using industry standards

While it may not be true that there's nothing new under the sun, there are a lot of proven metaphors available. As we've tried to point out in the preceding points, creating an effective metaphor requires a lot of effort. However, someone else has already done that work in many of the metaphors that you see over and over again—file cabinets and folders, book cases and books, artist palettes, scissors and glue, and so on. They work; most users with any amount of computer experience know them. So use them.

Further reading

Lopuck, Lisa, *Designing Multimedia* (Berkeley, CA: Peachpit Press, 1996).

Macintosh Human Interface Guidelines by Apple Computer, Inc. (Reading, MA: Addison-Wesley, 1992).

Mayhew, Deborah J., *Principles and Guidelines in Software User Interface Design* (Englewood Cliffs, NJ: Prentice Hall, 1992).

Siegel, David, *Creating Killer Web Sites* (Indianapolis, IN: Hayden Books, 1996).

Weinshenk, Susan and Sarah C. Yeo, *Guidelines for Enterprise-Wide GUI Design* (New York: John Wiley & Sons, 1995).

The Windows Interface Guidelines for Software Design (Redmond, WA: Microsoft Press, 1995).

12

Ensuring Accessibility

Although information delivered electronically is potentially more accessible than information locked into print documents, electronic information can present significant accessibility problems for users:

- Users are less familiar with online libraries than they are with physical libraries.

- Users have fewer practiced techniques to access online information than they have for physical books.

- Users have the feeling of being lost in the details (lost in cyberspace) when they try to find information online.

Consequently, users need a variety of ways to find the information they need to perform tasks, understand concepts, and learn the skills they will need on the job. In Chapter 5, *Recognizing the Implications of Design Research,* we discussed how the results of your preliminary research impact the accessibility methods you choose to implement:

- You might provide context-sensitive information directly related to a computer application.

- You might include "standard features" such as tables of contents or indexes.

- You might provide a variety of search facilities.

This chapter provides guidelines to consider for the accessibility methods you have chosen to implement.

Context sensitivity

When they are using software applications, users often choose to access information based on the location of their cursor on a particular screen, dialog box, input field, or button. They want to know what something is or how to perform the specific task enabled by the application. Your task is to anticipate the type of information your users might need in a particular context.

To make context-sensitive information systems most effective, consider the following guidelines.

Anticipate the information that users will want

More so than any other users, users who access information through context-sensitive help systems expect to find needed information upon entering the system, without navigating through a series of topics. This expectation makes it critical that you fully analyze the reasons they might access the help system from each screen or dialog box in the application. Do they need help completing a field? Do they need to understand the purpose of a screenful of information? Do they need an explanation about why they are where they are? Do they need to get out of trouble?

In the design of Apple's bubble-help system, the designers anticipated that users would need to know how to access a menu item or selection that was grayed out, meaning that it was inaccessible to them at that point. The designers wrote different help messages to display based on whether or not the menu items or selection options were active or grayed out. The designers tried to understand the users' most common questions at the point of need.

Use all the resources at your disposal to anticipate your users' questions. As much as possible, involve users in this research—find out what they want to know. Although no design of a context-sensitive help system will be foolproof, user involvement may help you come closer to useful solutions.

Provide information related to the current cursor (keyboard) focus

Many purported context-sensitive systems take users to high-level information based on their location in the application. Although the information they need may be in the high-level help topic, it is often buried in paragraphs of text describing the entire context of the application screen and therefore requires more work and closer reading than the user might be willing to do. Rather than immediately reaching the quick answer they are looking for, users must scroll through information about all aspects of the current screen.

The reason behind this approach is typically twofold. First, designers have not fully analyzed the information needed from every point in the system (see our earlier discussion). Second, the programming is more complicated to support unique, specific information based on cursor focus, because the programmer must include calls to each individual help topic related to a specific field or area of the screen.

Although more programming support may be required to provide lower-level context sensitivity, your help system will be more effective if you provide context-sensitive information related to the current cursor (keyboard) focus. For example, provide users information about buttons, menu items, input fields, display fields, error messages, or information messages that can be specified by the cursor. Cursor-specific help may be provided through abbreviated help bubbles displayed directly on the application screen (Figure 12.1) or through more extensive context-specific help in a supporting information window (Figure 12.2).

Ensure that users understand why they have accessed the topic

Despite your best planning, there will be users who do not find the information they expect when accessing context-sensitive topics. They may not understand why they have reached a particular topic, or they may not have reached the information they had in mind when they asked for help. Ensure that the connection of the help topic to the application context is clearly stated in the topic title and the purpose statement following the title.

Provide simple ways to change topics

If users need information that differs from what you anticipated, they need an immediate method for changing topics. If you can anticipate other topics users might want to access rather than the displayed topic, list them prominently as related or alternative topics. In addition, provide TOC, Search, or Index buttons as part of the help interface to allow users to modify their search for information.

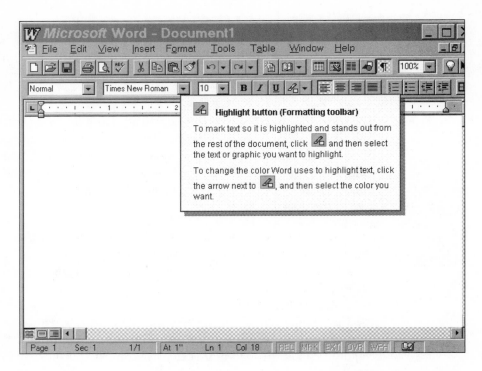

Figure 12.1: The help bubble is activated by the ? cursor and provides information about the highlight button.

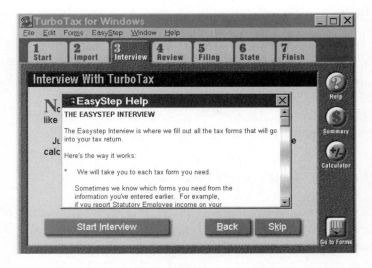

Figure 12.2: Users get context-sensitive information about the Interview tab in TurboTax by clicking the help button with that tab selected.

Determine how much navigational control to give users who access information via context sensitivity

In contrast to the previous guideline, one key factor in deciding to provide a context-sensitive system is the recognition that many users do not want to explore. Stage 1 and 2 users want an immediate answer to a question and then want to go back to work. In this situation, you need to decide how much you want to allow the user to explore. Exploring the entire field of topics may make users confused and lead them to distrust the usefulness of the online information.

Table of contents

A table of contents (TOC) provides users with a familiar way to locate topics of interest as well as a view of the overall structure of the electronic document or library and the topics or volumes it contains. A TOC establishes a hierarchical relationship among topics, listing subtopics related to a higher-level topic through a series of labels (1a, 1b, 1c, and so on), a system of indents, or icons. This set of structural cues is especially important because online documents do not provide readers with physical cues about information size and do not give readers the ability to thumb through the pages to get a feel for the information contained in the document.

The TOC is perhaps the simplest access method to create in online information. Most software designed to assist you in creating online information will automatically insert links between items in your TOC and the associated help topics. However, you typically still have much control over the TOC functionality and display, as described in the following guidelines.

Be readily accessible

Many online users will turn to the table of contents to find the information they need. As a result, the table of contents needs to be easily accessed from any help screen. Many online tools automatically place the table of contents in a secondary window that is present on the screen at all times; others open the contents through a button provided on all screens.

If you choose to display the table of contents at all times, you must carefully consider the design of the rest of the information space. The table of contents must not obscure the accessed topic, navigation aids, buttons, or menus. It must be large enough to be usable, but small enough to be out of the way.

Show hierarchical relationships

Although information topics should be designed to stand alone—that is, you can't assume a reader has read anything other than the current topic—topics can and should be grouped. The groups should show the hierarchical relationship of the topics from primary through secondary and tertiary. The heading for a group of topics should fully describe the relationship among the group (Figure 12.3).

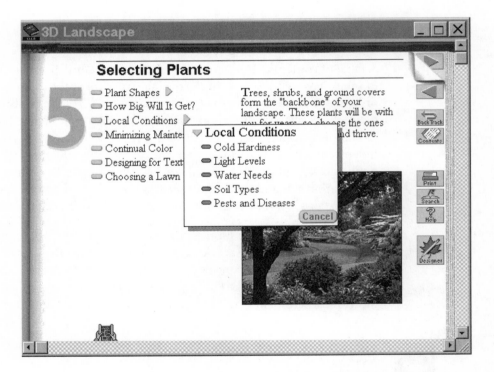

Figure 12.3: The relationship of the topics in this pop-up secondary table of contents is made clear through the grouping's title "Local Conditions."

An ideal online system has a two- or three-level hierarchy with no more than 12 to 15 choices for any group of topics. Balance the subtopic lists among the higher-level topics. Be certain that the users do not have extremely long lists to scan for a few topics and short lists for others. In general, follow guidelines for effective outlining of text topics such as those found in Brockmann or Price and Korman (see "Further Reading").

To emphasize the hierarchy you have selected for a particular set of topics, indent each level and identify the levels with different symbols or icons, as shown in Figure 12.4.

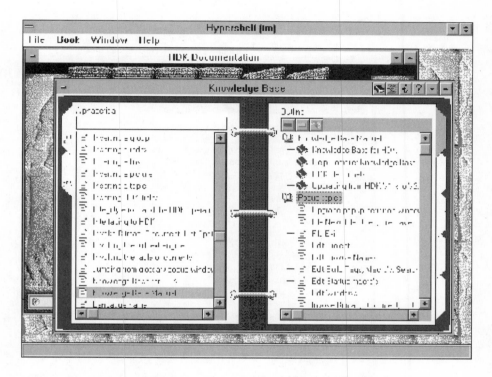

Figure 12.4: The table of contents has open and closed book icons to illustrate the first level of help and document icons to indicate the second level.

Create TOCs that are expandable and collapsible

To keep users from having to scroll through long topic lists, the table of contents should be expandable and collapsible. An expandable table of contents should allow the user to display subtopics for only the selected heading or headings or to display all the subtopics for the entire TOC. A fully collapsed table of contents should display only the highest level of information. Users should be able to expand a selected group to see the second-level topics and so on (see Figure 12.5).

In the most commonly used help systems, a single click selects a table of contents item, a second click expands the item, and a third click closes the item. A double click selects the item and opens the topic with the selected item remaining highlighted through color or reverse video (see the next guideline). However, an Expand/Collapse button set should be provided to minimize mouse clicks and facilitate access by users who do not understand the single-click/double-click requirements.

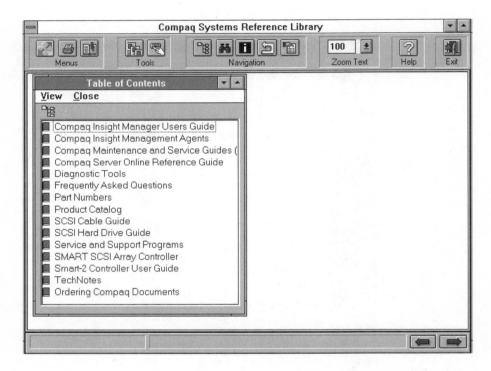

Figure 12.5: The button that looks like a flowchart acts as an Expand/Collapse button for the table of contents in this system. Not only does it appear in the menu, but on all topic screens as well.

 Highlight the current topic

When the user moves from one topic to another in the information space, the new topic in the table of contents should be highlighted (as in Figure 12.6). The highlighting reminds the users of the relative position of the topic they are reading to the whole online system, providing a context for the information they are reading.

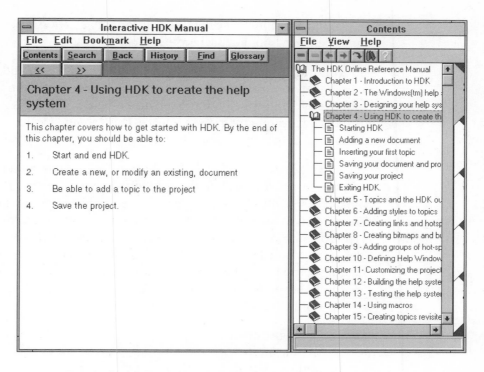

Figure 12.6: The highlighted table of contents item corresponds to the current topic.

Indicate the type of information provided

As much as possible, topic titles should indicate what type of information is provided in the topic and for whom it is written. For example, use gerunds to indicate task-oriented information (Establishing Loan Fees) and noun strings to indicate reference information (Documentation Policies). Avoid single-word titles, but also remember the limits of your tool; for example, some tools allow no more than 25 characters in a title.

Titles should be clear to both novice and advanced users. For example, the table of contents should help the novice user map general information to a specific task being attempted, and it should point advanced users to summaries or a quick reference.

Use informative and unique topic titles

When you plan your library presentation, remember that your users will first rely on the titles of each online document to decide if it might contain the needed information. Make the title as informative as possible, even if the number of words in the title becomes long.

Titles of online topics appearing in the table of contents should be specific enough that users can easily read the title and determine if the topic might contain useful information for their current needs. The terms used should be distinct and meaningful to the audience. Users should feel reasonably confident that they have made the right choice with each click of the mouse.

One organization created a CD-ROM to deliver its technical documentation to its customers. Included on the set of disks were more than 1000 titles covering 300 to 400 different aspects of the company's product line. The documentation on the CD-ROM was presented alphabetically by the title of each text. Unfortunately, many of the titles were nearly identical, such as "Reference Manual for the XXX78," "User's Guide for the RRR100," and "Getting Started with the MMM57." In addition, the system truncated the titles in the list of documents to the first 20 or so characters. Consequently, users saw only long lists of

> Getting Started…
> Getting Started…
> Getting Started…

Because the titles did not conform to the presentation limitations of the system, the CD-ROM was extremely difficult to use.

Topics and titles should be unique so that users can be sure which branch of the TOC to choose. Do not duplicate titles within the structure unless sections of the information contain identical content for different applications or products.

If you are working with a tool that truncates the titles of documents in the library contents list, consider providing bubble help (or Microsoft's tool tips) so that the user can view the entire title when the cursor pauses over it.

 ### *Use the terms your users will know to title the information topics*

As information designer, you have an obligation to understand how your users refer to the tasks they are trying to perform. If the users state their goals in terms that are familiar in their working environment, then you need to use the same terms to label the information topics you intend to create (Figure 12.7).

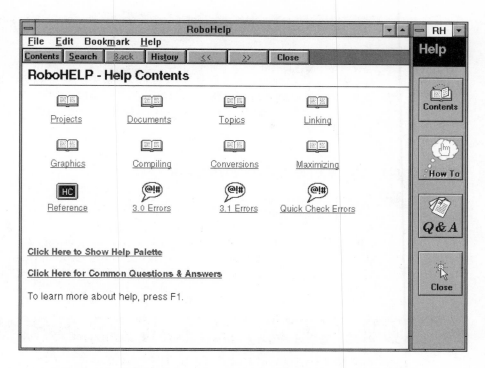

Figure 12.7: The RoboHelp table of contents uses language that will be familiar to users of an online help development tool.

 Ensure that the title in the TOC is identical to the name of the topic

Users confronted with a topic title different from the title used in the TOC may be confused. Many will return to the TOC fearing that perhaps they clicked on the wrong topic inadvertently. Having the same name in the topic title (perhaps in a nonscrolling region) provides additional reassurance that users have accessed the right information.

 Use double clicking to get the user from the TOC item to the help topic

Double clicking is the standard action in the TOC generated by most authoring tools. It is best to ensure that your online documentation maintains the standard.

Move from the TOC to the top of the selected topic

Access from the TOC should always be to the beginning of the selected topic, just as a paper-based TOC lists the page where the information begins in the book. Other access methods are designed to take users elsewhere in the topic; for example, full-text searches will jump users straight to the occurrence of the desired word.

Allow users to determine scope

TOCs may be document specific or may include a variety of information resources related to a particular subject. For example, you may want to include a high-level table of contents for related books in a library or for all the documents contained on a CD. Depending on your purpose for choosing a specific approach, you may want to allow your user to control the scope of the TOC, just as they may control the scope of a text search.

Pop-up tables of contents

Sometimes you may find it necessary to provide secondary views of portions of your TOC and make them available from inside individual help topics. For example, you may want to provide the user with more topic choices related to the primary topic. You may want to help them navigate by first taking them to higher-level information about a group of topics and then providing them with choices to move to more specific information. The higher-level information helps them make the choice to find the specific information they need.

For example, in Audio Help (Figure 12.8), the related topics link always takes the user to the subordinate TOC for that area of the information system.

A common implementation for secondary TOCs is the pop-up TOC. The following guidelines provide suggestions for this implementation.

Signal the presence of a pop-up TOC with a button or standard icon

Users will not use elements of your information system if they are not aware they exist. Be certain to indicate that a secondary TOC exists in a consistent and obvious way (Figure 12.9).

Pop-up tables of contents

Figure 12.8: The secondary table of contents lists subtopics of the main topic, "Using Sound in Stacks."

Provide introductions to secondary TOCs

Because pop-up secondary TOCs do not have a parallel in hardcopy documentation, users may not understand what to do with them. For this reason, you should not simply provide a list of additional topics, you should remind users of the purpose and direction of this topic list. What will users gain by reviewing the list and selecting another topic? Why are you providing this list outside of the primary TOC?

For example, rather than list all the related topics alphabetically at the end of a topic, group them under lead in paragraphs explaining why the topics are related—"To learn more about generating reports, see..." or "For information about a specific report, see..."

Allow the user to move back to the primary topic from the pop-up TOC without selecting an item

After reviewing a secondary TOC, users may decide that the information they need will not be found among the listed topics. Ensure that they are not forced to make a selection but can dismiss the pop-up as they do any other pop-up in the system.

Pop-up tables of contents

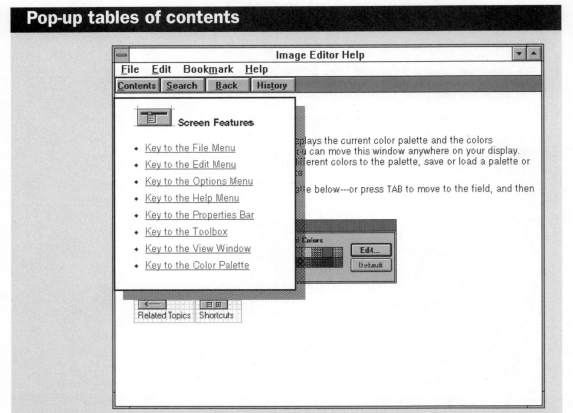

Figure 12.9: Clicking on the Related Topics button on the lower left brings up a pop-up secondary window containing the table of contents for that section of the help system.

Indexes

Many users prefer to use an index to search for information in online documents. Like its paper counterpart, an online index is an alphabetical list of terms that the designer or indexer has determined will help the users pinpoint the information they need. By selecting an index entry, users quickly reach the topics that best answer their questions.

An index search differs from a full-text search. Whereas a full-text search accesses every occurrence of specific words or phrases within a text, an index catalogs only the most significant instances of a word or phrase.

In some systems, index searches are referred to as keyword searches. However, an index is much more than a list of words; it is a filter for tasks and concepts. Users can consult the index to locate a task or a concept on which they want more information.

When creating an online index, keep in mind the following guidelines.

 ## *Be comprehensive in indexing topics*

The number of index entries should be three to four times the number of topics to be appropriate to the needs of both novice and experienced users. The recommended density for a good index for hardcopy text is one index item for every 100 words, or approximately four to five index items per printed page, but the index density for online access should be more comprehensive because more informal access methods (flipping through pages) are unavailable to the user of online information.

Indexing for online information is basically the same as indexing for print copy. The following suggestions summarize guidelines for choosing entries, but are not meant to be comprehensive. Refer to the variety of texts available for more complete advice on how to index effectively.

- **Start with keywords from the topic headings.** Identify the most important words in the heading text, not all the words. For example, if the heading reads, "Preparing the credit memorandum," index the keywords "credit" and "memorandum" rather than the word "preparing."

- **Add synonyms and competitor's terms.** Even though users might not know the specialized terms that refer to the concepts in your document, the index can lead them to the right information if you include synonyms or alternate entries that may occur to the user who is attempting to find specific information. Interview representative users to understand their goals and the language they use to express those goals. In addition, consult competitive products for terminology. Be certain to include words common to both beginning and advanced users.

- **Use phrases as well as single words.** The additional words in a phrase may provide the extra information users need to feel confident that choosing the entry will take them to the needed information.

■ **Include both acronyms and noun phrases.** Users may be familiar with either but not necessarily both.

Use detailed primary entries rather than secondary and tertiary entries

Even more so than paper documentation, each index entry requires its own unique wording so users (and the system) can determine which topic best meets their information needs. For example, you might have several topics all related to printing. Rather than use "Printing" as the indexed word for all the topics, include additional information, such as "Printing from a Macintosh," "Printing Reports," or "Impact Printing," to differentiate between the topics.

Reference only one topic

Just as on the printed page, it's best to reference only one page or range of pages for an index entry, index entries in your online system should reference only one topic. In this way, users don't have to hunt and peck through a long list of potential topics (page numbers) until they find the specific information they are seeking. Instead, they are able to tell from the detailed entry the type of information they will find.

In some cases, if you do use the same index entry in more than one topic, the system does not differentiate and takes the user to the first topic with that indexed word. Even if the system does provide a mechanism for distinguishing between the topics, it invariably adds an additional step before users can access the information they need.

This recommendation is not to say that you cannot provide for both contingencies. Consider including both general words that when chosen provide a list of potential topics, as well as detailed primary topics.

Link to meaningful occurrences of a subject

Avoid indexing every mention of a word. Instead, focus on referring users to information that they will find useful. Users don't come to an information system looking for words. Design your index to help users find the information they need to complete tasks, achieve goals, and find conceptual information. Index references should lead users to relevant information, not to incidentals.

Index nontextual elements

Your index should not be limited to the text of the online document, but should include graphics, animation, video, and sound. However, finding nontextual elements means that they must be indexed so that they can be referenced by the search system. Such indexing requires that you describe the nontextual element in ways that will be relevant to the needs of the user.

For example, if you include a video of the president of the company describing the company's mission, you will have to index the video in a variety of ways in which a user might search for such information, including the president's name and title, and the fact that he is describing the mission. You may even want to examine the text of the mission statement to decide if a relevant subordinate subject may be the subject of a future search.

Consider the implications of entering in the "middle" of a presentation

When users reach a topic, they may find themselves in the middle of a presentation that has begun at a previous help topic. To avoid the disorientation that often occurs, clearly indicate the relationship to higher-level topics or ensure that topics are independently presented and represent a viable chunk of information.

For example, in the help system shown in Figure 12.10, a sequence of four help topics that discuss how to complete four steps of a process are clearly labeled Step 1, Step 2, Step 3, and Step 4 so that users know exactly where they are upon entering the sequence.

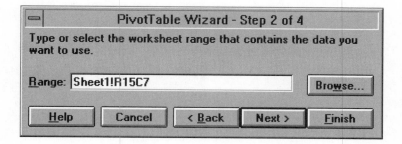

Figure 12.10: The Pivot Table help in MS Excel 5.0 specifies the number of total steps and the number the user is currently viewing (Step 2 of 4).

Allow domain-specific indexing

Rather than requiring users to view a master index listing all terms indexed in all pieces associated with your online system, allow users to specify which pieces they want to search; for example, they may only want to look in a specific book or only at the multimedia pieces.

Provide a browsing tool

An index for a large volume of information will obviously be rather lengthy. Try not to require users to scroll through the entire index, but enable them to easily browse the index entries. For example, a common implementation allows users to select the first letter of the keyword they are looking for (Figure 12.11).

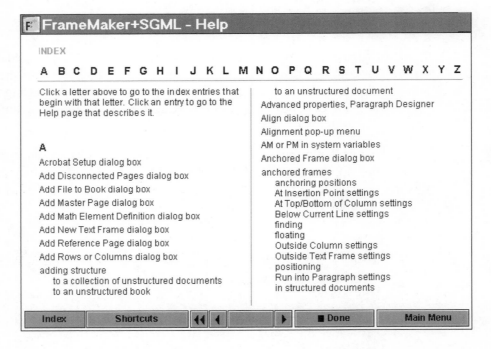

Figure 12.11: The alphabet is listed at the top of the help screen, allowing the user to move quickly to a subsection of the index.

An index search also allows users to browse the index. By typing a word or phrase, users jump to the closest match in the index. Selecting that entry displays a list of potential topics from which to choose. Users are more in control of where they will end up and are not simply choosing from a seemingly random list of words.

Be readily accessible

Because such a large proportion of users indicate a preference for using the index to find information, the index must be easily reached from any screen. Include a button or menu choice to provide this access.

Ensure accuracy

Just as in print documentation, where indexes must take users to the proper page, index jumps must be accurate and take users to the correct topic. It should be clear to users why they have jumped to the specific topic. Consider highlighting the word that caused the jump.

Avoid indexing pop-up and definition windows

Many systems will not allow you to index pop-up or secondary windows. Because this information should be supportive information to a main topic, it stands to reason that it would not be valuable information to reference in an index anyway.

Be consistent

Your index should reflect similar phrasing and a similar approach throughout the online system. This may often require that the creation of the index be done by one person perhaps in one sitting. Alternatively, you must ensure that your editor is thorough in ensuring this consistency.

Search methods

One of the advantages of online documentation is that users gain the power and speed of the computer to automate their search and retrieval process. Electronic searching enables users to query an electronic document for a specific word, phrase, pattern, or spatial configuration. However, without careful planning, this ability might cause more problems than it solves. Many users do not, or cannot, control their searches, ending up with enormous lists of possible topics that provide no information about their relevance to the original query.

Users value effective search mechanisms in the online libraries or help systems they try to use to meet their information needs. By definition, a successful search for a user is one that returns a high percentage of relevant topics (called hits) and a low percentage of irrelevant topics. A successful search allows the user to reach the needed information quickly, often within 3 minutes of initiating the search.

The tool you choose for your help system to some extent dictates the type of search engine you have available. Some tools support full-text searches; others provide only index or keyword searches, in which the author or indexer defines the terms on which users can search. To get exactly the system you want, you may need to program your own customized search engine. When programming a search engine outside a standard development tool, ensure that your end result works on all necessary platforms. If you have documents that need to be retrieved from mainframe, PC, and Unix systems, you need a search engine that can search multiple systems and return matches to the users' operating system environment.

The following sections discuss the various search mechanisms that might be available for the system and the library of information you are creating.

Full-text search

Full-text search is one of the easiest search mechanisms to define within an online library, although the actual underlying program structure may be quite complex, especially if the search must occur across many diverse operating environments. At its simplest, a full-text search matches strings of characters entered by the user with identical strings of characters in the source information. For example, when a user types the text string "online documentation," the system will locate every instance of the phase "online documentation" in the text that is being searched.

In reporting the results of a full-text search to the user, some systems provide a list of the titles of topics that contain the desired text string. Other systems display a small portion of surrounding text that contains the resulting text string in addition to the topic title. Still other systems simply take the user directly to the first instance of the text string in the searched text, usually showing some of the surrounding characters or the entire topic.

Unfortunately, many users, especially novices and advanced beginners often find a full-text search frustrating. In general, such searches are too complex and too broad reaching to be effective for most users. Full-text searches, on their own, require users to know the specific terminology used in the online system. Without such knowledge, users may find no hits or hundreds of hits on a word.

If you must use a full-text search, consider the following guidelines.

Couple the search with other types of searches

Full-text searches are best paired with thesaurus and Boolean searches (with some cautions—see *Boolean search* later in this chapter). These tools, properly used, overcome the terminology barrier, and help narrow the search.

For example, in a thesaurus search, the system extends the search to match synonyms of the words or phrases entered by the user. Similarly, some systems will account for spelling variations and typographic errors. Use your indexing skills when creating a thesaurus search to anticipate terms users might think of rather than the terms actually used in the online document.

Support wildcards, case insensitivity, and word variation

Full-text searches often expect exact matches. Plurals and other forms of a word, punctuation, and misspellings may adversely affect the search and return inappropriate topics or may miss relevant topics.

To compensate for the inherent problems in a full-text search, provide capabilities to users that prevent them from needing to know exactly how a term appears; for example, wildcards to allow a number of different endings to a root word or better yet, a smart enough search to show those different endings regardless of the one typed. Furthermore, it will be hard enough for users to know the exact terminology to search for, let alone the case in which the term appears. Be sure the search allows for any capitalization entered.

Provide limited contexts for the searches

Especially in intranet, Internet, and CD-ROM delivery, where you may have libraries of information, provide a means for users to limit the search to a certain part of the information system, such as text on a particular topic (service, application, product) or even an individual chapter or section with a larger context.

Allow searches on the results of a previous search

One way to narrow a search is to start with a general word or phrase and then add additional words to further specify the topic sought. Rather than ask users to define all the words to be searched at the origin of the search, allow them to add words after the results of the first search are completed, searching only those results for the additional words.

Retain the results of the previous search

Until a user begins a new search, retain the results of the previous search, even if the search results screen is dismissed by the user. Such retention of the search results requires little memory, but adds considerable usability. Too often users select a search result, only to find that they have not found the topic they want. Users must then rerun the search to obtain their original list of hits again.

A better technique is to provide an obvious and easy way for the user to return to the search results screen. From there, users have the option to initiate a new search, choose another hit from the results of the previous search, or quit the search.

Provide a way to print and/or save the results of the search

Users may want to retain for future reference the results of a search. Provide a means for them to print a search results screen or save it to a file for future reference.

Provide a way to cancel the search

Users often realize that a search is going in the wrong direction after it has begun, or they find that they have initiated what may prove to be a very lengthy search resulting in hundreds or thousands of hits. Provide a way for users to stop a search after it has begun. A cancel or escape keystroke may result in considerable time savings and more productive searching than having to wait for a clearly unproductive search to be completed.

Indicate your progress through the domain being searched

Provide a device that shows the progress of the search. Some search routines show the number of topics found (Figure 12.12) or the percentage of total topics searched. Such indicator devices assure the user that progress is being made, or that something is happening. Any action that results in a seemingly "dead" system causes the users considerable concern and may result in their initiation of keystrokes that lead to problematic actions once the search is complete.

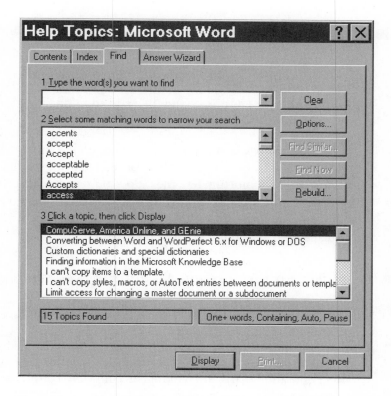

Figure 12.12: The Find topic screen indicates that so far 15 topics have been located that are related to the word "access." The indicator changes as topics are found.

Display search results as they are found

Many systems begin to display a list of topics as soon as they are located by the search. Such a list both assures the users that something productive is occurring and allows them to decide whether to halt the search before it is complete.

Jump to a topic immediately if only one match is found

If only a single topic is located in a full-text or index search, consider opening the topic immediately rather than requiring the user to select the topic first. Be aware, however, that such a move may confuse users who expect to review a list of relevant topics before proceeding.

Boolean search

In many systems, a simple full-text search can be enhanced through the addition of formal Boolean logic to the search process. In such searches, users begin with a key word or phrase and then add additional words or phrases to narrow or broaden their search.

To apply Boolean logic effectively, users need to understand the implications of their choices or be guided through those choices with an effective and well-designed interface. Unfortunately, most Boolean search tools provide little or no assistance to the users in refining their searches. The users try combinations of words and hope their choices have the desired affects. Keep the following guidelines in mind to avoid these issues.

Provide clear instructions for entering search parameters

So many approaches are used in Boolean searches today that even the most sophisticated user will need instructions for the idiosyncrasies of your system. Be sure users understand

- If quotation marks are required around words or phrases to invoke what is called a string search.

  We recommend avoiding awkward requirements like quotation marks because users frequently omit them and don't understand why the results of their searches are so incorrect

- If multiple words in phrases are automatically treated as if there is an AND or an OR relationship between them.

Many users are totally surprised when Boolean relationships are automatically inserted in what they thought were continuous phrases. Remember that the formal logic that is easy to program is extremely difficult for most people to understand.

 ## Use ordinary language to clarify the search logic

The Boolean terms AND and OR are confusing to most online users. Users usually assume that they mean exactly the opposite of what they actually mean.

For example, when users use an AND search, they usually assume that they are expanding their search to find every instance of both words. However, an AND search actually narrows the search by finding only those sentences or paragraphs that contain both the words. The result is fewer hits rather than more.

Similarly, an OR search is counterintuitive for people not trained in formal logic. An OR search actually works the way people think an AND search is going to work, by looking for sentences or paragraphs that contain one of the words or the other word. The result is more matches rather than fewer.

Rather than using these confusing terms and maintaining the purity of the formal logic, put the restrictions in terms the user will understand (Figure 12.13).

 ## Design your interface to guide users through this search

The most effective Boolean searches are essentially wizards or coaches designed to walk users through the search process. They provide users with prompts and menus to structure search requests and show examples of the results users will get with the structure created (Figure 12.14).

If you can redesign the search interface, consider using iterative usability testing to improve the guidance given for Boolean searches. Simplify the search scheme so that it is within the capacity of your average user to understand. Although some very technically astute users have a good grasp of formal logic to use the standard search interfaces, less technical users will often avoid using the options at all.

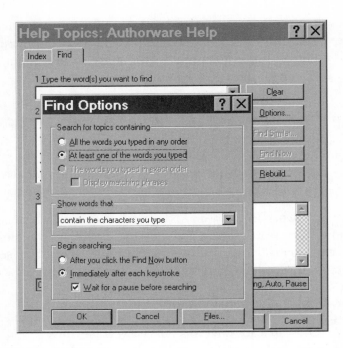

Figure 12.13: This Find Options screen explains the choices the user can make to organize the search.

 ### *Allow users to specify how close related terms need to be to each other to constitute a search hit*

A proximity search allows users to specify that the multiple words they enter in a search must occur within a certain distance of each other to qualify as a match. For example, if the users are looking for a subject that concerns reading CD-ROMs that only play music, they may want to specify that the words CD-ROM and music occur together in the same sentence for the search to produce a match. If the two words occur in the same paragraph, rather than the same sentence, the search would not be successful.

Priority search schemes can allow the users to specify the maximum allowable number of words between the two search words, the presence of both words in the same sentence or the same paragraph, or even the presence of both words in the same document, whichever is desirable.

In some systems, the only option is 0; that is, the words must appear right next to each other. In others, the option seems infinite—if the words appear

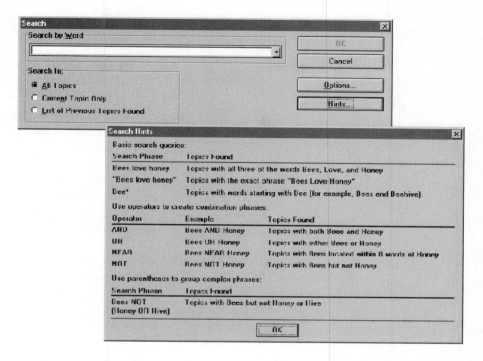

Figure 12.14: This full-text search screen indicates how to use the AND and the OR Boolean searches.

anywhere in the same document, a match is found. Allowing users to specify this distance helps them widen or narrow their search as needed.

In addition, you may want to control the default definition of proximity. Investigate the default proximity and decide whether it meets your users' expectation.

Parametric search

A parametric search is a special type of search used to find information stored in a database based on the value of certain parameters. At the present time, parametric search techniques are used primarily for catalogs. For example, a user looks in a department store catalog for all clothing that comes in Petite.

However, as the industry moves to design and construct information databases to store and retrieve information about products and organizations, parametric searches will become increasingly appropriate to include in our kit bag of search techniques. The following guidelines provide some beginning suggestions for including parametric searches in your system.

Structure your information into a database

Although the word "database" may be technically overwhelming to many, your work dividing information into modular topics forms the basis for creating a simple database—each topic is an entry in a large database table.

As you become more comfortable with a database concept, you'll see opportunities to subdivide your topics into smaller, related tables. For example, start by looking for information that is already organized as a database—a catalog or product specifications.

National Semiconductor has created an online catalog of the electronic components it sells (Figure 12.15). The information about the components is stored in a database that includes parameters identifying various characteristics of the components that engineers and others would use to locate the component they need.

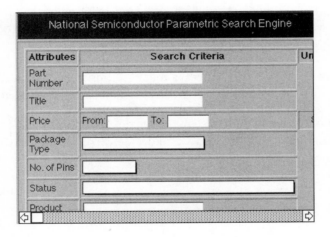

Figure 12.15: The National Semiconductor Web page uses a parametric search engine for users to locate and order their products.

If a user wants to locate a particular type of integrated circuit, for example, he or she is able to search the database for one or several circuits that match a set of desired characteristics. Using a parametric search engine customized specifically for the parameters stored in this particular database, the user can enter either a specific parameter required or a range of parameters into the various categories provided in the interface. The search engine searches the catalog for items with characteristics that match those requested and displays a table of matched items.

The table of matched items is linked to the pages in the catalog that describe in detail each of the items found. To view the catalog page, the user needs only to click on the item in the table and the catalog page with a picture of the item is displayed.

 ### Look for related characteristics

For each database table you create, look for common characteristics that users might use to narrow a search. For example, the National Semiconductor database includes parameters for price, size, and capacity. Users can look for all components within a certain price range or of a certain size or capacity.

In an information database, you might include parameters such as media type (graphic, video, sound, animation, CBT) or audience (system administrator, end user, programmer), depending on how you expect your audience might need to distinguish between entries. For example, you might use media type if you expect that users might come to the online system with the idea to work through all the CBTs available to them.

Natural-language search

Because of the inadequacy of search engines that have been built into the average online search system, many companies are developing proprietary, natural-language search engines. Natural-language searches allow users to type in questions or phrases in any form they choose using any words they find relevant. The search system interprets the query and looks for information that is most closely related to the concepts expressed. To create an effective natural-language search, consider the following guidelines.

 ### Learn how your user looks for information

Constructing a natural-language search system is not a simple task. You must know a great deal about how your users are likely to look for information, and you must code your information objects in terms of the content they contain and their relevance to the way your users might look for information.

When the natural-language search systems are well designed and the information objects thoroughly analyzed, the searches can be very powerful indeed. For example, in 1996, Microsoft released a tool for its popular word-processing system that also permits users to type in words or phrases of their own choosing (see Figure 12.16). The words or phrases need not exist in any form in the information topics to be searched. The topics themselves have been coded thoroughly so that their content and relevance is fully described. The user's question or phrase leads to topics that appear to be relevant to the information need at hand.

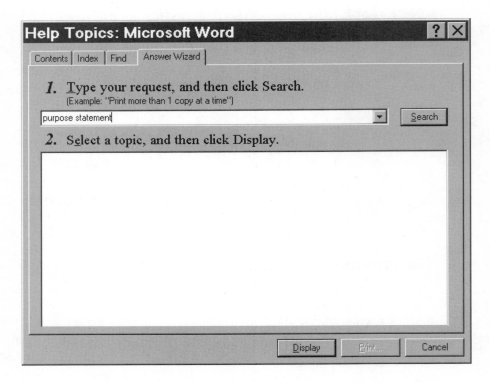

Figure 12.16: Microsoft's Answer Wizard allows the user to type a natural-language query to find a topic.

To produce such a natural-language query system, the designers required the participation of the customer support personnel, who were experts at the types of questions users typically ask and the information most likely to be relevant answers to those questions.

Prioritize the results

Develop a system to rank the likelihood that a topic answers the question posed (Figure 12.17). List the results in your prioritized order, or show a percentage or ranking indicating the likelihood the match is relevant.

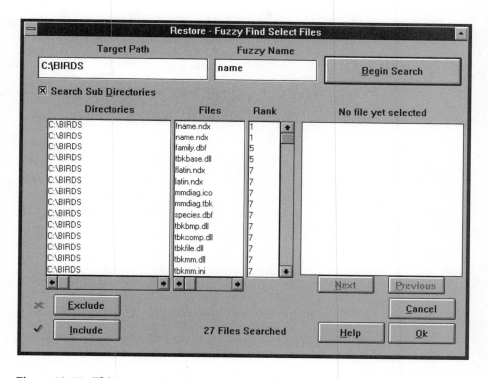

Figure 12.17: This system provides a ranking indicating how close the potential match is to the users' original entry. The lower numbers indicate a higher probability.

For example, one system, designed to handle all of the legal documents produced upon the breakup of AT&T, permitted attorneys to enter queries that contained a few words, a few sentences, several paragraphs, or even an entire document. The search system polled 12,000 documents of hundreds of pages each and produced a small list of relevant documents listed in priority order from the most likely to be relevant to the least.

Further reading

Bonura, Larry, *The Art of Indexing* (New York: John Wiley & Sons, 1994).

Earle, Ralph, Robert Berry, and Michelle Corbin Nichols, "Indexing Online Information," *Technical Communication*, Vol. 34 No. 2, pp. 146–156, 1996.

Horton, William, *Designing and Writing Online Documentation*, 2nd edition (New York: John Wiley & Sons, 1995).

Price, Jonathan and Henry Korman, *How to Communicate Technical Information: A Handbook of Software and Hardware Documentation* (Redwood City, CA: Benjamin/Cummings, 1993).

13

Providing Navigation Aids

Once your users have found a beginning point in their use of your information system, they will probably move from topic to topic as they search for information. As they do so, they have a high potential for getting lost in cyberspace. Unlike traditional books, online information systems do not give many cues about where users are in the overall design of the system. The online information has no obvious beginning or end; rather it is a potentially complex sequence of information that users may reach through a random set of hypertext links. Where users are, where they've been, and where they need to go may all be obscured by the lack of context.

It's your task to provide navigational aids that make moving around easy, but getting lost difficult. If you've created a meaningful structure, one that makes sense to your users, the most important part of your navigational problem has already been solved. Your next goal is to support movement within the system through a set of navigation aids and hypertext links that lead users to relevant additional information. This chapter discusses guidelines for meeting that objective.

Orient the user

A key way to keep your users from getting lost is to ensure that they always understand where they are. Just as maps and road signs help travelers find their destination, your online system should provide visual signals to your users so they understand their location in the system at all times. Use the following guidelines when choosing the signposts you will provide.

Provide a home base

A home base is typically a user's entry point into the system. For example, it might be a main menu or table of contents. Users should be able to return to that point from any other point in the system. A Home button or menu option is an escape if users are unable to retrace their steps through the system, and a shortcut if they are finished with the path they are traveling.

Provide navigational instructions

Regardless of the types of navigational tools you provide, you should explain how to use these tools within the online system. People may take some time to learn how to use the online library to retrieve information simply because the process is quite different from the one they learned for books.

A common way to orient the user to using online documentation is by providing an "About this system" topic. Other methods include providing instructions in the text itself. For example, you might direct the user to click on any of the highlighted topics for more information rather than explain in a centralized location that highlighted topics are hypertext links to related information.

There are advantages and disadvantages to either of these methods. "About" topics, like a book's preface, are unlikely to be read by most users. Providing instructions within the help screen ensures that all users understand how to navigate. However, as users become more skilled and comfortable with using the system, they may find that navigation instructions get in the way.

Research your users to determine if they need instructions for navigating through your information library. If they are experienced users of online information, such instruction may be unnecessary.

Provide navigational signposts

Clear markers in the online documentation give users the ability to identify where they are in the system and how to get where they need to go. A well-designed interface includes visual aids to provide this information. These aids should always be in the same place on the screen or window, and they should be visible at all times. They may include the following:

■ **Topic numbers (for example, 3 of 5).** If you are providing information about a topic on a series of screens, rather than requiring users to scroll through one long topic, you might number all the related topics. Users understand immediately where they are and how much information is available.

■ **Color.** You might present different categories of information using a color coding scheme. For example, users will learn that screens with blue backgrounds all have to do with printing, whereas those with green backgrounds are related to formatting.

■ **Icons.** As with color, you might indicate certain types of information with icons. For example, you might use an icon to indicate the presence of procedures, notes, examples, related information, and so forth. The icons in this book, for CD, Help, CBT, and Web, are examples of this point, as are the icons in Image Editor (Figure 13.1).

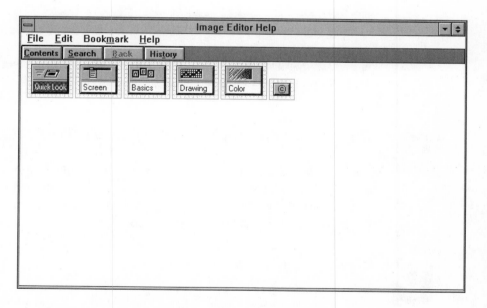

Figure 13.1: Image Editor uses icons to categorize its help topics.

■ **Maps.** In a concept similar to an ever-present table of contents, maps graphically depict the user's location in the system. For example, you might show a flowchart of the system with the user's location highlighted (Figure 13.2).

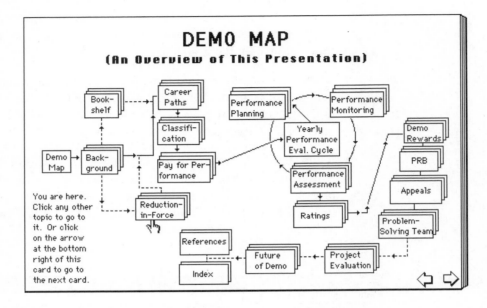

Figure 13.2: This Demo Map shows users where they are in the system and explains how to move to another location.

Show context through a table of contents secondary window

If possible in the tool you are using, ensure that the highlighted item in the table of contents changes whenever the users make a hypertext jump to another topic in the library. In this way, users continually see the topic they are consulting in the context of the table of contents.

Keep the title visible

If the topic accessed is long and users must scroll to read the text, ensure that the title of the topic is always visible in a nonscrolling region (Figure 13.3). This simple technique ensures that users remember which topic they are reading.

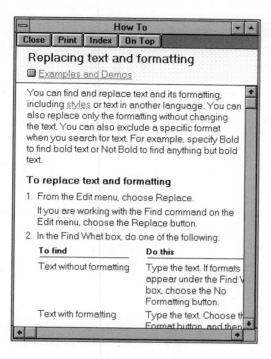

Figure 13.3: All help topics in Microsoft Word include a nonscrolling head. Users always know what topic they are reading even after scrolling several paragraphs. In addition, the designers have included a link to "Examples and Demos" in the non-scrolling region to give users continuous access to these important learning aids.

Point to related topics

Another way to orient users is to show them what other topics are related to the current topic. You might do this by listing related topics at the end of a topic or by defining a browse sequence through related topics. Browse sequences imply that topics are contiguous, just as they would be on previous or subsequent pages of a book.

Provide labeled links

You can assist navigation decisions by providing labeled links that indicate what kind of information users will reach if they select a particular link (Figure 13.4). If the users note that a link will take them to an illustration of the concept, they can actively decide whether they want to view that illustration. If a labeled link tells the users that they will receive more

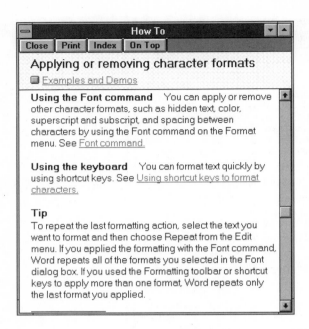

Figure 13.4: Microsoft Word provides a labeled link (Examples and Demos) in the nonscrolling region. Users know what kind of information to expect if they choose that link.

information about Step 3, they can actively decide whether they need that information.

Without labels on the links to aid the navigation decision, users are unable to anticipate the types of information that they might reach by selecting a link. The more information they have about the destination, the easier it will be for users to make choices about where they want to be.

Leave bread crumbs

Beyond the ever-present navigational signposts you provide in your system, you should also allow for other signposts that are not necessarily displayed or used throughout the entire system. The following guidelines suggest the types of bread crumbs you might offer to your users.

Allow users to mark frequently accessed topics

If users have had trouble finding information in your system, they will want a way to easily return to that information. Bookmarks allow users to mark topics and name them in a way meaningful to them (Figure 13.5). When they later select the bookmark, they move directly to the screen they marked without having to remember how they found the information in the first place.

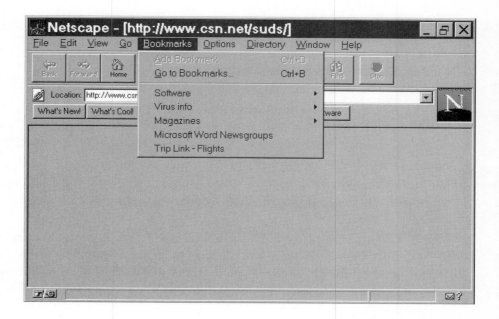

Figure 13.5: In Netscape, users can create bookmarks for URLs that they believe they will access frequently.

 Bookmarks should be stored on each single user's hard drive, rather than in a single location for all users, or the usefulness of an individual's bookmarks is lost. That is, if all users of a system create bookmarks in the same file, eventually the list becomes unwieldy and subject to all the difficulties of finding information in the original system file—the bookmark names are meaningless to everyone but the person who created them.

 Remember to warn your users that bookmarks stored on their hard drives are not updated when they access the Internet or an intranet. They have to press the Reload button to reach the actual file.

Record a history of all screens accessed

History buttons enable users to jump to a previously viewed screen or window. When pressed, the History button displays a list of topics the user has seen during the current session. The user clicks on the topic of interest and returns to that point.

Histories are especially important should users take a wrong path and want to return to the point from which they strayed rather than the very beginning.

Control the possibilities

Although you want to allow your users freedom to move through the system, you may find it necessary to control the number of paths they can take from a particular starting point. Use the following suggestions as guidelines for controlling the possibilities.

Provide a short path to information

In general, users should be able to navigate from the main menu to the topic of interest in two to four clicks of the mouse, depending on the complexity of the information. Users get tired and can lose their place if too many jumps are required to find the information.

Avoid overnavigating

The more paths through the information you provide, the greater the risk that users will get lost. As you map your system, ensure that there is a reason for each path. Don't provide links and related information just for the sake of appearing comprehensive. See Chapter 6, *Structuring Your Online System,* and Chapter 7, *Adding Hypertext Links,* for more information about structuring your document and choosing links.

Provide a browse sequence

Browse sequences, using Next (>>) and Previous (<<) buttons, enable users to page through a document one screen at a time, much as they might skim through a book. Typically, you define the path between these screens by linking logical chunks of related information—subtopics grouped under a more generally inclusive topic. By pushing the Next button, users move through the subtopics until they either reach a new main topic or return to the original main topic.

Ensure that the browse sequence is finite

The purpose of a browse sequence is to link related information together in a logical order. It is not to ensure that the online information can be read from beginning to end like a traditional book. If you take the latter approach, the sequence becomes infinite and meaningless to the user. Limit the sequence to a functional grouping. When the users have reached the end of a group, return them to the main topic rather than moving into a new topic.

Look for commonality among topics and group similar items. For example, you might choose to group topics such as sending output to a printer, sending output to a file, and sending output to a screen. At first glance, printer, file, and screen might not seem to have much in common; on second thought, however, you can see that they are all output devices.

Ensure that browse buttons make sense to the user

Unfortunately, traditional browse buttons can be quite confusing to users. Which is more understandable— Forward, >>, or Next? Backward, <<, or Previous? Where, if at all, do up and down arrows fit in?

There is much confusion, especially about the Previous (or <<) and Back buttons. Some compilers, including Windows Help and IPF, offer both options. Yet most users don't understand the distinction—the Back button returns the user to the last screen accessed; the Previous button moves one screen back in a predefined browse sequence, as illustrated in Figure 13.6. In some cases, these buttons may go to the same place; in others, they don't.

How you approach this problem depends on your audience. You may not need to address it at all if users are familiar with other systems. If not, consider renaming the buttons to more clearly convey where the user will be going.

Prevent wrong navigation choices

Ensure that topic titles and browse sequences are clearly distinct and helpful. Users should feel reasonably confident that the right choice is being made with

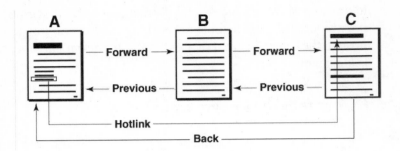

Figure 13.6: If users travel down the pre-defined path by pressing Forward, they move from A to B to C. If they then choose Previous or Back from C, they move to B. If, however, users move from A to C via the hotlink, they move back to A with the Back button, but to B with the Previous button.

each click of the mouse. For example, from the title, users should have a good idea of the type of information that will be displayed.

Provide escape routes

As stated earlier, provide a way for users to return to their starting point, be it the main menu (Home), the screen from which they just came (Previous), or any screen they have accessed in their current session (History). Don't force users through a sequence of screens, but allow them to escape or to Quit at any time.

Further reading

Horton, William, *Designing and Writing Online Documentation*, 2nd edition (New York: John Wiley & Sons, 1995).

Shneiderman, Ben and Greg Kearsley, *Hypertext Hands-On!: An Introduction to a New Way of Organizing and Accessing Information* (Reading MA: Addison-Wesley, 1989).

14

Composing Your Topics

The best access and navigation methods that you provide in your information design are of little use if the information your users finally find is unintelligible to them. Users may discover that the information they find has been written with the assumption that they know much more about the subject than they do. The information might contain words that they do not understand, acronyms that are undefined, or concepts that they do not have sufficient background or understanding to grasp.

On the other hand, if the users find information written appropriately for their needs, with neither too many words nor too few, they will be satisfied that they can use your information system to support their goals. If they can accomplish the tasks they want to complete by following the instructions you have provided, they will come back to the online information again and again.

In this chapter and the next, we provide guidelines for writing effective online documentation. In this chapter we concentrate on the approach you should take for the differing information types introduced in Chapter 4, *Categorizing Information Needs*. In the next chapter, we discuss the specific language, style, and tone you should use.

Writing procedural information

The rules for writing online procedural information are essentially the same as those for writing procedural information for paper. However, several guidelines will help you adapt your writing style for online reading. For example, users are more likely to read brief procedural text online than to print it, so you must accommodate the problems associated with reading from the screen.

The following guidelines apply to writing effective procedural information.

Phrase procedures in user terms

Because most users prefer to consult procedures only when they have a task to perform, ensure that the organization of the procedural information matches the way that users think about the tasks and goals they have for their activities. Remember that less experienced users are likely to state their task needs in their own terms, rather than in your terms or the terms of the system. Only as they gain experience will they learn enough of the specialized terminology to actually look for it.

Number each step that users have to perform

It might seem obvious to insist that each step in a procedure be numbered. However, we frequently find online procedures that bury action steps in paragraphs of text. Numbering each step, as in Figure 14.1, and using numbered lists only for procedures helps users to identify procedures visually. Users do not have to search through lengthy paragraphs to find the actions they need to take.

Limit each numbered step to a single action

Avoid putting several actions in the same numbered step, as in Figure 14.2. Users often skip steps that are embedded in other steps and continued as the second half of a compound sentence. Most users will want to perform a step immediately, thus turning away from the text for a few moments. When they return to the text, they are most likely to begin at the next step rather than to read the last half of the step they believe has been completed.

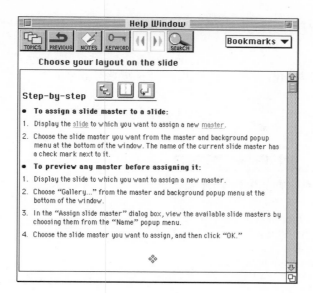

Figure 14.1: This example of steps from Aldus Persuasion Help shows that each step is numbered and contains a single action.

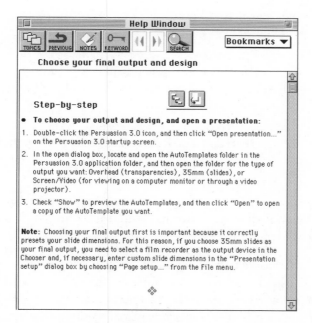

Figure 14.2: This example of numbered steps from Aldus Persuasion Help shows steps that contain multiple actions. Note Step 2 in which users must locate and open two folders to successfully complete the step.

Present steps in the order in which users must perform them

Action steps must always be presented in the order in which they are to be performed—another obvious rule that is often violated. We so often see text that violates the rules (Figure 14.3), in part because writers present information in the order in which they figured it out.

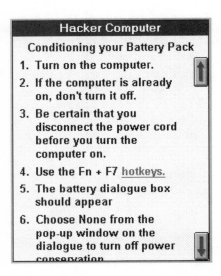

Figure 14.3: The steps in "Conditioning your Battery Pack" are not presented in a logical order. Note that step 5 is a feedback statement (a result) rather than an action step.

 ## *Try to write no more than five action steps for a single procedure*

If your procedure contains more than five or six steps, consider breaking the procedure down further, as shown in Figure 14.4. You may actually have two procedures written as one.

If it seems undesirable to create multiple procedures out of a single long procedure, consider creating subheadings for the procedures to provide stopping points at which the users can stop to evaluate progress and ensure they haven't made mistakes. Discretely placed feedback statements or suggestions that the users notice the results on the screen may help them ensure that they are at the right point in the process before they move on.

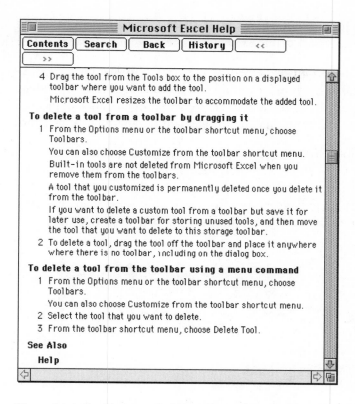

Figure 14.4: In this example from Microsoft Excel Help, the two optional methods for deleting a tool from a toolbar are presented as separate procedures, rather than combining them into one.

Start steps with imperative verbs

Each step within a procedure should read like a command—enter, press, select, and so on. This makes it obvious what action is expected of the user.

Some steps require that certain conditions or decisions be made. Place the condition before the action so that the user does not perform the action without reading the condition at the end of the sentence.

Distinguish among mandatory, conditional, or optional steps

Many procedures have alternative steps that the user might take under specific conditions. Often, such optional steps begin with an If clause that states the condition under which the alternative actions might be taken. We learn, for example, to stop if the red light appears or to proceed if we see the green light.

It is important to distinguish between steps that must be taken and steps that are taken only under certain conditions. The conditional steps might begin with an "If" clause and might be set off by a change in placement and font or by the inclusion of a graphic element that highlights the alternative path.

Optional actions may also be available for users to pursue if they wish (Figure 14.5). Options may include using a keystroke to make a menu selection rather than using the mouse and cursor. For novice users, optional paths to the same end are frequently confusing. If you have many novice users, strongly consider providing only one way to perform a step or complete a task.

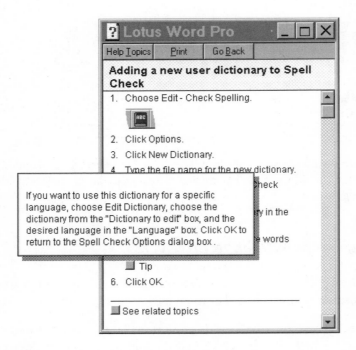

Figure 14.5: The pop-up explains that users have an option to use their new dictionary for a specific language. This information is kept out of the mainstream text of the procedure because users do not *have* to complete the task described.

The on-screen presentation of procedural steps provides enormous opportunities to use labeled hypertext links that simplify the basic presentation and hide the complications in layers. For example, keystroke options might be included through a pop-up link rather than by lengthening a sentence. Conditional steps might lead to a secondary window listing the conditional actions outside of the main stream of procedural steps.

 ### *Provide only one method for performing an action within a topic*

Trying to explain every possible way to complete a task makes a confusing procedure. If there are many ways to perform a task, decide which method you will present (the easiest to learn, the easiest to perform), and then be consistent. Refer to the alternatives in related topics through labeled links.

 ### *Be precise in your instructions*

Users are given the best chance for success when they know specifically what they are expected to do. As a result, your instructions should be explicit. For example, don't write "tighten the screw;" instead write "tighten until flush with the surface." Make the variables or values required readily available. Ensure that all conditions, such as time or location, are clearly stated within the procedure.

 ### *Keep steps short*

If at all possible, limit a step to one or two lines of text. Remember that reading on screen is more difficult than reading on paper. What looks quite short on paper will appear long and cumbersome on screen.

 ### *Enable users to move easily between procedure and application*

In context-sensitive applications, procedures should not require users to flip back and forth between the information and the application. Rather it's better to present this information in the form of a wizard or coach (Figure 14.6), or to program the information to remain "on top" so users can easily refer to it at anytime during the task.

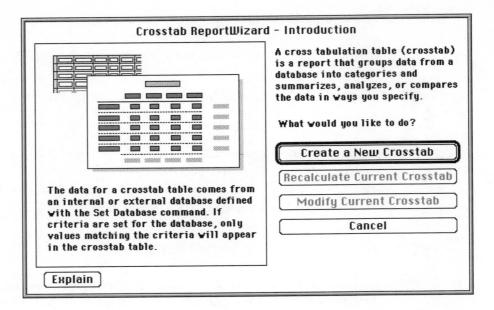

Figure 14.6: The Crosstab ReportWizard in Microsoft Excel 5.0 provides an instruction that also results in the completion of the task. A wizard functions as a combination of a help and application software interface.

Writing conceptual information

Writing conceptual information even for online presentation is more like writing paper-based documentation than any other type of online information. Because of the more narrative nature of conceptual information, users expect to read more and are likely to print the text for easier reading.

Consider the following guidelines as you write conceptual topics.

Develop a complete idea in a single topic

Although conceptual information may, of course, be divided into subcategories that we commonly refer to as chapters or sections of a book, users need information that is fully integrated rather than separated artificially into screen-sized short topics. Much conceptual information requires a continuous narrative to help users build a path of understanding from information they know to information they do not know (Figure 14.7). Breaking up the information into small chunks interrupts the flow of information, making it difficult to follow and understand. Instead, you should present conceptual information as scrollable continuous streams of text and illustrations.

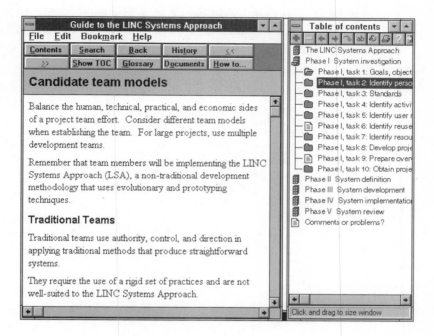

Figure 14.7: This conceptual discussion scrolls through many paragraphs of information in a single topic, as it leads users from information they know (traditional teams) to new information about candidate team models.

Include transitions

To help users get through this larger amount of text, you should provide transitions from one idea to the next. Such aids will help them understand the flow of information and assist in their overall understanding.

Watch out for large blocks of text

Although conceptual information is likely to be presented in larger chunks of information, a large block of text will look even more ominous on screen than it does on paper. Be sure to break up your text with graphics, bulleted lists, and subheadings to avoid the solid gray effect.

Relate new information to known concepts

When introducing a new concept, relate it to something similar from the users' experience. You might relate the information using similes, metaphors, or examples. For example, in Figure 14.8, Microsoft Excel provides a series of topics for Lotus 1-2-3 users that relate its functions to those of Lotus 1-2-3. The comparison between the two products is explicit because they are both spreadsheet programs.

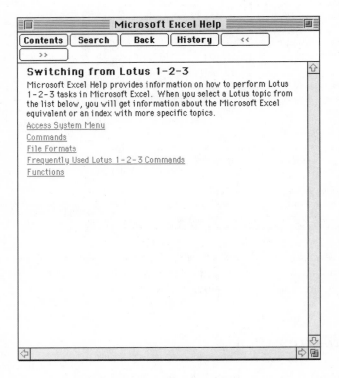

Figure 14.8: Microsoft Excel helps Lotus 1-2-3 users come up to speed by relating its features to those of Lotus 1-2-3.

Similarly, Quicken relates its product to a checkbook. This comparison is presented in a graphic metaphor because Quicken, a software program, is obviously not the same as a checkbook.

Both comparisons help users better understand the concepts behind the products. The target audiences relate to the examples chosen.

Use many examples and graphics

Conceptual information is best learned through explicit examples and illustrations. Graphics reinforce ideas and are often understood more quickly.

Make sure that it's clear that users are looking at an example or graphic and not the real thing; for example, users often mistake screen captures for the real application program and don't understand why they can't complete their tasks. See Chapter 16, *Adding Graphics,* for more information on designing graphics.

Put examples in context

Although users learn conceptual information best from examples, this doesn't mean simply dropping examples into your text at opportune times. You must talk about the examples and show how they relate to the topic at hand or they become background noise.

Discuss examples both in the surrounding text and in callouts on the example (perhaps implemented through hotspots on the graphic). Call attention to the specific details that apply to the concept being discussed.

Annotate examples thoroughly

Many users, especially experienced users at the higher stages of use, become frustrated when they find an example that looks relevant to the goal they want to achieve, but they cannot figure out how the example was developed. Thorough annotation of the example, explaining exactly how the example was developed and including the underlying code, completed fields, and so on, will greatly enhance the usefulness of the examples for these users (Figure 14.9).

Use continuing examples

Rather than provide individual examples for each point you present, build up case studies. Continue to revisit the same situation with additional or differing information to help users see how each topic relates to each other.

However, be cautious in overusing the same examples. Some users complain that examples are irrelevant to their specific application and prefer to see a variety of examples from many areas, assuming that their area of interest will

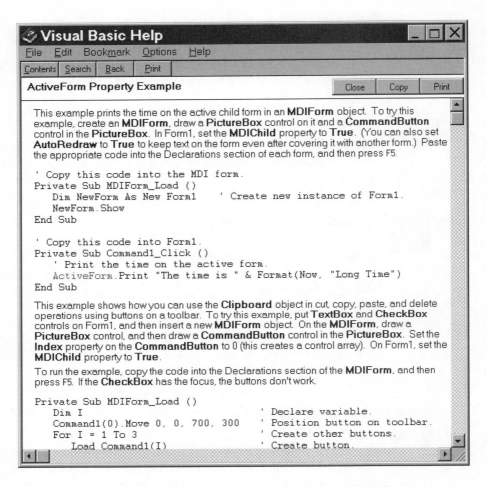

Figure 14.9: This fully annotated example of code in Microsoft Visual Basic is presented as an example in Visual Basic Help. Users may copy and paste the lines of code in the help text into code that they are creating.

be covered at least once. Your initial information plan should have identified your users' interests so that you can plan examples that will be appropriate and comprehensive.

 ## Define terms as they are encountered

When presenting new concepts, you will inevitably use terms that are new to your users. Provide definitions of those terms within the text rather than requiring users to link to the glossary.

However, keep in mind that users may not read topics in the order you expect. Words you believe they should have encountered previously may be new. Use pop-up definitions as a backup in those topics. If users already know the word, they never have to access the pop-up.

 ### *Make conceptual information printable*

Many readers prefer to read more lengthy and continuous conceptual information on paper. We have learned from observation and interviews that users looking for more conceptual knowledge about a subject are happy to receive up-to-date information electronically but prefer to print it for ease of reading. They often tell us of taking conceptual information home to read in the evening or on weekends or printing information to read quietly at lunch or on a break. They rarely want to read the information on the computer screen if it goes beyond a few paragraphs of text.

When forced to read lengthy conceptual information on the computer, users often find it easier to read by scrolling through the pages rather than turning virtual pages on the screen. Even the slightest delay produced by the rewriting of the screen at a page turn may break the reader's concentration. If sentences or paragraphs are extended from one page to the next, it may be difficult for even a very skilled reader to hold the beginning of the idea until the end of the idea appears. Going back to the previous page is, of course, just as slow and frustrating.

Writing reference information

Reference information is most often scanned rather than read in its entirety. When writing such information, therefore, use an approach that makes information the most predictable and accessible as possible, as described in the following guidelines.

 ### *Provide the same type of information about the same things*

Reference information is most often a collection of facts that distinguish similar things from one another; for example, the syntax, parameters, and return values of commands and functions in a programming language. Therefore, make sure that you include the same type of information about all the things you are documenting to help the user make these distinctions. For example, you might decide to include a purpose statement, syntax, a list of parameters, return values, and examples when documenting commands. Ensure that all commands have all this information.

Present the same information in the same order

Not only should you provide the same types of information, but in the same order for all items. For example, you might present syntax, then define parameters, and finally give code examples for each command in a language reference.

Because users are not expected to read reference information in one sitting, they may not immediately notice this consistency, but given time they will learn, for example, that the command examples are always at the bottom of the topic, quickening their search for information.

Use lists and tables

Data about products is most accessible if it is presented in lists or in tabular form (Figure 14.10) rather than embedded in lengthy paragraphs. Users are more easily able to scan for the information they need.

A tabular approach is also useful for parametric searches (see Chapter 13, *Providing Navigation Aids*). Users can ask the system to display all entries with a specific value in a column of information.

Use a telescopic style in tables

Depending, of course, on your audience, reference information can often be written telescopically; that is, you do not need to write in full sentences. Remember users are scanning, not reading, and need to pick out only a single fact. When you create tables and lists you may need to eliminate extra words that only get in the way of a rapid search.

Writing instructional information

In instructional information, you are the teacher. You must relate to your readers as an instructor relates to his or her students. Whether instructional information is written as formal training, such as a CBT, or informally in each

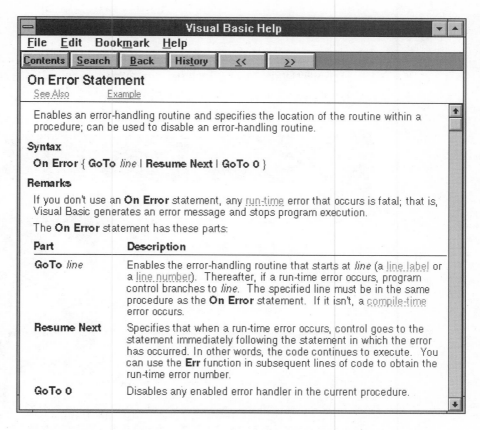

Figure 14.10: This help screen from Microsoft Visual Basic describes the parameters of the On Error statement in a table with part name and description visually differentiated. Programmers can quickly scan for information about the parameter they don't understand.

individual topic, you should consider the following training-based hints for writing effectively.

Provide motivation

Users have a greater willingness to learn if they are presented with the reasons they need to learn. Explain why users need to learn specific information in terms that will make them see the value behind the information and make them want to learn it.

Give users learning objectives

Indicate to users what you expect them to be able to do at the end of the instruction (Figure 14.11). Such information sets expectations and gives users something by which to measure their performance.

Figure 14.11: This screen from Hewlett-Packard's JetStore computer-based tutorial lists the behavioral objectives for the chapter on "Data Security & Backup Strategy."

 ## *Give users something to do*

Active interaction is required for effective learning. When possible, ask the user to do something during the course of the instruction. Depending on the context, this may be a simulated exercise, an action using the program, or simply answering an occasional question.

Don't blame the user

Although feedback statements are instrumental to instruction, they can be very traumatic to users when phrased incorrectly. Never blame users or make fun of their mistakes. Now is the time for more passive constructions. "You pressed the wrong key" sounds much more threatening to the user than "The wrong key was pressed."

However, you'll have even more success by not focusing on the mistake at all— "F7 saves the document. Try again to locate the key to quit."

Reassure the user

Novice users, learners of new information, require reassurance to know they are doing things correctly. Provide information that allows them to verify their recent actions. If a mistake is made and you are tracking mistakes, indicate if the mistake was a common one or easily overcome. If users do something correctly, congratulate them with a proverbial pat on the back (Figure 14.12).

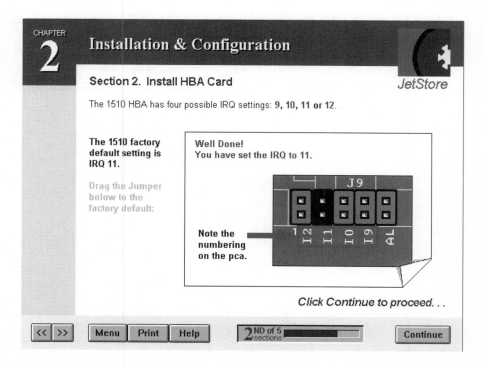

Figure 14.12: This screen from Hewlett-Packard's JetStore computer-based tutorial provides a "pat on the back" feedback statement after the user sets the jumper correctly.

Lead users to their own conclusions

Rather than simply presenting information, help users discover it on their own. If users feel they have figured out information themselves, they will more likely remember it and feel confident that they can develop their own solutions again in the future.

Further reading

Clark, Ruth Colvin, *Developing Technical Training* (Reading, MA: Addison-Wesley, 1989).

Gery, Gloria J., *Making CBT Happen* (Boston: Weingarten Publications, 1987).

Gery, Gloria J., *Electronic Performance Support Systems* (Boston: Weingarten Publications, 1991).

Horn, Robert, *Mapping Hypertext* (Lexington, MA: The Lexington Institute, 1989).

Jonassen, David, *The Technology of Text* (Englewood Cliffs, NJ: Educational Technology Publications, 1985).

15

Writing for Readability

In addition to the content of your topics, discussed in Chapter 14, *Composing Your Topics,* the characteristics of language choice, sentence structure, transitions from sentence to sentence—all influence the users' ability to make sense of the information you have provided and apply it to the tasks they want to perform. Your goal is to make the information you provide as readable as you can.

What exactly do we mean by readability? In earlier sections, we have discussed concepts that promote other aspects of the usability of online information. You have learned the importance of an interface design that makes the structure of the online information sources obvious to the user. You have learned about accessibility, the importance of a design that makes it easy for users to find information. Readability refers to the characteristics of the text itself, rather than to the design superstructure that surrounds the text. By readability, we mean a focus on text that most users will be able to read once and understand—text that contains sufficient explanation to help users clarify their understanding, but not so much information that they will feel compelled to skim or skip what seems superfluous.

Although we can describe the basic characteristics that have been widely understood to promote ease of reading, you will find that ensuring readability is not a trivial task. You will need to ask users to review the text, read it for meaning, and read it to perform tasks, to ensure that you have chosen correctly. Only with direct user feedback through usability studies will you ensure that the text you write is readable and ultimately usable.

You will also find it important to remember that no text, full of the myriad choices you will need to make, will be equally readable to all of your users. Some will find text you believed clear and transparent to be impenetrable. In many cases, that will be because the users lack the knowledge of the subject matter that you have assumed. In other cases, users may feel insulted by the simplicity of your explanations, in part because they may have a deeper command of the subject matter than you can hope to have. In short, you are unlikely to satisfy the needs of all your users. However, focusing your choices on the vocabulary of the field you are presenting, simplifying sentence structure, and layering information so that users can choose the level of complexity they need, all will assist you in meeting the needs of a wide variety of your users.

This chapter summarizes good writing practices and encourages you to establish style standards for your online project early. You'll save a lot of editing time with a little time spent up front.

Follow good writing practices

Despite the differences in the medium of presentation (on the computer screen rather than on paper), most of the rules that apply to paper documentation also apply to online documentation. However, if you believe that some or most of your users will read information on the computer screen rather than printing it out for themselves, guidelines that recommend brevity, concise presentation, effective use of white space, and so on must be applied more stringently than before.

The starting point is always good practice, as the following guidelines point out.

 ### *Understand your users*

It's extremely important to realize that gathering data about your users in your information planning was not a meaningless exercise. Not only does an understanding of your users help you plan the information objects needed, it also helps you decide about the details of your presentation. How familiar are your users with the information being presented? If there is a commonly used vocabulary of the subject matter, are they familiar with it?

Are the users international (multicultural and multilingual)? How thorough is their command of the language you are using? Will you need to avoid culturally specific allusions (metaphors especially)?

How much or how little information will your users need? How much of their time are they willing to spend reading your text? Will they simply skim, looking for actions and facts, or read at length, looking for understanding?

The more you know about your users as readers, the more effective you will be in making decisions that will enhance the readability of your text.

Follow minimalist writing principles

Given the smaller display available for online documents, presenting information succinctly and concisely is extremely important. However, it's important to remember that minimalism does not simply mean fewer words or incomplete text. Removing every other word or every other step is not the secret to minimalism.

Because many books have been written about minimalist techniques, we only highlight a few tips here:

- **Don't document the obvious.** A good user analysis will help you determine what you can expect your users to know already.

- **Layer information in additional and related topics rather than including information for all stages of use in one lengthy presentation.**

- **Get right to the point.** Don't include long introductions, especially one-sentence paragraphs that repeat the topic heading.

- **Replace text with pictures or tables whenever possible.**

- **Edit your text vigorously.** Take out unnecessary words. Remember that you are writing for a small space. Think like an advertising writer who has to convey a message in two or three sentences.

Ensure accuracy and completeness

Despite the high pressure to keep text to a minimum, you cannot leave out information needed by your users. Consider layering the information and providing access to more levels of information through well-labeled hypertext links.

Maintain consistent language in heading levels

The format defined for a heading level (font size, layout, space before and after) is not sufficient to make the headings distinguishable for the users. Headings at the same level (first order, second order, and so on) should be written using the same grammatical structure. For example, you may have a series of first-order headings that begin with an infinitive phrase, such as

- To complete an expense form

- To add a beneficiary

- To reconcile your account

Such consistency of presentation will help your users understand the structure of the information and find the type of information they need.

Use numbered lists and bulleted lists consistently

If they are consistent, numbered lists and bulleted lists can help users recognize different types of information. Such visual recognition occurs more quickly than if the users have to read the text and decipher its purpose. We recommend numbered lists for instructions that must be performed in the sequence described. Bulleted lists should be reserved for information that has no particular sequence of performance.

Use parallel structure in lists

When you create a list, be certain that all of the items begin with words in the same part of speech. For example, if you create a list of actions, begin each item with a gerund:

- handling files

- setting up directories

- changing directories

If you are creating a list of seminar topics offered during the month, use the name of the seminar for every item in the list:

- Discount usability testing

- Designing online help systems

- User interface design

Note that in these sample lists, the capitalization of the items is also consistent. In the first list, all the items begin with lower-case letters. In the second list, the first word of the seminar title is capitalized but the other words are not.

Punctuate lists consistently

Not only should lists be phrased and formatted consistently, they should also be punctuated consistently. A common practice today is to avoid any punctuation after the items in a list. Excessive punctuation can be distracting.

You should also decide on the punctuation to use in the phrase that introduces the list. Many writers use colons to introduce all lists. Others use no punctuation when the introductory phrase and each list item form a continuous sentence. Compare the following examples.

The following chapter discusses the contractual requirements of your department:

- How to handle employee objections

- How to resolve legal issues

- When to escalate problems to your supervisor

The following chapter discusses how to

- handle objections,

- resolve legal issues, and

- escalate problems to your supervisor.

Use positive statements

We have all learned that double negatives often make sentences incomprehensible. Statements such as "Negative statements are not unavoidable" have to be carefully deciphered before we recognize what is being communicated.

In the same way, expressions that contain other apparently negative elements can confuse users. For example, Patricia Wright found in her research that it is easier for someone to comprehend a statement that says,

> "Jane is taller than Joan."

than it is for them to understand the statement

> "Joan is shorter than Jane."

We all have a tendency to more easily comprehend a comparison if the comparative word we select is on the upper side of the comparison rather than the lower.

 ### *Conform to accepted style standards*

Many experts, through much research, have compiled golden rules of documentation writing. These rules apply regardless of medium:

- Use short, simple, familiar words.

- Avoid jargon.

- Use culture- and gender-neutral language.

- Use correct grammar, punctuation, and spelling.

- Use simple sentences, active voice, and present tense.

- Begin instructions in the imperative mode by starting sentences with an action verb.

- Use simple graphic elements such as bulleted lists and numbered steps to make information visually accessible.

For more suggestions, we recommend referring to one of many excellent books on writing style, especially technical style.

Develop your own online style guide

Just because users might not read all the topics within an online information system in one sitting, you cannot justify inconsistency in presentation. The best way to ensure consistency throughout your presentation is to make and follow a style guide.

In an online style guide, include

- Spelling and capitalization rules

- Guidelines for writing action steps

- Guidelines for writing headings at all levels

- Rules for handling acronyms

- Guidelines for optimal paragraph lengths

and many more. Consult editing guides such as Karen Judd's *Copyediting* for more ideas on creating project-specific style guides.

If at all possible, try to maintain a set of styles across all the information types that you have in your online system. Users find it disconcerting to open documents that differ dramatically from one another. Procedural text with step-by-step instructions should always look the same, as should conceptual material designed to be printed and read offline. We are not recommending that one style fits all, but that consistency within information types will make them more readily identifiable to your users.

Further reading

Judd, Karen, *Copyediting: A Practical Guide* (Los Altos, CA: William Kaufmann, Inc., 1982).

Strunk, William, Jr. and E. B. White, *The Elements of Style*, 3rd edition (New York: MacMillan Publishing Company, 1979).

Tarutz, Judith A., *Technical Editing: The Practical Guide for Editors and Writers* (Reading, MA: Addison-Wesley, 1992).

Williams, Joseph M., *Style: Ten Lessons in Clarity & Grace*, 3rd edition (Glen View, IL: Scott, Foresman and Company, 1989).

Wright, Patricia and A. J. Hull, "Answering questions about negative conditions," *Memory and Language*, Vol. 25, pp. 691–709, 1986.

16

Adding Graphics

Graphics in electronic media serve much the same purposes as graphics in print media—to convey messages more effectively than words, to clarify and enhance meaning, and to make information more enticing, interesting, and entertaining. Similarly, the basic concepts governing the design of effective graphics are parallel in the two media. Designers need to apply the same graphic design principles affecting layout, typography, color, and so on that have been developed for print media.

However, graphics in electronic media also provide an entirely new arena of opportunities for the information designer. Although instructional designers have frequently used other media, especially video, to convey concepts, teach technical subject matter, and create a persuasive mood for ideas, information designers are only now able to incorporate the advantages of video, sound, and animation into the world of traditional technical and business messages.

Electronic media allow graphics to move from the static and largely two-dimensional world of the printed page to the dynamic and three-dimensional world of the computer monitor. Images that once stood still can be made to move. Ideas that had to be conveyed only partially on the page can come alive to the viewer. The possibilities are enormous and are just beginning to be appreciated as users acquire the hardware needed to display dynamic graphic images on their desktops.

At the same time that the opportunities seem limitless, technical issues and constraints must be taken into account if more visual presentations of information are to be easy to use. Graphics can present many more difficulties both to designers and users than text alone. They can increase file size substantially and make information slow to load onto the computer screen. They can introduce color conflicts that will make information look peculiar and often be inaccurate representations of real objects. They can be expensive and time-consuming to produce.

The following guidelines give you a starting point to help you think more visually about your information and to plan carefully to avoid the problems inherent in electronic display. However, the best approach is to include graphic designers, video artists, animators, technical illustrators, and experts in the electronic display of visual images on your design team. Because the world of technical and business communication, especially information delivered electronically, has long been the province of those who communicate through words, we rarely see the potential for graphic communication fully realized. Many verbal communicators tend not to think visually or consider opportunities for conceptual and technical illustrations. They lack the basic skills needed to produce graphic images that communicate effectively. Only by enlisting the help of graphic professionals and giving them a central rather than a peripheral role to play in the design process will this change.

Deciding to include graphics

There are many reasons you might choose to include graphics in your system. As with all your decisions, however, first and foremost should be that users often learn more quickly and effectively through visual information. You will create more effective learning environments for a majority of your audience by including the following types of graphics in your system:

- **Technical illustrations** provide key information about products and processes. They include illustrated parts breakdowns, technical illustrations of various views of hardware, screen shots of software, and diagrams of processes.

- **Conceptual graphics** illustrate relationships among ideas, show rather than tell a story, represent motion, or make complex thoughts simple enough to be understood.

- **Design elements** are a vital part of the overall appearance of the online system. They are used to distinguish parts of the interface and to call attention to various items being presented.

■ **Aesthetic additions** brighten the visual environment. Visual designers are able to enhance the users' experience by expressing a mood, communicating a message, directing the users' thinking, adding focus and emphasis, and creating an atmosphere in which learning can best occur.

The following sections provide guidelines for when to include each of these graphic elements.

Using technical illustrations

Most information designers are familiar with using technical illustrations to portray physical objects that users are trying to learn to use effectively. Computer displays are an ideal environment for technical illustrations because they provide exciting opportunities to make two-dimensional images come alive. Technical illustrations can be rotated in space, color-coded, opened for inside views, zoomed into and away from, and more. Consider the following guidelines when you plan to include technical illustrations in your electronic information.

Use graphics to show what objects look like

Probably the most obvious use for graphics is to simply show an illustration of a physical object. The illustration might take the form of a photograph, line drawing, three-dimensional illustration, or even a video.

Information designers have long used static illustrations of hardware in print. On the computer screen, you can now make the illustrations come alive. Perhaps one of the most likely possibilities is to allow the user to drill down into a high-level illustration to uncover progressively more detail. For example, in the online help for a Hewlett-Packard laser-measurement tool, machine operators can view an illustration of the laser setup (Figure 16.1). By clicking on one part in the complete setup, they can view details of that part (Figure 16.2) and jump to a discussion of how the part might be adjusted (Figure 16.3).

Similarly, on the Apple service CD-ROM, technicians can select a high-level view of the machine they need to repair (Figure 16.4). By clicking on various parts of the machine, they can move progressively from the outside to the inside (Figure 16.5). Once they reach the mechanism that they want to replace, they can jump to a parts list to order the correct parts or to a removal and replacement procedure for the parts in question (Figure 16.6).

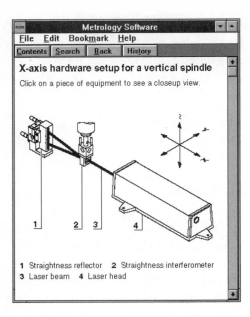

Figure 16.1: The first illustration of the laser mechanism in the help file shows the four parts of the mechanism in the required alignment. The user can click on any piece to see a closeup view.

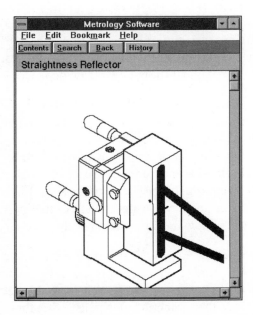

Figure 16.2: The closeup view of the straightness reflector shows the detail more clearly.

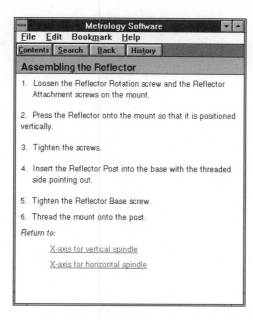

Figure 16.3: By clicking on the closeup view, the user jumps to the instructions for assembling the reflector.

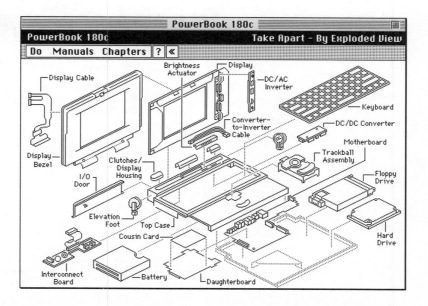

Figure 16.4: The exploded view of the Apple PowerBook 180c leads to "Take Apart" instructions for the technician.

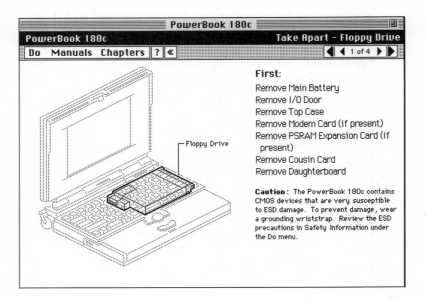

Figure 16.5: By clicking on the floppy drive, the technician sees its position in more detail and reviews the initial steps to access the floppy drive for repair.

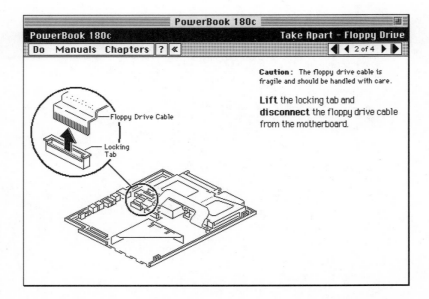

Figure 16.6: By clicking on the floppy drive again, the technician receives instructions for disconnecting the floppy drive cable from the motherboard. Subsequent instructions are reached by clicking on the directional arrows in the upper right-hand corner. Note that this step is the second of four.

Use graphics as examples

Examples that show how an action is performed can be conveyed through line art, animation (Figure 16.7), photography, or video, depending upon the capabilities of your user's hardware and software configuration. An animation can be used to illustrate a process that might be too difficult or dangerous to photograph or videotape. For example, an animation might be used effectively to show an event like cell division. An illustration might provide an example of what a part looks like before and after it is added to an assembly.

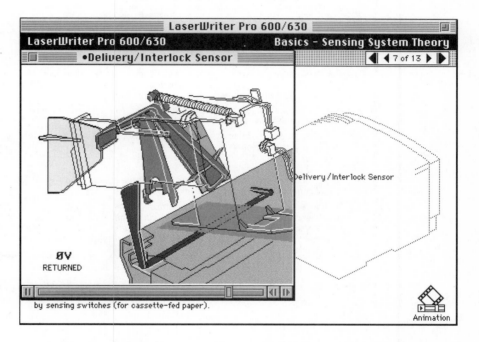

Figure 16.7: Animation used in the Apple Service Source CD demonstrates for the technician exactly how the Delivery/Interlock Sensor operates. In the animation, the various parts are color coded for easy interpretation.

 ## *Use graphics to verify*

To create effective procedures requires that you provide users with feedback to verify that they have completed a step correctly. Graphics can often be used effectively, in many cases, to provide the verification that users need. For example, you might provide a screen shot to illustrate what the computer screen should look like if the correct screen is open (Figure 16.8) or if the actions have been correctly performed. You might provide a illustration of what a part should look like if it has been assembled correctly.

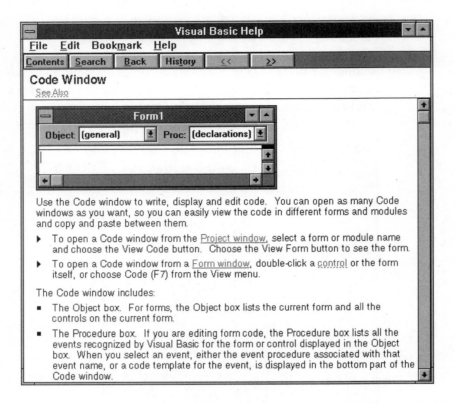

Figure 16.8: A screen shot in Visual Basic Help helps users verify that they have found the correct screen.

 ## *Distinguish images of the software screen from the actual software screen*

When you provide verification graphics, keep in mind that screen images can be especially confusing to application users. They may mistake the screen shot for the actual software screen. When they try to pull down a menu or select an item, nothing happens. They may conclude that the system is frozen and reboot.

Consider differentiating the screen images in your information topics from the actual software screens by some graphic differentiator. You may use a subtle color change, a border in a color or pattern, or a label at the top of the screen calling attention to the fact that the users are looking at an example, not the real thing.

Use graphics to show process

Graphics can more easily show the steps in a process or the sequence of a flow of information or product than can words. For example, through a series of photographs or line drawings, you can show a technician taking apart a machine. You may want to show the same process through an animated drawing, especially if the sequence of actions is difficult to envision from a static image (Figure 16.9).

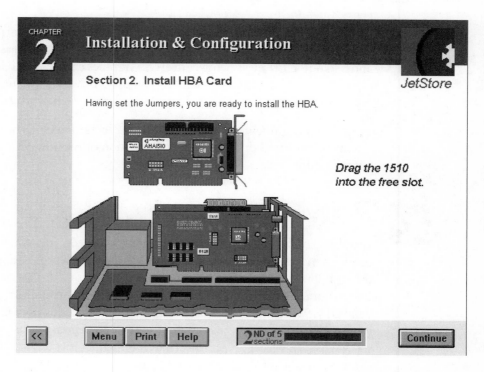

Figure 16.9: The graphic allows the user to move the HBA card into place in the correct slot. The user practices the action in the safe environment of the interactive tutorial before moving to the actual device.

You may even want to convey the same information through a video clip. Remember, however, that the medium you select should be the best way to convey the message at hand, not the most flashy way. It might be more cost effective to include a set of sequential still shots to represent a process. The stills present the same information but cost less and occupy less storage space on a CD-ROM.

You may also want to use a graphic and a sequence of callouts to indicate to a user how to perform a process that is associated with an on-screen or printed form. An illustration of a form or a dialog box accompanied by callouts that explain how to fill out the parts of the form provides a visual illustration of a process that may otherwise have required many verbal steps and many pages of text.

Using conceptual graphics

Conceptual graphics, including such graphic images as flow charts, diagrams, graphs, maps, and other pictorial representations of meaning assist the reader in understanding the ideas being conveyed. Graphics enable you to illustrate what is difficult to express in words alone. If you use only words, you neglect powerful expressions of meaning that are better or best understand through images.

The following guidelines suggest reasons for including conceptual graphics in electronic information, providing a dimension of meaning that enriches and expands upon text.

Use graphics to replace words

Graphics are capable of replacing hundreds of largely ineffective words to convey a message. The most obvious way to replace words with graphics is through illustration, pictures of the physical objects that the users need to understand. A technical illustration of a machine, a breakdown of its parts, detailed views from all sides convey information graphically that is impossible, or extremely awkward, to convey in words. But using graphics to show what a physical object looks like is only the most obvious choice. Consider using graphics to enrich the users' understanding of concepts and motivate them to become engaged in a subject that may, on the surface, appear boring and uninteresting.

Use graphic devices to clarify meaning

Graphics can be used to represent an abstract idea that may otherwise be difficult to grasp. The graphic may itself be abstract rather than representational; for example, a set of intersecting circles may effectively convey the relationship among three interrelated ideas. Diagrams of workflow can help users understand a sequence of events. Navigational maps help users recognize where they are within an information structure (Figure 16.10). Graphics can even portray movement in time through simple repetition of an image or through more complex animation techniques.

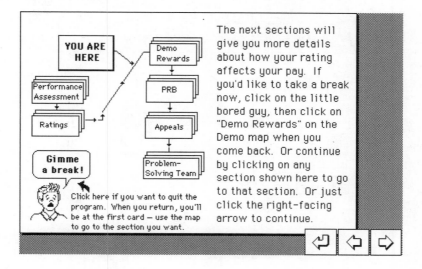

Figure 16.10: The map of a portion of the hypertext links provides a summary for the users of where they have been in the system and where they will go if they continue to move forward.

Use graphics as summaries

In addition to serving as a source of complex meaning itself, a graphic might also summarize information presented in words, providing a memorable image to begin or end a topic. Researchers have found, for example, that when readers first view a graphical representation of the concepts presented, they are better able to comprehend and recall the text explanation. A conceptual graphic that illustrates an idea before it is discussed in text enables users to absorb and remember more details about the concept. As a result, users learn the concept more thoroughly.

For example, in the Unisys LINC online documentation, the information designers used a graphic image to introduce the systems approach on a single screen (Figure 16.11). In addition to using the graphic to summarize the approach described in the accompanying online documentation system, the designer also included graphic hotspots to provide more conceptual details about the system while anchoring the user to the original graphic.

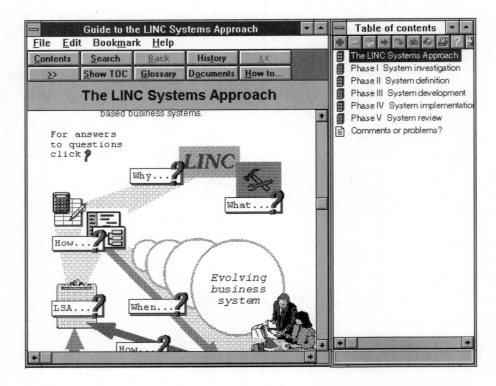

Figure 16.11: The introductory screen in the LINC documentation set introduces the system approach before users begin reading about it in depth. The graphic hotspots provide answers to users' questions about the system without leaving the context of the graphic image.

Using graphics as a design element

As discussed in Chapter 11, *Designing the Information Interface,* graphic elements are an integral part of the overall look and feel of your system. Selecting fonts, establishing a grid, laying out the information screens, choosing colors for type and other design elements, sizing graphics appropriately for on-screen viewing—all these elements of design must be considered as you plan your online information. A consistent design enables users to rely on the design elements to find what they are looking for; innovative elements break from your consistent design framework to grab attention (Figure 16.12). In each case, you must consider what the impact of the design elements will be upon the user. Refer to Chapter 11 and use the following guidelines when adding graphics as design elements.

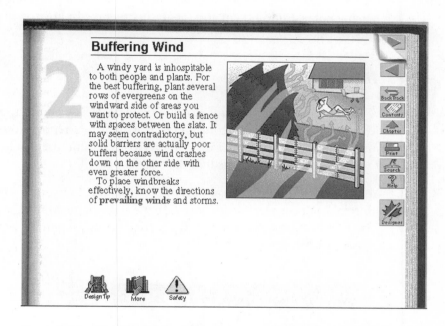

Figure 16.12: The grid in this online book dictates that text always appears on the left half of the screen with a graphic on the right side. Navigation buttons always appear on the right border of the page, just as users would move to the right side of a hard-copy manual to navigate a book. The large chapter number establishes a scan column for the rest of the page. The bottom portion of the screen is reserved for icons indicating special topics associated with the current one.

 ## *Establish a functional grid for the screen*

Grid-based design provides a standard layout that functions across multiple information topics to maintain a consistent appearance for the information library. Within the standard grid, you may create standard modifications for special information types. For example, you may want a variation on the grid to handle a procedural topic and another to handle a conceptual topic.

Create a grid by dividing the page into a small number of units. The columns should define the columns of text and graphics, the gutters (space between the columns), and even the vertical space between major elements, such as the steps in a procedure.

By establishing a grid, you establish a consistent alignment among various meaningful elements in your design. In many instances, the grid itself is defined by the relationship of text blocks or chunks and the white space around them. However, you can also define relationships among elements by placing boxes around them and separating them with horizontal and vertical lines or rules.

Include icons

A great deal of work has been done in the past decade on the application of icons to interface design. Icons function as signs that represent something outside of the immediate visual context. Icons remind users of actions that they might take or concepts that they want to recall.

You may want to use icons as part of the visual field of your information objects. For example, information designers at Microsoft use the Open File icon to remind users to perform that action as one step in the process (Figure 16.13).

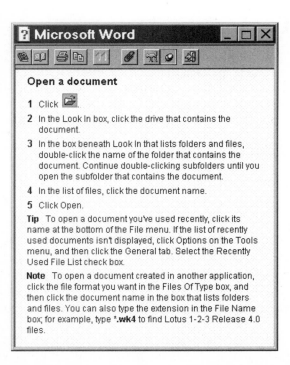

Figure 16.13:   The Open File icon is used as part of a procedure in Windows 95 Help for Microsoft Word.

Icons might also be used to help users categorize information or select particular segments to read. The visual cues provided by icons help users immediately recognize the type of message being conveyed. The icons provide visual anchors that remind users that they are reading a particular type of information. For example, as shown in Figure 16.12 earlier in this chapter, 3D Landscape designers use a variety of icons—Steps, Tools, Related Topics, and so on—to indicate the type of information users will access if they click on the icon.

 ## Add graphic devices to make ideas more visual

Even simple graphic devices, such as tables and lists, help break up text and convey ideas more visually (Figure 16.14). A list, whether bulleted (unordered) or numbered (ordered), clarifies the relationship among details far more easily and effectively than dense paragraphs of text. Icons and symbols provide a shorthand method of evoking a concept. Arrows or other pointing devices emphasize what is most important or what should be noticed.

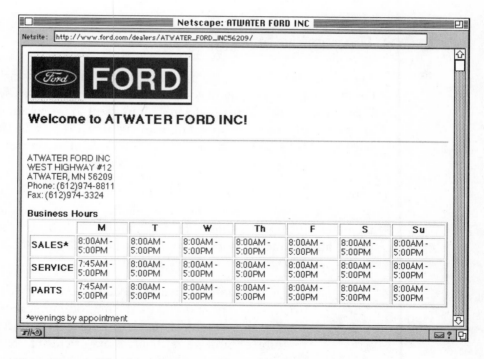

Figure 16.14: Although this Web page uses very few graphics, the tabular structure of the text makes it appear graphical.

Use type position to differentiate text elements

The position of the type will affect how your information is interpreted by the reader. For example, you may want to center type above an area of text or position all your headings at the left margin to ensure that they are easy to see when users scroll through a screen.

Variations in the primary type elements—style, size, and position—help to create the structure of the information on the screen. The structure you use conveys information to the reader that makes meaning clear.

Using graphics to add aesthetic appeal

No matter how well-written your information, if you don't grab users' attention and then provide a pleasant atmosphere within your system, users may never return to the system. As described in the following guidelines, graphics serve a very important role in providing interest and setting mood, even if they have no other functional use.

Use graphics to maintain interest

Marketing communication and advertising has traditionally included graphic design as a primary means of communicating information to users. The visual images in advertising are usually more important to the communication than are the words. The visual appeal of the image draws the readers in, creating an interest, even a level of excitement, that tempts them to pay closer attention to the message, or even to notice the message at all.

Traditionally, business and technical communication has not made much use of graphic design to enhance the visual quality of the presentation. However, the move from ordinary online help systems to the Web has opened the possibilities of adding more interesting design elements to the information that people have to or are supposed to read.

 Much of the information included in corporate Web sites is oriented toward sales and marketing communication. As a consequence, graphic design is prominent in the best Web sites. A tradition of more visual and less text-oriented information on the Web appears to be emerging, suggesting that a more visual presentation of technical and business information may become increasingly appropriate.

Use graphics to motivate users

Graphic images that are attractive, interactive, and entertaining can motivate otherwise bored users to pay attention. You must be able to gain the users' attention before learning can take place. If you are presenting instructional information, graphics in the form of illustration, photography, animation, and video will help you grab your users' attention and motivate them to participate in their own learning (Figure 16.15).

Graphics used effectively can set the stage for the concepts you want to introduce while still providing an element of fun to what otherwise might be a dull subject.

Figure 16.15: A school bus speeds down the road in the Lotus Word Pro tour. The bus serves as a motivator to users who may be otherwise bored learning about another word processing package.

Use graphic elements to entertain users

Depending on your topic and purpose, you might include graphic elements that are simply entertaining to users, for example, brief animations of cute characters interacting with your product. However, as in the use of humor in technical writing, always carefully consider the appropriateness of such entertainment pieces. Keep in mind the translation of any implied humor in such graphics, as well as the impact of such an event when viewed regularly due to frequent use of the information.

Use graphics to set the mood

Some of the graphic elements you incorporate into your system may serve no functional purpose at all. They simply set a mood (Figure 16.16). For example, a more spartan interface implies formality—the information being presented should be taken seriously. In the opposite case, confetti borders imply a more relaxed environment.

Including color as a design element also helps to convey meaning and emotion. In western cultures, red often connotes danger and green passivity. In some eastern cultures, red means joy and white is used for mourning.

Designing your graphic presentation

It is certainly not within the scope of this book to teach you to become a graphic designer. However, the following guidelines can help you check that the graphics that are designed serve their purpose.

Make graphics easy to understand

Users should not have to spend a lot of time analyzing a graphic to understand it. Rather graphics should convey their meaning within seconds. Simplicity of presentation, including eliminating unnecessary elements, makes the message more immediate and vivid to the intended audience.

Notice how the introductory screens used in several of the Windows 95 help systems are difficult to understand (Figure 16.17). The screen capture, the labels, and the background art complicate the space. The users do not know how to organize the visual information into a coherent message.

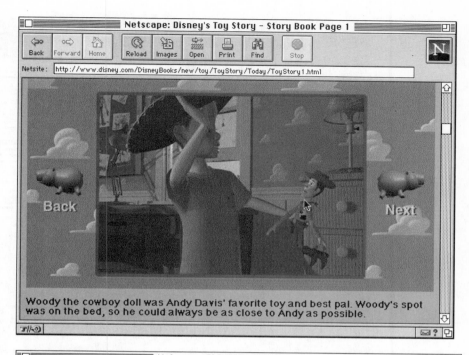

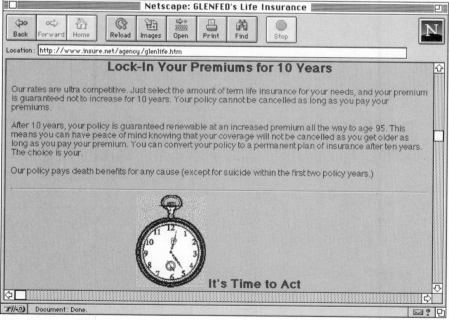

Figure 16.16: Contrast the mood set by these two Web pages. In the first, flying pigs add an element of fun. In the second, an ominous stopwatch reminds users that time is running out to buy life insurance.

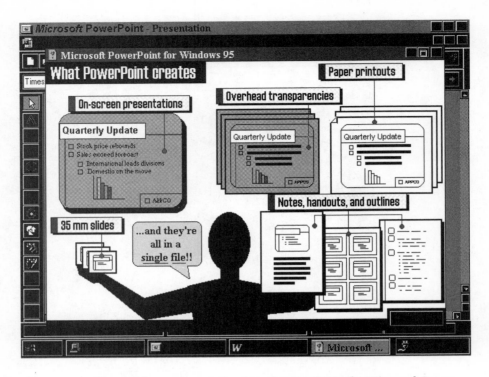

Figure 16.17: Graphic images are used to introduce topics in the Microsoft Power-Point for Windows 95 help system. In this case, what PowerPoint creates is presented visually, including graphic hotspots to define On-screen presentations, Overhead transparencies, Paper printouts, and 35 mm slides.

Ensure that images focus on their primary message

Especially with technical illustrations, you need to make sure that drawings are simplified by eliminating elements that are not part of the primary message. Because of the reduced resolution of the computer screen, details that could be included in print will make the illustrations less visible and clear on the screen.

Don't cover the text or work area

If you have included graphics in pop-up windows, be sure that they do not cover the text area to which they refer. Align the graphics so that they always appear under, next to, or above the text, depending on the size and positioning of the information on the viewers' screen.

Fully annotate the graphics

Use figure captions and callouts to explain the purpose of the graphic and enhance its use as a medium to express ideas. Use captions to direct the reader to the graphic and focus the significance of the graphic on the discussion at hand. Use callouts to point to significant areas of the graphic and explain how they should be interpreted. You might also choose to talk to the graphic within the body of the text itself (Figure 16.18).

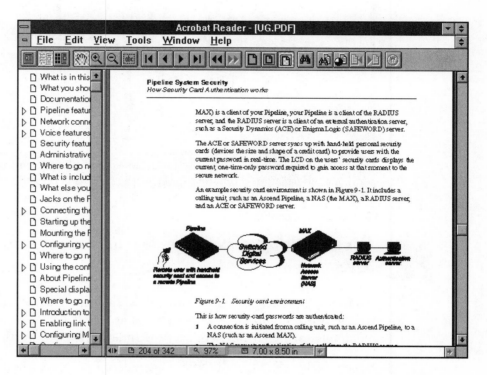

Figure 16.18: The figure in this CD-ROM book is fully explained in the text immediately above it.

Use graphic hotspots to explain elements of a graphic

If your online information tool allows it, add hotspots to your graphics that provide links to other information. For example, you might use graphic hotspots to label parts of a graphic using pop-up definition topics. Users click on part of the graphic and they view information explaining the graphic. Compare the effectiveness of Figure 16.19 which uses all hotspots with Figure 16.20 which uses no graphics at all.

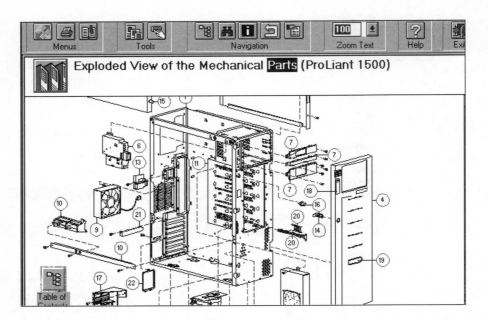

Figure 16.19: Numbered callouts on the exploded view of this Compaq server link to additional information about the part, including part numbers and ordering information.

Consider using stock images to reduce the cost of development

Many graphics packages come with CDs of stock images that you can use in your information products without licensing fees. If a stock picture fits the requirements, the savings in budget and time may be well worthwhile.

Be certain, however, that the images are indeed free to use. Many images, such as clip art, can only be used internally in an organization, not for products that will be sold. For example, you cannot use much of the available clip art in your help system when it is a part of a software application for sale outside your company. You cannot use a photograph that was taken for the company annual report on a Web site without the written permission of the photographer, and often payment of a royalty fee. You cannot include a video that you had shot for a training film on a training CD-ROM unless your arrangements with the video producer and the actors specifies this additional use.

Be certain to check with your legal department and read the fine print of the use contracts on any clip art, stock photographs, or stock video that you may have available.

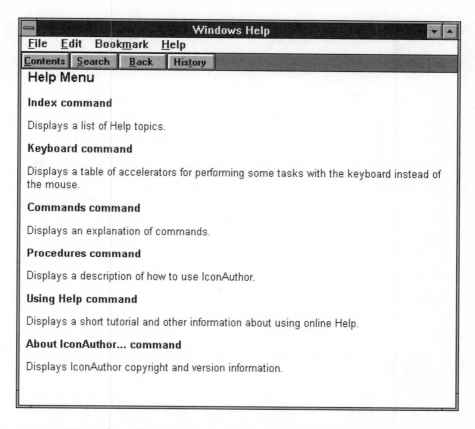

Figure 16.20: This verbal description of the items on the help menu provides no context for the user. By using graphic hotspots on an image of the help menu, the information designer would have helped the user visualize the information more easily.

Controlling graphic appearance

Many graphics that look good in print, fall apart on a monitor where the resolution is much, much lower. Lines that looked straight become jagged. Details disappear in smeared images. Animation breaks down into discrete frames and the feeling of movement is lost. Video slows to a snail's pace, images decompose into their underlying pixels, and sound that was once synchronized with video no longer is. Voice that matched lip movements now lags behind or moves ahead of the visual image. Good planning of the graphic elements you will include and how you will include them will help avoid these issues. Use these guidelines as you plan.

Ensure that graphics are readable and attractive

A graphic style that works well on paper may not work when displayed on a computer screen. Use the following techniques to adjust the style for graphic display:

- **Adjust line weights.** Use heavier lines than are appropriate on paper because fine lines often disappear from view.

- **Adjust font stroke width.** Use fonts with wider strokes when displaying dark text on a light background. Choose fonts where the stroke has a more uniform thickness rather than a stroke that varies from thick to thin.

- **Use anti-aliasing to rid your lines of jagged edges.**

- **Use white space generously.** White space helps users to separate elements into relevant groups and immediately recognize differences among information types.

Be consistent in your graphic style

Establish and use a consistent style throughout all your graphics. Use similar color schemes, font sizes, and scale (Figure 16.21 and Figure 16.22). Do not change the type of graphic you use for the same purpose. For example, don't switch from line drawings to photographs or from cartoon figures to real people.

If you decide to use video to convey information, use video every time you present a similar message. Remember that it is often best to use the simplest graphic image that will convey the message effectively.

Select type fonts carefully

The number of type faces available for your interface can be overwhelming. You can select a serif or sans serif type, a type that has weights from extra bold to light, italic or roman type, and many other variations. All of these are the physical characteristics that make type readable and visually interesting, as well as provide appropriate emphasis. Type that works well on paper often does not work well on the computer screen.

Most designers recommend using simple, sans serif fonts at larger sizes than you would ordinarily select for paper for on-screen reading. Many readers will

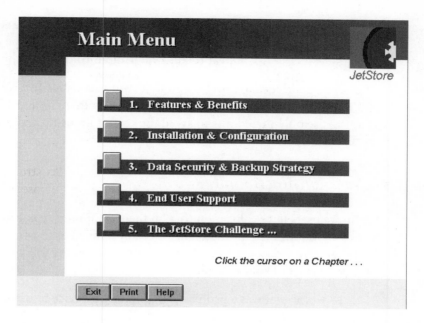

Figure 16.21: The Main Menu of the JetStore tutorial provides an attractively presented list of the user's choices among the learning modules.

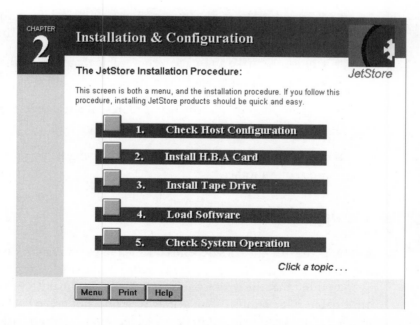

Figure 16.22: The second-level menu of the Installation & Configuration module maintains the same look as the main menu.

find type less than 12 point difficult to read. In addition, leave adequate space between the lines of text (2 points of leading, depending on the font itself) so that the text does not appear too crowded and forbidding to the reader.

It is also a good idea to select a font that your users already have on their systems. The standard screen fonts on many PCs are Ariel and Times. You may want to use only these fonts to avoid the cost of licensing and distributing additional fonts.

Use color functionally

As more users have color monitors on their computers, you can use color in more of your information design, especially applied to illustrations, photography, video, and animation. Color provides the following enhancements to your system:

- Color that was a prohibitively expensive device to use on paper becomes easy to use on the screen.

- Color makes a screen easier on the eyes, reducing the glare of a white background.

- Color added to an illustration allows you to isolate important features and encourage the user to pay particular attention to them.

- Color may make an image recognizable that would otherwise be difficult to comprehend.

- A color photograph may better represent a real object than a black and white drawing.

- Color allows us to label information, distinguishing parts of an image from one another.

Use appropriate contrast

Legibility of your graphics depends on adequate contrast between the graphic and its background. Increasing contrast can make smaller type more legible. Keep in mind that the wrong background color can make type or illustrations unreadable. For example, a hot yellow type on a hot green background will provide insufficient contrast to be readable. Darker type on dark backgrounds ensures that type will disappear for all but the best viewing conditions. Keep in mind that no color combination has greater contrast than black and white.

Contrast is determined by the hue, saturation, and value of the colors you
choose. Hue refers to the name of the color, such as red, green, or blue.
Saturation refers to a color's intensity or how bright or dull it looks. Value
refers to how dark or light a color appears. Typically, you use a light type on a
dark background or a dark type on a light background. However, be certain to
consider the saturation of the color as well as its value. Just because you think
of yellow as a "light" color and blue as a "dark" color does not mean that all
yellows are light and all blues are dark—a yellow may be very bright and
unreadable against a dark blue background.

Size graphics appropriately

When importing a graphic into your system, choose an appropriate size to
ensure clarity of the information being conveyed. The lower resolution of
online information compared to paper dictates that graphics be larger so users
can make out detail (Figure 16.23).

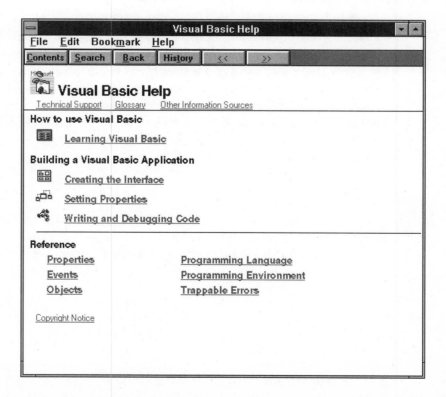

Figure 16.23: Considering all the space available in the main menu of the Visual Basic
Help, the icons are too small.

Decide if you need an entire graphic to make your point. A partial graphic, including partial screen images, may be just as useful, require less space and less scrolling, and enable the user to see the important elements easier.

For online help, the screen images you provide may not need to be large to achieve your purpose. Users often have access to the actual software screen in another window. They can compare overall appearance without having to distinguish words.

To provide more detail for an illustration, without requiring a huge graphic, allow users to zoom in and out of the graphic using hypertext jumps. That is, starting from an overall view of the objects, allow users to select an area to enlarge for more detail (Figure 16.24). In this way, you do not clutter the high-level graphic with too much detail.

Recognizing graphic constraints

Despite all the obvious advantages they provide to users, graphics add another level of complexity to your online system, creating issues that you don't have to worry about if you design a text-only environment. However, many of the technical issues you will need to consider are beyond the scope of our discussion here. We point out only the most significant issues as a starting point. Be certain to consult the many useful texts available for details on the use of graphics in the particular medium you have selected for your information library.

Watch the file size

Graphics make your document files larger, and users are less likely to install large document files if hard disk space is limited. The following factors affect file size:

- **Color.** Color graphics files are at least four times as large as black and white. Sixteen colors are four times larger than two colors; 256 colors are two times larger than 16 colors; 16M colors are three times larger than 256 colors.

- **File format.** GIF (Graphics Interchange Formats) formats in general are much smaller than the same graphic in other formats, such as TIFF (Tagged Image File Format) or BMP (Windows Bitmap). GIF is

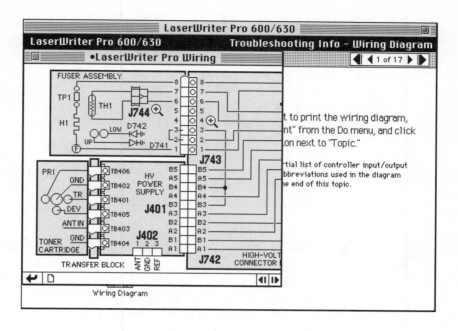

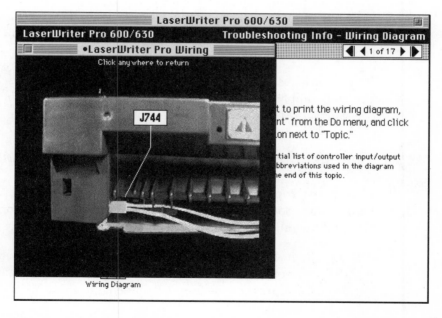

Figure 16.24: The Apple Service Source provides a wiring diagram for the LaserWriter Pro 600/630. By clicking on the "zoom in" icon (the magnifying glass with the plus sign), the technician views a photograph of the machine showing the actual location of the referenced wiring.

effective for almost all images except large photographs because little information is lost in the compression process. The expanded image will look very close to the original image before compression.

JPEG (Joint Photographic Experts Group) format is most often used to compress photographs. However, information is lost in a JPEG compression, although usually not enough information to make any difference to the viewer.

- **Compression.** Certain graphic and file types compress more than others. BMP files may compress up to 50%; GIF files will result in very little size difference when compressed.

Know the differences among file types for graphics

There are a wealth of possible file formats in which your graphics may be created. The variety of formats provides a lot of flexibility for the graphic artist, but they can cause a big headache for the online developer. Each online development tool, each monitor resolution, each platform, and every combination of these factors, supports only certain formats. Each format compresses in a different way, responds to resizing in a different way, handles color in a different way, and so on.

It's not the focus of this book to outline the best file types to use in each situation, simply to recommend that you become fully versed in your options. See "Further reading" for a selection of books to read about file types.

Consider the restrictions of your users' equipment

How graphics appear on your users' monitors is very much a factor of their hardware and software. Know the lowest common denominator of monitor type and resolution that you will need to support.

Some help compilers, such as those for Windows 95, have dropped support for low-resolution monitors such as CGA and VGA. Consider not only users' equipment but the formats that your tool will support.

In addition, be sure that your users' equipment can support color if you plan to include it. Consider not only if the monitor supports color, but how many colors are supported, especially if only 16 colors are supported. The displays are governed by a concept called color palettes, which refers to the way colors are identified within the computer and displayed on the screen. To ensure that color translates effectively and you need to understand how to select the correct color palette, perhaps supply a custom palette if necessary. Refer to several of the texts in the "Further reading" section at the end of the chapter for complete information.

Consider cross-platform issues

If you will be providing cross-platform information, you need to recognize the differences in graphic interpretation. Although some file formats translate well across platforms, others do not. Compression options also differ. Furthermore, the various platforms treat color very differently. Color images that look fine on one platform can look terrible on the other platform. Fully research your options before you begin and test your choices early in your development process on all platforms.

Reference graphics

Depending on the constraints of your users' equipment, you may want to provide a link to your graphics rather than automatically displaying them. For example, if graphics require a long time to load, provide a link. Users expect a delay after clicking a button, but if they are simply scrolling, they expect a more instantaneous display.

Remember that whether or not you link to the graphics must still depend on the purpose of the graphic. Can users understand the information being discussed without the graphic, or is it a key component to their successful understanding? If you are simply concerned that the users will have to scroll within the topic, consider loading the graphic into a secondary window when the topic is displayed.

Further reading

Deaton, Mary, "Working with Graphics: Parts One and Two," *The WinHelp Journal*, Vol. 1, Nos. 2 and 3, 1994.

Horton, William, *Illustrating Computer Documentation* (New York: John Wiley & Sons, 1991).

Horton, William, *The Icon Book* (New York: John Wiley & Sons, 1994).

Marcus, Aaron, *Graphic Design for Electronic Documents and User Interfaces* (New York: ACM Press, 1992).

Mullet, Kevin and Darrell Sano, *Designing Visual Interfaces* (Englewood Cliffs, NJ: Prentice Hall, 1995).

Rimmer, Steve, *The Graphic File Toolkit* (New York: Addison-Wesley, 1992).

Siegel, David, *Creating Killer Web Sites* (Indianapolis, IN: Hayden Books, 1996).

Tufte, Edward, *Envisioning Information* (Cheshire, CT: Graphics Press, 1990).

Weinman, Lynda, *Designing Web Graphics* (Indianapolis, IN: New Writers Publishing, 1996).

White, Jan V, *Graphic Design in the Electronic Age* (New York: Watson-Guptill, 1988).

17

Moving Forward with Multimedia

In addition to the two static media we ordinarily include in documentation (that is, text and graphics), electronic media may include other dynamic components:

- Sound, including voice and music

- Animation

- Photography

- Video

- Interactivity

Guidelines for these dynamic features could easily form the foundation of another entire book. In this chapter, we simply highlight some of the most important guidelines, without exploring the intricacies of each medium.

Choosing to include multimedia

Before using any dynamic medium, you must be able to justify its use. Will users understand information more quickly if other media are included in the presentation? Is the information clearer? Will users be willing and able to use it? Will the system display the information in a useful way? Use these guidelines in making your decisions.

Choose the medium that represents the best and most logical choice to communicate a concept

The use of each medium is justified only if it communicates or supports a substantial message that cannot be communicated as effectively in any other way. Don't get caught up in the hype. Multimedia isn't only a matter of keeping up with the computer game industry. Everyone is *not* doing it. Use multimedia only if it helps you get a point across more effectively than less costly media.

For example, when Apple Computer added the sound of a correctly operating disk drive to its service CD-ROM, they were adding information that could not be duplicated by text or graphics. When the Department of Veterans Affairs allowed its physicians to view ultrasound test results over their intranet, they were adding a video effect that could not be provided in any other way.

Don't rely solely on one group's opinions

Everyone has an opinion on whether to include multimedia in an online system. Marketing and sales may push for special effects to impress buyers or keep ahead of the competition. Programmers, or even your information-development group, may negate the idea because of the extra work development. The finance people may be afraid of increasing development costs.

You need to balance the variety of opinions with reality. If in doubt, do some market research. Ask potential users whether they want or need multimedia, and determine if they'll use it. However, don't believe everything they tell you. One company heard over and over that they should present their documentation online, but observations of the work environment showed that users had no available computers to access the online information and never used the online information available through other products.

Observe users' work environments to decide whether a different, more attractive, or more dynamic presentation of information will assist in learning and performance. For example, will it encourage people to spend time learning because their experience with the tool keeps them motivated and interested?

Balance effectiveness against cost

Even if your research shows that users will be positively affected by the use of multimedia, you still need to consider the cost of the multimedia and determine if the positive reaction balances that expense.

Remember that the cost of multimedia extends beyond the immediate costs of the development tools and the time to develop. It includes file size and memory required to run. It also includes increased customer service time to support customers who can't get the information product to work, let alone the application itself.

Assess the compatibility of the users' systems with multimedia

Although the statistics become more favorable every day, we know that users may still not have the right hardware to receive the best value from multimedia. Users will not necessarily have a computer that is fast enough, has enough memory, or includes the right sound card, CD-ROM drive, or video card to run dynamic multimedia effects.

Consider file size and storage space required

When users install software, one of the most common ways to minimize installation time and space is to eliminate the online documentation. Keep this problem in mind as you create online information. Keep file sizes and required space at a minimum to limit the temptation never to install the online documentation.

Remember as well that viewing multimedia-rich files may impose an enormous burden on your network. You will need to investigate just how much multimedia your network can support.

 File size is especially important when designing documentation for the Web. Consider how long it will take users to download information, or how long the effect will take to display at their screens. Many elaborate multimedia-rich systems are huge and require considerable time to load even over very fast telecommunications lines. Users are very impatient when it comes to access time, especially when they are charged by the minute by their communications carrier.

Consider the user's environment

Multimedia effects can be very distracting in some workplaces. For example, some workplaces are quieter than others or use cubicles rather than private offices. Sound may distract people around the users or vice versa. It may also be embarrassing for users to have their neighbors hear sounds that point out mistakes.

 ### *Allow enough time for development*

Multimedia will take longer to develop than a more traditional presentation of information. If you don't have enough calendar time or staff to complete the multimedia development effort, don't rush to add it by the current release dates. Instead begin planning for the next release of information now.

Using multimedia effectively

If you have determined that multimedia is the right approach for your users, keep the following guidelines in mind.

 ### *Integrate the media into the entire presentation of information*

Integrate the various media you have decided to include into a coherent whole. Design your online information so that dynamic media are synchronized and balanced with traditional media and present compatible and supportive messages. No one medium should overwhelm another.

Be certain to integrate the multimedia effects throughout the information library. We have seen many instances in which it was obvious that the developers ran out of steam. They developed multimedia effects enthusiastically at the beginning but ran out of time, money, and enthusiasm before the end. The entertaining and motivating tunes that accompanied the first part of the presentation became fewer and farther between until they disappeared altogether. Unfortunately, users' expectations had been raised. They had come to expect the same effects throughout and were disappointed to find them missing.

Be consistent in your use of multimedia effects

Try to use multimedia consistently throughout the system. For example, use voice-over for all your feedback statements, but nowhere else. Use a video or animation to introduce a new concept. Users will learn what to expect from each effect and therefore absorb the information more effectively.

Do not rely solely on multimedia effects to convey information

Especially if you are in doubt about your users' equipment capabilities, ensure that the online information functions effectively without the multimedia. Also provide users with the option of turning off the multimedia effects if they don't want to view them. They should be able to view a video or listen to the sound only if they choose to do so.

Many users still have systems that are character based and do not permit them to view more than text and simple line drawings. Design so that such users can turn off the media and still retain a substantial part of the message.

Give users control

Users must have control over the multimedia effects that you provide. You cannot guarantee that users will understand the information the first time through. Users must be able to replay a video or a passage of sound. They must to able to start and stop a sequence at will and review segments as needed.

Furthermore, if users are in a crowded workspace, they may need to adjust volume to avoid disturbing their neighbors. Make these controls obvious and easy to use, as demonstrated in Figure 17.1.

Keep it simple

Multimedia effects should be simple enough that the user can follow them without missing critical information. Small but important details should not go unnoticed or unrecognized because users are distracted by the effects.

Figure 17.1: A control panel associated with this video allows the user to start and stop the viewing at will, to select individual frames, and to move forward and backward; in short, to maintain control over the extent of the multimedia experience.

 ## Make multimedia effects interesting and relevant

Multimedia information is potentially more interesting, entertaining, and motivating than other online information. Users expect significant opportunities for interaction and changing displays on their computer screens. Be sensitive to these expectations. Don't keep users staring at an unchanging visual display for more than 10 to 15 seconds.

Don't use multimedia in ways that are potentially boring for many users. Is it really more interesting to watch a talking head than to simply hear a voice next to a still picture of the speaker? What value is there really to a voice reading the exact text that appears on the screen unless you anticipate having many users who are visually impaired?

In addition, don't use multimedia simply to add interest. Often multimedia effects are added to online documentation for no apparent reason, other than that the author could do it. Carefully consider whether the effect supports the presentation of information. For example, does that little animated character, cute as it may be, really help convey your message?

 ## Be culturally neutral

Just as you try to maintain cultural and gender neutrality in your text and graphics, you should be culture and gender neutral in your multimedia effects. Consider accents of voice-overs, racial and ethnic mix in videos, types of music, and so on. Because pictures and sounds convey so much more information than words alone, they can also convey many more subtle insults. Getting it right for everyone is extraordinarily difficult.

Furthermore, consider whether your information system will be localized for other cultures and languages. For voice-overs, you'll need to re-create the sound files for each language in which your product will be localized. You may even have to reshoot video if the content is in some way inappropriate for other cultures.

Don't cut corners

Because of their experience with professionally created television and film, contemporary audiences are sufficiently sophisticated to recognize poorly executed special effects. If you're going to include multimedia, do it right. Ensure that your effects look professional, not thrown in at the last minute or produced by a friend of your spouse's second cousin (who happens to own a video camera and was available late one Thursday night).

One key is to involve professionals on your team. If you do not know how to create animations, don't decide that you can learn while creating your online information; find someone who produces animation professionally.

On the other hand, well-done effects don't have to be elaborate. For example, simple video stills accompanied by voice-over can create the same effect as full-motion video and will be viewable by many more members of your audience.

Test thoroughly

Multimedia has the largest potential for not working the way you thought it would. Users find it highly annoying to call customer support and find the answer to be something to the effect of "It worked in our lab." In fact, we have all had the experience of attending presentations run by multimedia professionals in which all the embarrassing problems are accompanied by the muttered phrase "It worked during rehearsal."

If you include multimedia, you must allow adequate time for testing on all possible platforms and configurations that your users will employ. Even then, you're bound to miss some—"I'm using a TRS-80 that I've had in my garage since I was in high school."

Providing interactivity

Multimedia gives you the power not only to show users how to do something but to let them try it themselves through simulations. In a simulation, you give users a safe environment to practice what they've learned without risk to their actual work environment or their company's data.

When providing simulations, consider these guidelines.

Allow users to go down wrong paths

The simplest simulations require that users give the right responses at each decision-making point. If they don't, they receive a message helping them get to the right answer before moving on.

Although it requires more programming and anticipation on your part, a more effective design allows users to do something incorrectly, following the wrong path until they recognize their error. Then, the system provides guidance to help them recover. Simulations of this sort help build users' confidence that they can recover from mistakes in the real world as well.

Provide plenty of feedback

The primary reason to provide interactive simulations is to teach users through trial and error. To do so, you must provide adequate system responses to their actions. You cannot afford to use a simple beep to indicate that an action is incorrect. The feedback you provide must tell users what might have happened if they took that action and provide hints about the correct action. Then the users should have the chance to try again, as many times as they need.

Teach users to rely on the tools available to them

One danger of simulation is that users begin to expect that they will get guidance when they get lost, and they can rely on that guidance rather than learning how to recover on their own. When you can, provide pointers to the user guide or online help system in your feedback rather than giving help directly. Users learn that tools are always available to them even outside the simulated environment.

Further reading

Lopuck, Lisa, *Designing Multimedia* (Berkeley, CA: Peachpit Press, 1996).

Macintosh Human Interface Guidelines by Apple Computer, Inc. (Reading, MA: Addison-Wesley, 1992).

Siegel, David, *Creating Killer Web Sites* (Indianapolis, IN: Hayden Books, 1996).

The Windows Interface Guidelines for Software Design (Redmond, WA: Microsoft Press, 1995).

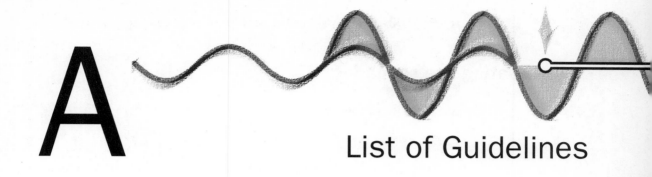

A List of Guidelines

This appendix summarizes the checklists and guidelines presented throughout this book.

Learning About Your Users' Information Needs (Chapter 2)

Conducting your research

- Rely on fact, not opinion
- Talk to the right people
- Ask the right questions
- Use the right methods

Creating user profiles

- Categorize users by job titles
- Categorize users by demographics
- Categorize users by attitudes

■ Categorize users by subject-matter knowledge and experience

Creating use scenarios

■ Start with routine tasks

■ Add exceptions

■ Focus on the users' goals, rather than the tasks performed with tools

■ Don't get bogged down in low-level tasks

■ Avoid defining tasks in terms that only experts will understand

■ Turn the scenarios into lists of questions users are likely to need information to answer

Determining the Stages of Use (Chapter 3)

Identifying and addressing Stage 1: Novices

■ Novices have no previous experience

■ Novices experience concern about their ability to succeed

■ Novices don't want to learn, only accomplish a goal

■ Novices don't know how to respond to mistakes

■ Novices are vulnerable to confusion

Identifying and addressing Stage 2: Advanced Beginners

■ Advanced beginners try tasks on their own

■ Advanced beginners have difficulty troubleshooting

■ Advanced beginners want information fast

Identifying and addressing Stage 3: Competent Performers

- Competent performers develop conceptual models
- Competent performers troubleshoot problems on their own
- Competent performers seek out expert user advice

Identifying and addressing Stage 4: Proficient Performers

- Proficient performers want to understand the larger conceptual framework
- Proficient performers are frustrated by over-simplified information
- Proficient performers correct previous poor task performance
- Proficient performers learn from the experience of others

Identifying and addressing Stage 5: Expert Performers

- Expert performers are primary sources of knowledge and information
- Expert performers continually look for better methods

Responding to multiple stages in one audience

- Determine the percentages of each stage of use among your user communities
- Decide if your information design must support each stage of use
- Determine how you will support each stage of use in your information design
- Decide if you will tailor information for specific stages of use
- Consider other media options in your approach

Categorizing Information Needs (Chapter 4)

Procedural information

- Include user, not system tasks
- Show the big picture
- Include only procedures that are appropriate for online presentation
- Include simple purpose statements
- Tell users what to do
- Present field definitions to help users complete online forms or fill in dialog boxes

Conceptual information

- Tell the users only what they need to know
- Write abstracts that explain the content and purpose of conceptual information
- Provide enough information for all the stages of use in your target audience who need conceptual information
- Provide information topics that help users understand why they might want to follow a particular course of action
- Provide definitions of terms to increase understanding
- Provide information topics that assist users in making decisions
- Provide information topics that help users understand the technical theory behind a product
- Provide information topics that include typical scenarios users might follow to achieve a goal
- Include information about the authors, if appropriate

- Provide publication dates for all information in the information system

Reference information

- Provide information that will be used repeatedly

- Provide information that will be used rarely

- Provide discrete pieces of data that will aid in understanding and support decision making

Instructional information

- Enable users to actually complete a task while following the procedures

- Use relevant, easily understood examples

- Include simulated exercises to allow practice in a safe environment

- Provide positive and negative feedback

- Use demonstrations to show how a procedure works

- Give users tools to build experience and skills

Mixing information types

- Consider user needs

- Analyze other information sources available

- Do not repeat everything from paper-based information

- Decide how you will combine information types

Recognizing the Implications of Design Research (Chapter 5)

Identifying design implications

- What media are required?
- How should the information system be structured?
- How should information be accessed?
- What interface design features should be included?
- How will users move through the system?
- What writing style is appropriate?
- What graphics are required to communicate effectively?
- What level of interactivity is required?

Making trade-offs

- Put user needs first
- Consult your users
- Consider available resources
- Get expert advice

Structuring Your Online System (Chapter 6)

Providing context sensitivity

- Is the information related to a computer application?

- Can the information you provide be accessed through the computer to support and improve employee performance?

- What types of information will you provide?

- How will the information be used?

- How will the information be marketed?

- What is the source of your legacy information?

- What platform are you delivering on?

- What are your user needs?

- Who are your users?

Partitioning the subject matter

- Is the information related to the products that you sell to customers?

- Is the information related to the services you provide for your customers?

- Is the information related to the services you perform within your organization?

- Is the information related to the activities performed by your users?

- Is the information related to the tasks that your users need to perform?

Organizing your topics

Alphabetical

- How many topics are you listing?

- Can information in the alphabetical list be grouped?

- Will users know what they are looking for?

- Are information topics uniquely named?

- Is information reference oriented?

Sequential

- Is the information time based?

- Are users aware of the required sequence?

- How will you prevent users from jumping into the middle of the presentation?

Logical

- Is the structure apparent to the users?

- Does the application structure suggest an organization?

- Will users access certain information more often than other information?

- Will certain users have access only to certain types of information?

Adding Hypertext Links (Chapter 7)

Determining when to use links

- Use links to address different audiences

- Use links to point to related information

- Use links as cross-references

- Use links to define browse paths

- Use links to control topic size and appearance

- Use links for common topics

- Use links to display graphics

- Use links to zoom in on graphics

- Use links to call other support

Choosing the type of link

- Consider the type of information you want to provide
- Consider the amount of information you want to provide
- Consider navigational issues
- Use expansion links
- Avoid links that produce changes between primary and secondary windows

Choosing a link structure

- Reinforce the information structure
- Meet the users' goals
- Layer information appropriately for the user
- Limit the number of links per topic
- Provide sufficient links to relevant additional information
- Avoid excessive branching
- Construct a map of the link patterns you are designing
- Avoid arbitrary links
- Avoid dead ends
- Ensure ease of navigation

Indicating the availability of links

- Consider industry standards
- Make links recognizable
- Distinguish between link types
- Consider the physical size of the links
- Instruct users what to do

Definition links

■ Select terms that are likely to be new to your user

■ Avoid providing definition links for every instance of a term

■ Provide another way for users to access definitions

■ Link to different definitions of the same term if the context is different

■ Don't nest other definitions

■ Repeat the term being defined in the definition window

■ Ensure that the pop-up window does not obscure the original linked term

Structuring Your Topics (Chapter 8)

Planning information flow

■ Plan the design of each information type

■ Ensure that each information type contains only the building blocks that you have assigned to that type

■ Consider carefully how the building blocks should be ordered within the information type

■ Hide secondary information until it is needed

Choosing your building blocks

■ Will you explain step-by-step instructions?

■ Will you list the conditions associated with an action?

■ Will you present data and other factual information that users need to support actions and decisions?

- Will you define key terms?

- Will you demonstrate a procedure?

- Will you provide descriptions that introduce or explain concepts?

- Will you explain the results of an action or event?

- Will you provide illustrations or real-life examples of a procedure or concept?

- Will you require interaction from the user?

- Will you explain how to move through the system?

- Will you provide purpose statements to support an action or decision?

- Will you provide optional ways of performing a step or a task?

Constructing an information topic from building blocks

- Are your users primarily novices?

- Are users experienced?

- Does the information provide background material that provides a context?

- Does the user need to make a decision?

- Does the information describe how to complete a task?

- Do users need to learn the information being presented or simply perform an action?

Testing your design and implementation (Chapter 9)

Testing functionality

- Create a test plan
- Exercise every link, button, and menu choice
- Use someone outside of the development team to perform the test
- Allow enough time to test and respond to the results
- Test on all platforms and configurations
- Anticipate nonstandard access
- Know when to stop testing

Evaluating usability

- Plan iterative testing throughout the development life cycle
- Define your testing goals
- Define your expectations
- Recruit the right test participants
- Create test scenarios
- Conduct a pilot of each test
- Make careful observations
- Debrief the users at the end of each test session
- Analyze your results
- Decide on changes you will make to the design and implementation of your system
- Go back for more information if necessary
- Allow enough time to test and respond to results

■ Retest solutions or changes

Choosing the Right Tools (Chapter 10)

Writing a Specification

User needs

- Include your interface requirements
- Describe the system's organization
- List the ways users will access the system
- Discuss your security requirements
- Describe how users will move through the system
- Describe the type of feedback you will provide
- List the ways users can interact with the information system
- Describe the ways users can control the system
- List any special effects you intend to include
- Describe how users will be able to print files

Compatibility

- List your minimum hardware requirements
- List your minimum software requirements
- List the file types that must be supported
- Discuss your compression plans
- Specify your printing needs
- List your productivity requirements for the final system
- Plan for updates

Conversion requirements

- Describe characteristics of your legacy documents
- Decide if, when, and how you will add hypertext links to legacy documents

Author needs

- Describe who will do the development
- Describe the workflow and support expected
- Describe development logistics
- List peripheral products that you might require
- Describe your expectations for training
- Describe your tracking needs
- List the statistics you will need
- Plan for updates
- Describe how information will be stored

Cost

- Consider the cost of the tool
- Consider the cost of hardware
- Consider the cost of training

Choosing among tools

- Distinguish between wants and needs
- Prioritize wants and needs
- Balance cost with features
- Don't take the vendor's word
- Request a trial of the product functionality
- Consider personal preferences

Designing the Information Interface (Chapter 11)

Text

- Select readable on-screen fonts
- Use larger font sizes for on-screen display
- Avoid too many font changes
- Keep line lengths short
- Distinguish important elements from normal text
- Avoid excessive emphasis techniques

Layout

- Be consistent in the format and design of display screens
- Create standards for your information interface
- Follow industry standards when applicable
- Establish conventions for the use of each element
- Use negative space
- Avoid horizontal scrolling
- Make the interface easy to remember

Window placement

- Do not obscure important information
- Place pop-ups in the center of the action
- Size secondary windows to fit the information
- Use cascading windows

Incorporating color

- Use color sparingly
- Consider limitations of the hardware
- Consider limitations of users

Choosing an effective metaphor

- Choose from the users' experience
- Ensure that the metaphor fits the task
- Explain the metaphor
- Don't overdo it
- Don't force the metaphor
- Don't forget the metaphor
- Test metaphors
- Consider using industry standards

Ensuring Accessibility (Chapter 12)

Context sensitivity

- Anticipate the information that users will want
- Provide information related to the current cursor (keyboard) focus
- Ensure that users understand why they have accessed the topic
- Provide simple ways to change topics
- Determine how much navigational control to give users who access information via context sensitivity

Table of Contents

- Be readily accessible

- Show hierarchical relationships

- Create TOCs that are expandable and collapsible

- Highlight the current topic

- Indicate the type of information provided

- Use informative and unique topic titles

- Use the terms your users will know to title the information topics

- Ensure that the title in the TOC is identical to the name of the topic

- Use double clicking to get the user from the TOC item to the help topic

- Move from the TOC to the top of the selected topic

- Allow users to determine scope

Pop-up tables of contents

- Signal the presence of a pop-up TOC with a button or standard icon

- Provide introductions to secondary TOCs

- Allow the user to move back to the primary topic from the pop-up TOC without selecting an item

Indexes

- Be comprehensive in indexing topics

- Use detailed primary entries rather than secondary and tertiary entries

- Reference only one topic

- Link to meaningful occurrences of a subject

- Index nontextual elements

- Consider the implications of entering in the "middle" of a presentation

- Allow domain-specific indexing

- Provide a browsing tool

- Be readily accessible

- Ensure accuracy

- Avoid indexing pop-up and definition windows

- Be consistent

Search methods

Full-text search

- Couple the search with other types of searches

- Support wild cards, case insensitivity, and word variation

- Provide limited contexts for the searches

- Allow searches on the results of a previous search

- Retain the results of the previous search

- Provide a way to print and/or save the results of the search

- Provide a way to cancel the search

- Indicate your progress through the domain being searched

- Display search results as they are found

- Jump to a topic immediately if only one match is found

Boolean search

- Provide clear instructions for entering search parameters

- Use ordinary language to clarify the search logic

- Design your interface to guide users through this search

- Allow users to specify how close related terms need to be to each other to constitute a search hit

Parametric search

- Structure your information into a database

- Look for related characteristics

Natural-language search

- Learn how your user looks for information

- Prioritize the results

Providing Navigation Aids (Chapter 13)

Orient the user

- Provide a home base

- Provide navigational instructions

- Provide navigational signposts

- Show context through a table of contents secondary window

- Keep the title visible

- Point to related topics

- Provide labeled links

Leave bread crumbs

- Allow users to mark frequently accessed topics

- Record a history of all screens accessed

Control the possibilities

- Provide a short path to information
- Avoid overnavigating
- Provide a browse sequence
- Ensure that the browse sequence is finite
- Ensure that browse buttons make sense to the user
- Prevent wrong navigation choices
- Provide escape routes

Composing Your Topics (Chapter 14)

Writing procedural information

- Phrase procedures in user terms
- Number each step that users have to perform
- Limit each numbered step to a single action
- Present steps in the order in which users must perform them
- Try to write no more than five action steps for a single procedure
- Start steps with imperative verbs
- Distinguish among mandatory, conditional, or optional steps
- Provide only one method for performing an action within a topic
- Be precise in your instructions
- Keep steps short
- Enable users to move easily between procedure and application

Writing conceptual information

- Develop a complete idea in a single topic
- Include transitions
- Watch out for large blocks of text
- Relate new information to known concepts
- Use many examples and graphics
- Put examples in context
- Annotate examples thoroughly
- Use continuing examples
- Define terms as they are encountered
- Make conceptual information printable

Writing reference information

- Provide the same type of information about the same things
- Present the same information in the same order
- Use lists and tables
- Use a telescopic style in tables

Writing instructional information

- Provide motivation
- Give users learning objectives
- Give users something to do
- Don't blame the user
- Reassure the user
- Lead users to their own conclusions

Writing for Readability (Chapter 15)

Follow good writing practices

- Understand your users
- Follow minimalist writing principles
- Ensure accuracy and completeness
- Maintain consistent language in heading levels
- Use numbered lists and bulleted lists consistently
- Use parallel structure in lists
- Punctuate lists consistently
- Use positive statements
- Conform to accepted style standards

Adding Graphics (Chapter 16)

Deciding to include graphics

Using technical illustrations

- Use graphics to show what objects look like
- Use graphics as examples
- Use graphics to verify
- Distinguish images of the software screen from the actual software screen
- Use graphics to show process

Using conceptual graphics

- Use graphics to replace words
- Use graphic devices to clarify meaning
- Use graphics as summaries

Using graphics as a design element

- Establish a functional grid for the screen
- Include icons
- Add graphic devices to make ideas more visual
- Use type position to differentiate text elements

Using graphics to add aesthetic appeal

- Use graphics to maintain interest
- Use graphics to motivate users
- Use graphic elements to entertain users
- Use graphics to set the mood

Designing your graphic presentation

- Make graphics easy to understand
- Ensure that images focus on their primary message
- Don't cover the text or work area
- Fully annotate the graphics
- Use graphic hotspots to explain elements of a graphic
- Consider using stock images to reduce the cost of development

Controlling graphic appearance

- Ensure that graphics are readable and attractive
- Be consistent in your graphic style
- Select type fonts carefully
- Use color functionally
- Use appropriate contrast
- Size graphics appropriately

Recognizing graphic constraints

- Watch the file size
- Know the differences among file types for graphics
- Consider the restrictions of your users' equipment
- Consider cross-platform issues
- Reference graphics

Moving Forward with Multimedia (Chapter 17)

Choosing to include multimedia

- Choose the medium that represents the best and most logical choice to communicate a concept
- Don't rely solely on one group's opinions
- Balance effectiveness against cost
- Assess the compatibility of the users' systems with multimedia
- Consider file size and storage space required

- Consider the user's environment
- Allow enough time for development

Using multimedia effectively

- Integrate the media into the entire presentation of information
- Be consistent in your use of multimedia effects
- Do not rely solely on multimedia effects to convey information
- Give users control
- Keep it simple
- Make multimedia effects interesting and relevant
- Be culturally neutral
- Don't cut corners
- Test thoroughly

Providing interactivity

- Allow users to go down wrong paths
- Provide plenty of feedback
- Teach users to rely on the tools available to them

B

Bibliography

Bailey, Robert W., *Human Performance Engineering: Designing High Quality Professional User Interfaces for Computer Products, Applications, and Systems,* 3rd edition (Saddle River, NJ: Prentice Hall, 1996).

Boggan, Scott, David Farkas, and Joe Welinske, *Developing Online Help for Windows 95* (Carmel, IN: Sams Publishing, 1996).

Bonura, Larry, *The Art of Indexing* (New York: John Wiley & Sons, 1994).

Brockmann, R. John, *Writing Better Computer User Documentation: From Paper to Hypertext* (New York: John Wiley & Sons, 1990).

Carroll, John M., ed., *Scenario-Based Design: Envisioning Work and Technology in System Development* (New York: John Wiley & Sons, 1995).

Clark, Ruth Colvin, *Developing Technical Training* (Reading, MA: Addison-Wesley Publishing, 1989).

Deaton, Mary, "Working with Graphics: Parts One and Two," *The WinHelp Journal,* Vol. 1 Nos. 2 and 3, 1994.

Deaton, Mary and Cheryl Lockett Zubak, *Designing Windows 95 Help: A Guide to Creating Online Documents* (Indianapolis, IN: Que Corporation, 1996).

Dreyfus, Hubert L. and Stuart E. Dreyfus, *Mind over Machine* (New York: The Free Press, 1986).

Dumas, Joseph S. and Janice C. Redish, *A Practical Guide to Usability Testing* (NJ: Ablex Publishing Company, 1993).

Earle, Ralph, Robert Berry, and Michelle Corbin Nichols, "Indexing Online Information," *Technical Communication,* Vol. 34, No. 2, pp. 146–156, 1996.

Ehn, Pelle, *Work-Oriented Design of Computer Artifacts* (Stockholm: Arbetslivscentrum, 1988).

Gery, Gloria J., *Making CBT Happen* (Boston: Weingarten Publications, 1987).

Gery, Gloria J., *Electronic Performance Support Systems* (Boston: Weingarten Publications, 1991).

Hackos, JoAnn T., *Managing your Documentation Projects* (New York: John Wiley & Sons, 1994).

Horn, Robert, *Mapping Hypertext* (Lexington, MA: The Lexington Institute, 1989).

Horton, William, *The Checklist* (Boulder, CO: William Horton Consulting, 1994).

Horton, William, *Designing and Writing Online Documentation,* 2nd edition (New York: John Wiley & Sons, 1995).

Horton, William, *Illustrating Computer Documentation* (New York: John Wiley & Sons, 1991).

Horton, William, *The Icon Book* (New York: John Wiley & Sons, 1996).

Jonassen, David, *The Technology of Text* (Englewood Cliffs, NJ: Educational Technology Publications, 1985).

Judd, Karen, *Copyediting: A Practical Guide* (Los Altos, CA: William Kaufmann, Inc., 1982).

Lopuck, Lisa, *Designing Multimedia* (Berkeley, CA : Peachpit Press, 1996).

Macintosh Human Interface Guidelines by Apple Computer, Inc. (Reading, MA: Addison-Wesley, 1992).

Marcus, Aaron, *Graphic Design for Electronic Documents and User Interfaces* (New York: ACM Press, 1992).

Mayhew, Deborah J., *Principles and Guidelines in Software User Interface Design* (Englewood Cliffs, NJ: Prentice Hall, 1992).

Mullet, Kevin and Darrell Sano, *Designing Visual Interfaces* (Englewood Cliffs, NJ: Prentice Hall, 1995).

Nielsen, Jakob, *Usability Engineering* (Cambridge, MA: Academic Press, 1993).

Nielsen, Jakob, ed., *The Interface Design Handbook* (New York: John Wiley & Sons, 1997), in press.

Nielsen, Jakob and Robert L. Mack, eds., *Usability Inspection Methods* (New York: John Wiley & Sons, 1994).

Petrauskas, Bruno, "Online Reference System Design and Development," *Perspectives on Software Documentation: Inquiries and Innovations,* ed. Thomas T. Barker (Amityville, NY: Baywood Publishing Company, 1991).

Price, Jonathan and Henry Korman, *How to Communicate Technical Information: A Handbook of Software and Hardware Documentation* (Redwood City, CA: Benjamin/Cummings, 1993).

Raven, Mary Elizabeth and Alicia Flanders, "Using Contextual Inquiry To Learn About Your Audiences," *The Journal of Computer Documentation,* Vol. 20, No. 1, pp. 1–13, 1996.

Redish, Janice, "Reading to learn to do," *The Technical Writing Teacher,* Vol. 15, No. 3, pp. 223–233, 1988.

Rimmer, Steve, *The Graphic File Toolkit* (Reading, MA: Addison-Wesley, 1992).

Rubin, Jeffrey, *Handbook of Usability Testing* (New York: John Wiley & Sons, 1994).

Senge, Peter, *The Fifth Discipline: The Art and Practice of the Learning Organization* (New York: Doubleday, 1990).

Shneiderman, Ben and Greg Kearsley, *Hypertext Hands On!: An Introduction to a New Way of Organizing and Accessing Information* (Reading, MA: Addison-Wesley, 1989).

Siegel, David, *Creating Killer Web Sites* (Indianapolis, IN: Hayden Books, 1996).

Strunk, William, Jr. and E. B. White, *The Elements of Style,* 3rd edition (New York: MacMillan Publishing Company, 1979).

Tarutz, Judith A., *Technical Editing: The Practical Guide for Editors and Writers* (Reading, MA: Addison-Wesley, 1992).

Tufte, Edward, *Envisioning Information* (Cheshire, CT: Graphics Press, 1990).

Weinman, Lynda, *Designing Web Graphics* (Indianapolis, IN: New Writers Publishing, 1996).

Weinshenk, Susan and Sarah C. Yeo, *Guidelines for Enterprise-Wide GUI Design* (New York: John Wiley & Sons, 1995).

White, Jan V., *Graphic Design in the Electronic Age* (New York: Watson-Guptill, 1988).

Wiklund, Michael E., ed., *Usability in Practice* (Cambridge, MA: Academic Press, 1994).

Williams, Joseph M., *Style: Ten Lessons in Clarity & Grace,* 3rd edition (Glen View, IL: Scott, Foresman and Company, 1989).

The Windows Interface Guidelines for Software Design (Redmond, WA: Microsoft Press, 1995).

Wright, Patricia and A.J. Hull, "Answering questions about negative conditions," *Memory and Language,* Vol. 25, pp. 691–709, 1986.

Zubak, Cheryl Lockett, "Choosing a Windows Help Authoring Tool," *WinHelp 96 Conference Proceedings* (Seattle, WA: 1996).

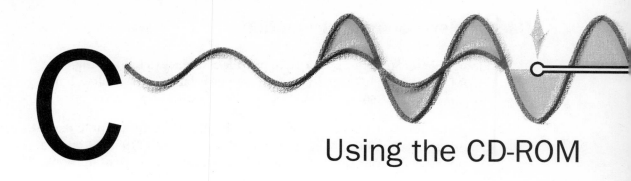

Using the CD-ROM

This appendix provides instructions for downloading the help files from the CD-ROM.

How to install and use the CD-ROM

The CD-ROM you have received contains the online help file for the *Standards for Online Communication* book. You will find one .HLP file named STAND.HLP.

To run the help files you will need

- an IBM PC or compatible

- a CD-ROM player

- Windows 95 or later

Installing the software

1. Start Windows on your computer.

2. Place the CD-ROM into your CD-ROM drive.

3. From Program Manager, Select File, Run, and type X:\INSTALL (where "X" is the correct letter for your CD-ROM drive).

User assistance and information

John Wiley & Sons, Inc. is pleased to provide assistance to users of this CD-ROM. Should you have questions about the installation, please call technical support at (212) 850-6194 weekdays between 9 AM and 4 PM EST.

To place orders for additional copies of this book or the software, or to request information about other Wiley products, please call (800) 879-4539, email at compbks@wiley.com, or use the business reply card at the back of the book.

If you are installing the help files on a LAN, of if your Windows files are on a LAN the install program may not be able to create a program group window in Program Manager. If this problem occurs, you will get an error message. You should still be able to run the help files by opening File Manager, finding the STAND.HLP file, and double-clicking on it.

Help file design

You will find that the help file we have designed follows many of the guidelines in the book. We selected Windows help for two reasons: the lack of a licensing fee and our need to meet the publishing deadline. We developed the help files using HDK, a Windows help tool available from Virtual Media Technology, available in the United States through DEK Software International of Cherry Hill, New Jersey. HDK provided us with a particular functionality that we wanted: a table of contents window that remains synchronized with the help topic in the primary window.

A few other features of the help file are noteworthy:

■ The browse paths allow you to move easily from one checklist item to the next but only within a particular topic. You cannot browse from one end of the book to the other without referencing the table of contents. This restriction of the browse sequence helps to keep you from getting lost.

■ Because the text is conceptual rather than procedural, we chose to allow long help topics to scroll. In this way, we have kept a complete topic intact rather than artificially splitting into shorter sections simply to avoid scrolling.We have also placed the many screen captures into secondary windows so that you can view them side-by-side with the related text—no scrolling in this case.

- You'll also note that we have customized the non-scrolling region with labeled links—buttons that take you to particular categories of information. The labeled links are an effective replacement for unlabeled, and often uncontrolled, hypertext jumps.

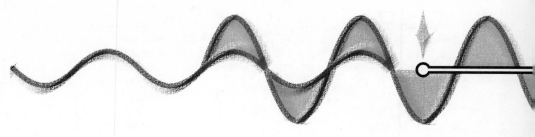

Index